Combining Methods in Educational and Social Research

Conducting educational research

Series editor: Harry Torrance, University of Sussex

This series is aimed at research students in education and those under-taking related professional, vocational and social research. It takes current methodological debates seriously and offers well-informed advice to students on how to respond to such debates. Books in the series review and engage with current methodological issues, while relating such issues to the sorts of decisions which research students have to make when designing, conducting and writing up research. Thus the series both contributes to methodological debate and has practical orientation by providing students with advice on how to engage with such debate and use particular methods in their work. Series authors are experienced researchers and supervisors. Each book provides students with insights into a different form of educational research while also providing them with the critical tools and knowledge necessary to make informed judge-ments about the strengths and weaknesses of different approaches.

Combining Methods in Educational and Social Research

Stephen Gorard
with **Chris Taylor**

Open University Press

Open University Press
McGraw-Hill Education
McGraw-Hill House
Shoppenhangers Road
Maidenhead
Berkshire
England
SL6 2QL

email: enquiries@openup.co.uk
world wide web: www.openup.co.uk

and Two Penn Plaza, New York, NY 10121-2289, USA

First published 2004

A catalogue record of this book is available from the British Library

ISBN 0335 21307 3 (pb) 0335 21308 1 (hb)

Library of Congress Cataloging-in-Publication Data
CIP data applied for

Typeset by YHT Ltd
Printed in the UK by Bell & Bain Ltd., Glasgow

S6965564

Contents

Preface

Why have we written a book about combining research approaches in education and social science at this time? Because there is growing interest in the possibilities, as dissatisfaction grows with the limitations of traditional mono-method studies – all very well in their way but unable to address fully the most complex research questions – and with the methodological schism and internecine 'warfare' that divides our field. This interest is clear among the funders of research. It is exemplified by two projects funded in 2002/3 as part of the ESRC Research Methods Programme, both of which are devoted to exploring issues of combining methods – specifically those methods traditionally termed 'qualitative' and 'quantitative'. For more information on these, see www.prw.le. ac.uk/research/qualquan/ and www.ccsr.ac.uk/methods/projects/posters/ bryman.shtml.

The new training guidelines for ESRC-funded research students (1 + 3) require for the first time that all students are able to undertake relatively high-level tasks within both traditions of research. The combination of such methods is also one of five particular priorities for the ESRC-funded Teaching and Learning Research Programme Capacity Building Network (see www.cf.ac.uk/socsi/capacity).

However, there are very few sources that the interested researcher can turn to for practical guidance on the conduct of research that employs multiple mixed methods. This book provides a conceptual and methodological guide to mixing or combining methods in education research (and in social science more widely), by situating, outlining and evaluating methods that are currently used both within and beyond these fields. The book is not easy reading, will not be comfortable for some existing researchers, and certainly cannot be expected to overcome the convictions of those researchers who are avowedly mono-methodic. But perhaps we should not expect anyone who believes that it is impossible to combine methods to be reading this book anyway. We hope, if nothing else, that it gives many others an opportunity to think about mixing the simple use of numbers with their qualitative work, or strengthening their numeric data with textual or visual illustrations. We believe that all research has an overarching logic and that, within this, the fruitful combination of methods *is* possible. We develop the idea of the 'new' education researcher, for whom the combination of approaches is a representation of a diverse skills base, and part of the development of a fuller multi-perspective on any research topic, rather than a matter of ideological or theoretical allegiance.

The authors would like to express their thanks to many colleagues, especially John Fitz, Jonathan Gorard, Eamonn Kelly, Laurence Moore, Ken Prandy, Gareth Rees, Karen Roberts, Katie Rushforth, Barry Sloane, Emma Smith, Harry Torrance and Patrick White for their help in formulating some of the ideas in this book.

A third methodological movement: challenging the dominance of single methods

The purpose of this book is relatively simple given the potentially complex nature of the subject matter. It is aimed at an audience of upcoming education and social science researchers, and suggests ways in which it is practical and relatively easy to combine evidence collected using a variety of different methods. The chief focus is on the combination of evidence derived from both what are traditionally termed 'qualitative' and 'quantitative' methods. This is in distinction to the wider issues, such as those about the triangulation of methods of data collection *within* a qualitative tradition, as discussed by Meijer *et al.* (2002), or what Tashakkori and Teddlie (2003) refer to as 'multi-methods approaches' using two methods from the same earlier traditions (e.g. ethnography and case study), or cross-disciplinary triangulation of the kind envisaged by Scholz and Tietje (2002). The book assumes that the reader is interested in the possibility of combining methods, and therefore considers such simple combination to be feasible. It is not intended here to persuade avowedly mono-method researchers, who use the same method again and again, that they have something to gain from using more than one method, if they do not, for example, believe that both 'qualitative' and 'quantitative' methods are valuable in their own right. Nor is it intended to deal at the outset with sweeping claims such as those of Sale *et al.* (2002: 43) that: 'Because the two paradigms do not study the same phenomena, quantitative and qualitative methods *cannot* be combined for cross-validation or triangulation purposes'.

The premise of the book is that both approaches have strengths, and that even greater strength can come from their appropriate combination. It is not the purpose of this book to become involved in a consideration of the differences in terminology used by various commentators – we mean by 'combining methods' the same thing as 'mixed methods research' (Teddlie and Tashakkori 2003), and sometimes 'multi-method' or 'integrated' research (Cresswell 2003). However, interested readers are encouraged to pursue the references provided in this book and consider the more varied, and more complex, models and terminology of combining methods described therein.

What is combined methods research?

As we shall make clear in the following chapters, there is a pressing need for education researchers to overcome any rigid methods identities supported by terms like 'qualitative' and 'quantitative', and to learn more about a wider range of methods as users, consumers and critics of each others' research. Perhaps we therefore need to reconfigure our methods classifications in some way to make it clearer that the use of qualitative and quantitative methods is a *choice*, driven largely by the situation and the research questions, not the personality, skills or ideology of the researcher. For example, we might think rather of methods of investigation being largely 'direct' or 'indirect'.

Imagine that someone takes three identical upturned cups and, in full view, hides a coin under one of these, and then shuffles the cups around quickly. They state that you cannot lift the cups, but ask you to decide where the coin is now. In theory, the foolproof way for an observer to pick the correct cup is to follow all of the moves of that cup from the start. They then know the answer. This would be a *direct* approach. In practice, whether it is foolproof depends on a number of factors such as the attention of the observer, the speed of the cups, the number of cup moves and so on. The more complex the situation the less likely it is that the direct approach of creating a narrative of the entire set of moves is foolproof. This is where an *indirect* approach gains. It may be more effective to complement the narrative of the cup moves with an indirect approach, and in the most complex situations (where the direct approach tends towards a 1 in 3 guess) it may be better to replace it entirely. For example, you might try shining a light through the cups to look for shadows, or weighing them in some way for a differential, or listening for differences in the noise they make when tapped. Properly done, since they can be replicated, such indirect approaches can be more accurate than the direct narrative approach.

With the direct approach we simply observe what is going on or ask people direct questions about the phenomenon. This is like much current qualitative work, such as interviews, but also simple questionnaire and measuring techniques. If this approach is available, then it is clearly easier and better. If you want to find out what someone wants for a birthday present and you have reason to believe that they know what they want, and they are willing and able to convey that to you, then the best thing to do is ask them. An indirect approach is more like a heuristic for the answer to the research question, rather than an algorithm. It can be based on the logic of hypothesis generation and testing, known as 'diagnosis' in other fields. If it is not possible to answer the question directly, then we can imagine an answer, calculate the implications of this answer, and then check for evidence or symptoms of that answer. This approach includes statistical modelling and attitude testing but also perhaps conversational analysis.

Both the direct and the indirect approaches are scientific. Both can involve what are currently termed qualitative and quantitative techniques. But put in this way, political arithmetic, for example (see Chapter 4), is more like straightforward observation analysis, since these both involve a relatively direct assessment of the phenomenon of study (involving manifest variables). On the other hand, factor analysis is more like discourse analysis since both use the surface data collected as a proxy for something else (latent variables). We do not say this classification is perfect (since combining manifest and latent variables is far from straightforward, according to Gray and Densten 1998), but it provides an example of how we could escape our history of strife between qualitative and quantitative approaches. Similarly, we could use classifications like 'active' (including action research, experiments and some evaluations) and 'passive' (including statistical modelling and in-depth observation) that cut across qualitative/quantitative divides. Or we could use terms like 'descriptive' and 'explanatory' for the same purpose. 'What is happening?' would be a descriptive question that could be answered using official statistics, documentary analysis or observation. 'How or why is this happening?' is a causal explanatory question, that could be answered using experiments, archive material or interviews. If we were to reclassify and teach methods on a basis like this, then several points may become clearer to all concerned:

- qualitative or quantitative represents only one way of classifying methods;
- our choice of method is determined by the needs of the investigation not the personal preferences or fears of the investigator;
- we all need to be able to use a range of techniques;
- completely different methods can have the same research aim (e.g. to find the coin).

As the cup example makes clear, direct and indirect approaches and, by implication, quantitative and qualitative methods, can all have the same overall aim and can use the same overall rules of logic (see Chapter 10). Therefore, they *can* be combined. Combined approaches such as we describe in this book accept the theory-ladenness of facts, the fallibility of knowledge and the under-determination of theory by data. These are not in dispute. Quantitative and qualitative methods are, in this model, merely tools for researchers to use as and when appropriate. But we suggest that they are nearly always more powerful when used in combination than in isolation. We do not mean by combining methods simply that both the qualitative and quantitative traditions should be in evidence in any one department, research group or project. In fact the identification of *separate* qualitative and quantitative elements within a project can be one of the biggest obstacles to their proper integration. Rather, we are referring to work in which different forms of data are put together to make a more coherent, rational and rigorous whole.

Combined methods work is not that new, appearing in the work of Campbell and Fiske (1959), for example. Teddlie and Tashakkori (2003) claim that there have always been studies using mixed methods, citing the early twentieth-century work in the Hawthorne factory as a case in point. They also claim that until the 'paradigm wars' of the 1980s such an approach was unproblematic and completely unremarkable (see Chapter 9). Erzberger and Prein (1997) trace combined methods approaches in sociology back to at least 1855. However, there has recently been an increase of interest in combined approaches from a number of sources. The combination of methods has only recently been covered in texts for training new researchers, and is only now being used more widely (Cresswell 2003). There is a growing recognition of the need to move beyond the use of mono-method research in both the social sciences and those disciplines where social science research methods have been applied (e.g. Debats *et al.* 1995 in psychology, Rogers and Nicolaas 1998 in sociology, and Barbour 1998 in medicine). Perhaps most notably, in the UK Economic and Social Research Council (ESRC) Research Methods Programme there are, at the time of writing, two funded projects solely and explicitly about developing models for combining methods. In education, this trend has been linked to concerns about improving both the skills base of educational researchers and the quality of educational research (NERF 2001), as well as recognition that the methods chosen to conduct research should fit the research question being posed (National Research Council 2002). In general, the debate has, for the most part, moved away from *whether* data from different sources should be combined, to a much greater focus on *how* (e.g. National Institute of Health 1999).

Although work using mixed methods is far from common (Hausman 2000), it is also not that rare. In fact, such combination goes on in social science all the time in many relatively uncomplicated ways, such as literature reviews or ad hoc field notes (Gorard 2002a). Everything observable during fieldwork is potentially informative, and the successful researcher attempts to answer research questions by whatever means it takes. There may be long letters attached to uncompleted questionnaires from respondents in a survey design. These are generally fascinating and useful, and a researcher would, presumably, not dream of claiming that these, or the pencilled comments on the margins of a form, were of no use since they were qualitative in nature and not foreseen as part of the survey. Similarly, in conducting interviews with headteachers one would not refuse to accept a school brochure of exam results proffered during the interview, or some school statistics sent on after an interview. When conducting a series of household structured interviews, the notes taken on the appearance of the house and its occupants can be very valuable. Once on the road to conduct research, everything is potentially informative and the researcher becomes a 'Hoover' of data, as far as possible. The research starts with draft research questions, and continues with an attempt to answer them by whatever means it takes. It is difficult to imagine why anyone would do anything very different.

Once you set your mind to it, opportunities for combining approaches are plentiful. We can conduct an experiment in which an independent variable is manipulated and the impacts of this are studied qualitatively over time. As early as the 1970s, work was being conducted on the *social* psychology of the experimental setting (Adair 1973). In designing a questionnaire, standard textbooks advocate the prior use of in-depth approaches, such as focus groups, to help identify and modify the relevant questions (Oppenheim 1992). Qualitative work does not have a monopoly on researching meanings, and the widespread use of attitude measures shows that many other researchers are interested in understanding meanings. We have no independent way of knowing whether in-depth work is actually better at divining meanings than questionnaires. Often the attitude questions are in any case based on prior in-depth work – what Hammersley (1996) calls 'facilitation' where one method is used to help another. Qualitative work has traditionally been used in several fields as the basis for the preliminary phases of other quantitative studies, perhaps to generate hypotheses to be tested by subsequent larger-scale work (Erzberger and Prein 1997). Q-methodology is usually seen as quantitative in origin, but it attempts to reveal subjectivity in psychology, so having some qualitative aspects as well (Dennis and Goldberg 1996; Brown 2003).

Even 'pure' statistical analysis is misunderstood by observers if they do not consider also the social settings in which it takes place, and the role of 'qualitative' factors in reaching a conclusion (MacKenzie 1999). The measurement of all useful quantities requires a prior consideration of theory leading to the identification of a quality to be measured (see Chapter 2). Normal statistical textbooks describe ideal procedures to follow, but several studies of actual behaviour have observed different common practices among researchers. 'Producing a statistic is a social enterprise' (Gephart 1988: 15), and the stages of selecting variables, making observations and coding the results take place in everyday settings where subjective influences arise. Gephart takes a clearly qualitative approach to quantitative work.

We can observe behaviour, such as classroom interaction, and include in our report a numeric summary of our observations. The similarity-contrast principle guiding the traditional analysis of narrative data is similar to the principle underlying numeric factor analysis (Tashakkori and Teddlie 2003). In analysing interview data, standard textbooks describe a quasi-statistical approach to counting responses, in order to establish patterns. A limited amount of quantification of all qualitative data – such as how many people said something like this – helps to overcome anecdotalism (Silverman 1985). Content analysis, using the common constant comparison method for example, uses both quantitative and qualitative operations on the text. Programme evaluation and case studies, including some action research, routinely involve both observation and measurement, usually regardless of their specific design (Scholz and Tietje 2002). Evaluation work often asks a variety of questions including those about effects, and why and how they occur (National Research Council 2002). Case studies can easily involve the results of written tests given to participants. The methods of history have to cope with primary and documentary evidence, with information from genetics, archaeology and linguistics, for example. In psychology, approaches such as personal construct theory explicitly advocate the mixing of numeric and 'qualitative' data.

To some extent, then, all methods of social science research deal with qualities, even when the observed qualities are counted. Similarly, all methods of analysis use some form of number, such as 'tend, most, some, all, none, few' and so on. This is what the patterns in qualitative analysis are based on (even where the claim is made that a case is 'unique' since uniqueness is, of course, a numeric description). Chioncel *et al.* (2003) take a realistic position on the reliability and validity of qualitative research that suggests that its practical separation from quantitative work is minimal. Words can be counted, and numbers can be descriptive. Patterns are, by definition, numbers and the things that are numbered are qualities (Popkewitz 1984). Paulos (2000) presents both stories about mathematics and the hidden maths of stories, and in this way draws a fascinating link between the logic of numbers and of narratives.

In fact, Gray and Densten (1998) suggest considering the two approaches of qualitative and quantitative as being on a continuum rather than in the form of a dichotomy that researchers have to select between. 'Qualitative and quantitative evidence', therefore, refers to a false dualism (Frazer 1995), and one that we are probably better off without. One practical reason would be that we could cease wasting time and energy in pointless debates about the virtues of one approach over the other. We do not need to be imprisoned by other people's ideas about 'incommensurable paradigms' and the like, at least until we have learnt a lot more about research in general. This supposed distinction between qualitative and quantitative evidence is essentially one between the traditional methods for their analysis rather than between underlying philosophies, paradigms, or even methods of data collection.

What's so good about combined methods research?

Combined methods research, and the combination of data derived through the use of different methods, has been identified by a variety of authorities as a key element in the improvement of social science, including education research. One of the key reasons advanced for this is that research claims are stronger when based on a variety of methods (National Research Council 2002). While requiring a greater level of skill, the routine combination of methods creates researchers with an increased ability to make appropriate criticisms of all types of research. Combined research often has greater impact, because figures can be very persuasive to policy-makers whereas stories are more easily remembered and repeated by them for illustrative purposes. It can also lead to less waste of potentially useful information (see Chapter 3).

Combined approaches can be particularly useful when the background theory for an investigation is minimal, and where one of the main purposes of the study is to generate useable theory (Geurts and Roosendaal 2001, see also Chapters 7 and 9). Some commentators claim that by combining methods in one study we can confirm and explain, verify and generate theory, all at the same time (Teddlie and Tashakkori 2003). Above all, if social phenomena tend to have multiple empirical appearances, then using only one method in each study can lead to the unnecessary fragmentation of explanatory models (Faber and Scheper 2003). Using combined approaches is, in these circumstances, most appropriate.

Why is there so little combined research?

The main reason that there is so little education research that routinely combines numeric and other evidence appears to be that there is so little education research involving numbers, and, apparently, so few researchers prepared to work with numbers (but see Chapter 8). There is now a system-wide shortage of expertise in large-scale studies, especially field trials derived from laboratory experimental designs. Over the last 20 years, there has undoubtedly been a move towards much greater use of 'qualitative' approaches (Hayes 1992), even in what were traditionally numerate areas of research (Ellmore and Woehilke 1998). In addition, acceptance rates for 'qualitative' publications are higher than for 'quantitative' pieces, by a ratio of around two to one in one US journal (Taylor 2001). In some fields, the 1990s were dominated by generally small-scale funding leading to predominantly qualitative 'thinking' (McIntyre and McIntyre 2000), entailing a considerable potential for bias when conducted in isolation (Dyson and Desforges 2002).

This imbalance is a general concern within UK social sciences, with the recent Commission on the Social Sciences (2003) describing 'a deeply worrying lack of quantitative skills' (p. 8). Funders, such as the ESRC want to see the pendulum swing back towards a more balanced portfolio of skills (e.g. Sooben 2002), and at the time of writing the ESRC has at least 14 separate initiatives in place to increase the use of quantitative approaches among social scientists. Similar sentiments have been expressed in other developed countries (Diamond 2002). In education, especially, there have been a succession of reports showing a shortage of quantitative skills, and the pressing need for capacity-building measures targeted at overcoming this shortage (Taylor 2002; Rendall 2003). Indeed, the problem is not simply one of shortage, but also of what Mortimore and Sammons (1997: 185) call 'crude anti-quantitative attitudes' among some commentators. This may be partly why the opponents of combined methods work so frequently identify themselves as 'qualitative' researchers.

There are, in turn, a variety of reasons for this situation. It stems from researchers' bad experiences of mathematics at school, leading to generally negative attitudes towards numeric issues and relatively low levels of numeracy among students. In fact, Meehl (1998) suggests that there is considerable self-selection for poor ability with numbers among students electing to study social science subjects. This may then be reinforced by superficial or poor teaching at university level, crowded courses and a lack of perceived relevance to one's own study or practice (Murtonen and Lehtinen 2003). Students in many disciplines, including social work, psychology, sociology and education now dread their compulsory statistics courses. These are always reported as the most anxiety-inducing courses, and this is despite the growth in readily available statistical information and the tremendous power of the computer to process it all, because the anxiety is not merely about maths. There is also a common philosophical confusion about what statistics is and what it represents (see Chapter 2), and this is found to be greatest for those students with the lowest ability, not merely with numbers but also in terms of creativity and reading (Onwuegbuzie and Wilson 2003).

A second major related reason why there is so little combined methods work is the existence and reproduction of single-method identities among new researchers. There is, among some researchers who use only qualitative methods, an assumption that adopting a method automatically means adopting an entire 'paradigm'. Students have been heard to exclaim, before deciding on a topic and research questions, that they intend to use 'qualitative' methods of data collection or analysis. The reverse, of course, also applies. There are mono-method researchers who use only quantitative techniques, although for the reasons given above these are fewer in number. They are perhaps most common in relatively established disciplines such as psychology, economics or medicine, where there used to be a tradition that only numeric data was of relevance (Lawson 2003). Students are therefore, perhaps unwittingly, encouraged to count or measure everything, even where this is not necessarily appropriate. Forms of evidence not based on numbers are despised, while evidence based on numbers is accepted somewhat uncritically. One outcome is that statistical analysis is done badly and so gets a bad press. Part of the problem here may be the 'cronyism' among reviewers that in-depth knowledge of advanced statistical procedures tends to generate, which leads to poorly explained and over-technical reports. In this book, we argue strongly against this tradition, and propose instead a simpler concept of quantitative work based more fully on a consideration of the relationship between the behaviour of numbers and the object of study.

Perhaps 'it comes as no particular surprise to discover that a scientist formulates problems in a way which requires for their solution just those techniques in which he himself is especially skilled' (Pedhazur 1982: 28), but to understand this temptation is not to condone it. There is a story of a person searching the ground late at night under the circle of light thrown by a street lamp. When asked what they were doing, they replied that they had lost their keys somewhere in the darkened bit of the road and were trying to find them again. Asked why, if the keys were lost somewhere else, they were looking in the wrong place the person replied that the lit area was the only part where it was *possible* to search. Absurd though this is, it is how many researchers apparently conduct their own 'searches'. We advocate here instead the selection of the research topic and the questions you are curious about *first*, and only then a consideration of how best to answer them. Do not fit your proposed study to your favourite approach (a case of the cart pulling the horse), and then try to disguise this as a philosophical, rather than a methodological, decision. Guidelines from the British Educational Research Association (BERA) urge that 'it is important to emphasise that there is no one strategy which is always going to be appropriate for every piece of research undertaken. It is very much a matter of ... fitting the method or technique to what is being investigated' (Campbell *et al.* 2003: 5). To do anything different is not only poor research, it is also unethical.

A third reason, according to Gray and Densten (1998), is that despite its long-standing nature and the debate over mixing methods, there is very little literature to suggest *how* it can be done. Of the three reasons this is probably the most easily overcome, and that is part of what we hope to do in this book.

The structure of the book

This chapter raises the issues that are the substance of the rest of the book – the consequences of allowing the notion of fitness for purpose to drive the choice of methods in educational research, and consideration of whether this will result in higher quality research, leading to reduction in the waste of potentially useful evidence, and the greater impact of research findings. As this introduction has implied, there do not appear to us to be insuperable philosophical or technical difficulties involved in combining different forms of data (for that is the assumption underlying the book). One of the purposes of this book is to illustrate to readers how combining different findings can be an 'everyday' occurrence. Another is to present some more developed models for the formal combination of data that readers are less likely to be aware of.

Chapter 2 discusses the nature of both quantitative and qualitative research, and some of the limitations of both, as currently understood. It shows that both approaches require considerable subjective judgement. The chapter then considers work such as the development of measuring instruments, which involves moving from in-depth study to a larger scale (and is therefore in contrast to Chapter 4 where the model moves from large-scale to in-depth). It continues by arguing that all measurements, by definition, require prior theoretical consideration and in-depth observation and that, therefore, the qualitative/quantitative distinction is almost impossible to sustain. It sets the scene for a consideration in later chapters of particular techniques that have been used when combining research by type and scale.

Chapter 3 explores the apparently simple notion of 'triangulation' between different research approaches. It then considers the formal combination of data across or between studies, starting with the traditional process of a narrative review of the literature and the more recent systematic reviews. It highlights a common problem in all of these models – namely that we have no agreed method for *systematically* combining evidence of different sorts. The bulk of the chapter is a description of a practical, and so far successful, way of overcoming this problem, utilizing subjective probability and Bayes' Theorem for combining evidence. This part of the chapter is concerned with what Teddlie and Tashakkori (2003) refer to as 'multi-strand conversion mixed methods' – the collection of data of one type and its conversion to another.

Chapters 4 and 5 describe the combination of type and scale of education research, as used within a single study, and in the context of real examples. Chapter 4 involves a 'new political arithmetic' model of our work on social segregation in the compulsory school sector. Chapter 5 uses a similar, but more complex, model from our research on participation in the post-compulsory education sector. Both chapters involve moving from evidence that is large in scale and predominantly numeric, to work that is smaller in scale and predominantly in-depth. This is what Teddlie and Tashakkori (2003) refer to as 'sequential mixed-methods work'.

Chapter 6 discusses the potential of a Medical Research Council model for complex interventions in education research, as a means of combining randomized and non-randomized data of different types, to test the effects of interventions and to illuminate the processes involved in generating these effects. Chapter 7 explores the use of design experiments in education, drawing on our work conducted as part of an international collaboration supported by the National Science Foundation of the USA. In these new kinds of studies, both qualitative and quantitative components are involved from the start, and in an iterative model. Chapters 6 and 7 provide examples of what Teddlie and Tashakkori (2003) refer to as 'concurrent mixed-methods work'.

Chapter 8 uses a variety of data sources, including our large-scale survey of researchers and our re-analysis of published work from 1997 to 2001, to illustrate the current prevalence of qualitative, quantitative and combined methods research in the UK. This helps to show the considerable potential that exists for combined methods work, and also some of the problems facing its development in the near future.

Chapter 9 examines the role of theory in research. It criticizes the development of a mono-method culture, and the consequent creation of lifelong 'methods identities' supported by a notion of paradigms. These alleged paradigms have led education and social science researchers to characterize themselves as much by the methods that they use to conduct their research as by the subject area that they have chosen for their research speciality. The chapter explores the origins of the 'paradigm wars', and the erroneous belief that use of a particular research method also involves a commitment to a particular theoretical worldview. In many ways this penultimate chapter, which tends to focus on problems in stand-alone 'qualitative' work, should be seen as the complement to the second chapter which tends to focus on problems in stand-alone 'quantitative' work.

Chapter 10 rehearses the argument that there is an overarching logic for all modes of research, considers the ethics of combined methods work, summarizes the findings of the book so far, and discusses their implications for the training and development of new researchers.

Simple numeric and textual data: querying the divide

This chapter provides a critique of the traditional quantitative and qualitative approaches to research, highlighting some of their limitations when conducted in isolation. The notion of research 'paradigms' alluded to in Chapter 1 is discussed further in Chapter 9. For the present, the book assumes a very simple definition of the two approaches, such as that in Gray and Densten (1998). 'Quantitative' work refers to counts and measures of things, while 'qualitative' work predominantly uses words (and increasingly visual images) as data. These different types of data often require different forms of analysis, but this is very far from saying that they therefore have a different underlying logic, or refer to different realities, or that either approach is better in any way than the other. Quantitative work here is based on numbers, but not necessarily on traditional statistical theory or the standard 'frequentist' approach. Qualitative work here is based on words, but is not necessarily 'interpretive' or social constructivist (or any other kind of 'ist). The chapter starts by considering one of the most natural and common ways in which researchers routinely combine these supposedly distinct methods, sometimes without even realizing it. We argue that even the process of measurement – the foundation of quantitative work – is based on qualitative work.

The meaning of measurement

We use this section to expand a little on the idea presented in Chapter 1 that even very basic operations of quantification, such as measurement, are heavily dependent on qualitative observation. To attempt to separate the two in the way usually done in textbooks does justice to neither, and could encourage dangerous misunderstandings.

Obviously, anyone can simply assign a number to an object or to the gradations within a concept. In this case we are using numbers as convenient labels – such as the serial numbers allotted to examination candidates for anonymity. What we must not do is mistake this process for real *measurement*. Unfortunately, such a basic misunderstanding of the idea of quantity is quite common, and leads to widespread practices that can only be described as 'pseudo-quantification' (Prandy 2002). The most notorious example of this might be IQ and the claim that 'intelligence is what IQ tests measure'. The problem, though, is not, as is usually argued, whether IQ tests measure intelligence, but whether they really measure anything at all, in the sense of establishing a quantity. The emergence of a number used as a proper quantity depends on a clear relationship between the properties or behaviour of the thing being measured and the properties or behaviour of the numbers used. This emergence is said to have three distinct stages (Berka 1983).

The first thing we need for true measurement is to be able to compare accurately the characteristics of a set of objects. Imagine that the characteristic we were concerned with was a very simple one such as length – then we would need to be able to make accurate relative comparisons of the length of different objects. We might start with a theory of length or 'longness', based on extensive qualitative observations of the fact that some objects stick out more than others, especially when laid side by side. We should be able to sort a set of objects in terms of this theory of length, so that each object in a sequence sticks out more than its neighbour (Prondy 2002). We would then have produced a relationship of order, and could use rankings (ordinally) rather than simply assigning numbers as identifiers (nominally). This process is basic to all measurements, and these simple scales are still found in the natural sciences, such as the Moh scale of the hardness of materials based on the qualitative observation of scratching. If we can then select one or more reference objects to act as a standard length (like a metre rule, or the human 'foot' in less sophisticated times) then we can base our numbers on multiples of that standard. In this case, the numbers become a proper measurement, and the concept of number begins to emerge independently of the reference set. The numbers emerge inductively to represent the sizes of various sets of things.

Of course, when we measure things ordinarily we tend to ignore this complex pedigree (of Berka's three stages). It seems easy and obvious to read the data from our measurement tools, because we ignore the theoretical and empirical presuppositions underlying them. But we do need to recall, when discussing the combination of research methods, that measurement is a process of assigning numbers that reflect the amount of a property possessed by an object. The property, such as length, does not really exist independently of the measurement. It is true that the ordering of objects that is associated with any quantity has a parallel with the ordering of numbers. This can be very useful, because it is usually more convenient to work with numbers than with objects; dividing by two is easier than sawing a log in half. However, quantities and number systems are two quite distinct structures; the utility derives from the fact of the parallel between the two, their isomorphism. However, it is the establishment of a quantity that assures the isomorphism, not the mere assignment of numbers. No amount of 'quantification' will, by itself, establish a quantity. Of course, length is a relatively simple scientific measurement. In education and other social science research we are usually concerned with concepts and variables that are more complex to handle. As Prandy (2002) points out, answering yes to a question, being a member of a group, engaging in an activity and so on may well be elements of a putative quantity, but they are also likely to be influenced by other individual characteristics. It is not usually possible for us to create objects like the standard metre. As a result, our quantifications are subject to considerable 'error'.

Measurement, the basis for all quantitative analysis is, therefore, predicated on prior qualitative work. It is not possible to conduct one without the other (see also Chapter 1). The impact of errors in measurement, and so the need for judgement when working with numbers, are the subjects of the next section.

Simple quantitative approaches

As explained in Chapter 1, one of the key reasons why there is not more combined work is that there is, apparently, relatively little work using numeric techniques in any case. And because combining methods requires numeric techniques, this chapter has a greater focus on these. This chapter should be seen as a complement to the penultimate chapter which has a correspondingly greater focus on 'qualitative' work. More importantly, because both chapters taken together show that the actual process of conducting research is the same whatever methods are employed, we hope that readers will read both in full. The level of arithmetic required for this chapter is minimal, but the conclusion is rather radical. The key issue for new researchers to realize is that the routine use of numbers in their research does not need to be complex or frightening (any more than it means that they must subscribe to an outmoded philosophy such as 'positivism'). Nor do they need to be convinced by the traditional statistical theory taught in their methods courses.

We cannot hope to present here a full, clear and unambiguous summary of the methods of data collection and analysis suitable for use with numbers. Nevertheless, we have argued elsewhere that with a good dataset, numeric analysis is usually rather easy (Gorard 2003a). It is what the analysis yields in terms of useful knowledge that is tricky, not the analysis itself. For example, given data for a population there are no probabilistic calculations necessary, no tests of significance, no confidence intervals, and so on. Similarly, running a simple experiment with two large, randomly selected groups and one outcome measure means that all you need to do is compare the scores of one group with the scores of the other in order to produce an effect size. The key is to have the comparator to make the comparison with, for without a comparison we end up, inevitably, with an incomplete consideration of the plausible alternatives (Dawes 2001). But at present, despite this simplicity, statistical training for new researchers is made far more complex, more frightening and less pragmatic than is needed. Researchers wishing to do simple work with numbers do not need all of the paraphernalia they are routinely presented with in training. So, in our experience, one of the easiest ways to encourage more researchers to work with numbers is to try and undo some of the 'damage' caused by those scary courses on supposedly elementary and essential statistics.

The rhetorical power of numbers

Of course, part of the danger of a technical approach to quantitative work that most people do not follow (and may feel is 'cleverer' than it actually is) is that it allows numbers to retain considerable rhetorical power for a wide audience. For example, figures for the USA in 1999 suggest that around 25 per cent of adults smoke, and that around 1 in 10 of these develops lung cancer compared to around 1 in 200 of non-smokers (Gigerenzer 2002). What, therefore, is the strength of the relationship between smoking and lung cancer? If we were to sample 800 adults we might get 200 smokers (25 per cent) of whom 20 (10 per cent) get lung cancer (see Table 2.1).

Table 2.1 Relationship between smoking and lung cancer (1)

	Cancer	No cancer	Total
Smoker	20	180	200
Non-smoker	3	597	600
Total	23	777	800

If, on the other hand, we sample 400 smokers and 400 non-smokers, we would expect 10 per cent of the smokers (40) and 0.5 per cent of the non-smokers (2) to have cancer, as in Table 2.2.

Table 2.2 Relationship between smoking and lung cancer (2)

	Cancer	No cancer	Total
Smoker	40	360	400
Non-smoker	2	398	400
Total	42	758	800

From Table 2.1 we can see that smokers in general represent 20/23 of those with cancer. So, if we sample 400 people with lung cancer, we expect 20/23rds (348) of them to be smokers. If we sample 400 people without lung cancer then we expect only 180/777ths of them to be smokers. These are the figures in Table 2.3.

Table 2.3 Relationship between smoking and lung cancer (3)

	Cancer	No cancer	Total
Smoker	348	93	441
Non-smoker	52	307	359
Total	400	400	800

Note that each of these tables, quite properly, has the same row and column headings. And the figures within them are based on exactly the same frequencies. But each gives an entirely different impression. Most notably, the first two tables appear to suggest that smoking is considerably more benign than the third. The relationship between smoking and cancer (the leading diagonal) appears stronger after the event (working back from cancer) than before (working forward from smoking). Which version is used in a presentation might depend on the prejudice of the researcher, or their funder. This might lead to different conclusions because of the more general weakness among academics in the understanding of quantitative methods. Even many 'quantitative' researchers are unable to see that Tables 2.1 to 2.3 describe the same basic findings, because such 'simple' but crucial things are not taught in traditional research training. The current focus on significance testing does not leave time.

A study of 280,000 women in Sweden assessed the impact of a screening programme for breast cancer. Over ten years, there were 4 deaths per 1000 among the over 40s without screening, and 3 deaths per 1000 with screening. There are several different ways the gain from screening could be expressed (Dawes 2001). The absolute risk reduction is 1 in 1000 or 0.1 per cent. The number needed to treat (to save one life) is 1000. The increase in average life expectancy is 12 days, and the relative risk reduction is 25 per cent. It is the last that is routinely used by advocates and those standing to gain from screening programmes, perhaps because it sounds like a saving of 25 lives per 100. All versions are correct – but the relative risk is more likely to get funding and headlines. Information leaflets about the screening procedure mostly do not discuss the danger of false positives or other costs. Some even give the illusion that screening can reduce the incidence of the cancer. But to achieve even the level of success above requires a high proportion of false positives in which the test results state that an individual has cancer, even when they do not. These false positives are the downside of the testing regime, and can lead to considerable distress and unnecessary operations. To these we must add the danger of cancer from the radiation in the screening itself, and the financial cost of the programme (and therefore the lost opportunity to spend this money on reducing the risk in some other way). So viewed dispassionately, and with alternative ways of looking at the same data, a 1/1000 risk reduction may not seem worth it for this group.

In judicial proceedings (and media reporting), forensic evidence (such as a fingerprint or DNA profile) is used to make a match with a suspect. Prosecutors tend to use the probability of such a match (e.g. 1 in 10,000) as though it were the reverse of a probability of guilt (9,999 in 10,000). However, they have to argue also that there is no human error in the matching process, that the match signifies presence of the suspect at the crime scene, that presence at the scene necessarily entails guilt, and so on (Gigerenzer 2002). Above all, they have to demonstrate that the number of potential suspects is so small that a 1 in 10,000 chance is the equivalent of 'beyond reasonable doubt'. If the crime took place in a city of 1 million people, and if we make the favourable assumption that potential suspects are limited to residents only, then 1/10,000 means that 100 residents will have just such a forensic match. Thus, the suspect actually has a 1/100 probability of guilt (on this evidence alone). This is much higher than for an average resident of that city (and therefore germane to the case without being conclusive), but much lower than 9,999/10,000. The importance of this error, and others like them, is hard to overestimate in law, medicine and beyond. The same error occurs regularly in statistical testing in education research, where researchers treat the inverse of the probability of their null hypothesis as identical to the probability of their conclusions. The gravity of this error would be hard to overestimate but is, again, largely neglected in traditional quantitative methods teaching.

We routinely face scares about health, food, the environment, and education of course, with the figures presented by their peddlers in the most rhetorically convincing way possible. Media reports of research studies tend to use the rhetorical power of numbers to make research reports appear more alarming or more flattering. We are unlikely to be able to change this directly. But our ability to see beyond the presentation, and to consider other equally valid presentations *is* under our control. Improving the ability of the research consumer is our best defence, and will harm only those for whom the ideology is more important than the evidence (or those who otherwise stand to benefit in some way from continued confusion). This improvement will be *most* marked in the apparently simple kinds of problems discussed in this section (for further examples, see Gorard 2003b). The lessons could perhaps be summarized as: be aware of the potential weakness of the measurements themselves, demand a base rate or comparison group for any claim, and be prepared to rework the figures yourself in different ways to lessen their rhetorical power. Anyone can do this, using only primary-school arithmetic techniques. Part of the move towards combined approaches is to lessen the dominance of the traditional statistical theorists who unintentionally prevent it by scaring students with complex and largely unnecessary detail.

There is a misconception among social scientists that statistical analysis is somehow a technical, essentially objective, process of decision-making, whereas other forms of data analysis are judgement-based, subjective and far from technical. This section focuses on the former part of the misconception showing, rather, that statistical analysis relies on judgement of the most personal and non-technical kind. Therefore, the key to reporting such analyses, and persuading others of one's findings, is the clarification and discussion of those judgements and their (attempted) justifications. In this way, statistical analysis is no different from the analysis of other forms of data, especially those forms often referred to as 'qualitative' (see the final section in this chapter). By creating an artificial schism based on the kinds of data we use, the misconception leads to neglect of the similar logic underlying all approaches to research, encourages mono-method research identities and so inhibits the use of mixed methods. The chapter starts from the premise that all statistical analyses involve the format: data = model + error, but where the error is not merely random error but also due to non-response, estimation, transcription and propagation. This total error component is an unknown and there is, therefore, no technical way of deciding whether the error dwarfs the other components. However complex the analysis, at heart it involves a judgement about the likely size of the error in comparison to the size of the alleged findings (whether pattern, trend, difference or effect).

This section alerts readers to the role of judgement in statistical decision-making via an imaginary example. It introduces the three common kinds of explanations for observed results: error or bias, chance or luck, and the plausible substantive explanations. It then reconsiders standard practice when dealing with each of these types in turn. Our standard approach to these three types needs adjusting in two crucial ways. We need to formally consider, and explain why we reject, a greater range of plausible substantive explanations for the same results. More pressingly, we need to take more notice of the estimated size of any error or bias relative to the size of the 'effects' that we uncover. The chapter then continues with an extended example, considering work on the school-mix effect as a possible example of 'pathological science' in light of the foregoing. This leads to a summary of the advantages of using judgement more fully and more explicitly in statistical analysis.

An example of judgement

Imagine trying to test the claim that someone is able mentally to influence the toss of a perfectly fair coin, so that it will land showing heads more than tails (or vice versa) by a very small amount. We might set up the test using our own set of standard coins selected from a larger set at random by observers, and ask the claimant to specify in advance whether it is heads (or tails) that will be most frequent. We would then need to conduct a very large number of coin tosses, because a small number would be subject to considerable 'random' variation. If, for example, there were 51 heads after 100 tosses the claimant might try to claim success even though the probability of such a result is quite high in any case. If, on the other hand, there were 51 tails after 100 tosses the claimant might claim that this is due to the standard variation, and that their influence towards heads could only be seen over a larger number of trials. We could not say that 100 tosses would provide a definitive test of the claim. Imagine instead, then, 1 million trials yielding 51 per cent heads. We have at least three competing explanations for this imbalance in heads and tails. First, it could still be an example of normal 'random' variation, although considerably less probable than in the first example. Second, it might be evidence of a slight bias in the experimental set-up such as a bias in one or more coins, the tossing procedure, the readout or the recording of results. Third, it might be evidence that the claimant is correct; they *can* influence the result.

In outline, this situation is one faced by all researchers using whatever methods, once their data collection and analysis is complete. The finding could have no substantive significance at all (being due to chance). It could be due to 'faults' in the research (due to some selection effect in picking the coins perhaps). It could be a major discovery affecting our theoretical understanding of the world (a person can influence events at a distance). Or it could be a combination of any of these. We now consider each solution in turn.

The explanation of pure chance becomes less likely as the number of trials increases. In some research situations, such as coin tossing, we can calculate this decrease in likelihood precisely. In most research situations, however, the likelihood can only be an estimate. In all situations we can be certain of two things – that the chance explanation can never be discounted entirely (Gorard 2002b), and that its likelihood is mostly a function of the scale of the research. Where research is large in scale, repeatable and conducted in different locations, and so on, then it can be said to have minimized the chance element. In the example of 1 million coin tosses this chance element is small (less than the 1/20 threshold used in traditional statistical analysis), but it could still account for some of the observed difference (either by attenuating or disguising any 'true' effect).

If we have constructed our experiment well, then the issue of bias is also minimized. There is a considerable literature on strategies to overcome bias and confounds as far as possible (e.g. Adair 1973; Cook and Campbell 1979). In our coin tossing example we could automate the tossing process, mint our own coins, not tell the researchers which of heads or tails was predicted to be higher, and so on. However, like the chance element, errors in conducting research can never be completely eliminated. There will be coins lost, coins bent, machines that malfunction, and so on. There can even be bias in recording (misreading heads for tails, or reading correctly but ticking the wrong column) and in calculating the results. Again, as with the chance element, it is usually not possible to calculate the impact of these errors precisely (even on the rare occasion that the identity of any error is known). We can only estimate the scale of these errors, and their potential direction of influence on the research. We are always left with the error component as a plausible explanation for any result or part of a result.

Therefore, to be convinced that the finding is a 'true' effect, and that a person can mentally influence a coin toss, we would need to decide that the difference (pattern or trend) that we have found is big enough for us to reasonably conclude that the chance and error components represent an insufficient explanation. Note that the chance and error components not only have to be insufficient in themselves, they also have to be insufficient in combination. In the coin tossing experiment, is 51 per cent heads in 1 million trials enough? The answer will be a matter of judgement. It should be an informed judgement, based on the best estimates of both chance and error, but it remains a judgement. The chance element has traditionally been considered in terms of null-hypothesis significance-testing and its derivatives, but this approach is seen as increasingly problematic, and also involves judgement (see below). But perhaps because it *appears* to have a technical solution, researchers have tended to concentrate on the chance element in practice and to ignore the far more important components of error, and the judgement these entail.

If the difference is judged a 'true' effect, so that a person can mentally influence a coin toss, we should also consider the importance of this finding. This importance has at least two elements. The *practical* outcome is probably negligible. Apart from in 'artificial' gambling games, this level of influence on coin tossing would not make much difference. For example, it is unlikely to affect the choice of who bats first in a five-match cricket test series. If someone could guarantee a heads on each toss (or even odds of 3:1 in favour of heads) then that would be different, and the difference over 1 million trials would be so great that there could be little doubt it was a true effect. On the other hand, even if the immediate practical importance is minor, a true effect would involve many changes in our understanding of important areas of physics and biology. This would be important knowledge for its own sake, and might also lead to more usable examples of mental influence at a distance. In fact, this revolution in thinking would be so great that many observers would conclude that 51 per cent was not sufficient, even over 1 million trials. The finding makes so little immediate practical difference, but requires so much of an overhaul of existing 'knowledge' that it makes perfect sense to conclude that 51 per cent is consistent with merely chance and error. However, this kind of judgement is ignored in many social science research situations, where our over-willing acceptance of what Park (2000) calls 'pathological science' leads to the creation of weak theories based on practically useless findings (Cole 1994; Davis 1994; Platt 1996a; Hacking 1999). There *is* an alternative, described in the rest of this section.

The error component

My son is 6 years old, and growing fast – a fact recorded on my parents' kitchen wall. On this wall my parents record the heights of all of their grandchildren, and the first thing my son does on arrival at their house is to go to the wall for an up-to-date measurement. The measurement is taken by placing a book or ruler on his head and drawing a line underneath with a date beside it. My parents are not scientists and do not insist on standard conditions for each measurement. The book or ruler is one variable, the child's stance is another, the wearing of shoes or socks might be another, and so on. Therefore, we should conclude that each measurement of height contains an unknown error. When my son was 1 metre tall, we might expect the measurement to have an error component of the order of magnitude of 1 centimetre either way. The 1 centimetre can only be an estimate, and could easily be twice or half that. It is unlikely to be 0 or 1 metre, however. This ratio of error to the measurement (1:100) is probably acceptable for everyday purposes when estimating a child's height.

However, my son shows little interest in his height, as such. He is more concerned with how much he has grown since his last visit, and with whether he is catching up with the height of his nearest cousin. Both of these questions require a calculation, subtracting one height from another. For a visit occurring one month after the previous visit, my son might only be expected to have grown 1 centimetre or less. To estimate this growth, he visually subtracts the previous height from the current one. Both the past and present measurements of height have an error component of the order of magnitude of 1:100. Subtracting the two measurements may eliminate their two error components if, by chance, they are in the same direction, or it may double them if they are in opposite directions. This leads us to an estimate of growth of 1 centimetre, with an estimated maximum error component of 2 centimetres either way. This ratio of measurement error to the measurement (2:1) is probably not acceptable for the purposes of estimating a child's growth. In this case, the error clearly dwarfs the finding, and to insist that the finding is meaningful would be 'pathological' (see above).

Two important points emerge from this consideration. There is no standard acceptable amount of error in any measurement. The relevance of the error component is a function of scale, and of the use to which the measurement is put. Also, the relative size of error in the growth result is not determined solely by the ratio of error in the original measurements. It depends on the precise steps in the ensuing computation. Of course, it helps if the initial readings are as accurate as possible, but whether they are accurate enough depends on what is done with the readings, and how the error component propagates as it is used in calculations. It is important to recall that every statistical, arithmetic or mathematical operation conducted with measurements is also conducted with their error components. If we square a variable, then we also square its error component, and so on. The more complex the calculations we conduct the harder it is to track the propagation of errors (even if we are aware of them at source), and so make an informed judgement of the ratio of error to final result. In extreme cases, the manipulation of variables leads to results almost entirely determined by the initial errors and very little influenced by the initial measurements (as is the case in some forms of weather forecasting – see the section on 'ill-conditioning' in Gorard 2003a).

To recapitulate: all research faces the problem outlined in the introduction, of having at least three types of explanation for the same observed data. The first is the explanation of chance. The second is an explanation based on error such as bias, confounds and 'contamination'. The third is a substantive explanation, from a range of plausible explanations. Null-hypothesis significance tests cater for only the first of these, and only under very unrealistic conditions. What are the alternatives?

Do we need statistical tests?

In a recent study of the teaching of quantitative methods, 'the statistical test for significance [was rated] as the most difficult subject' (Murtonen and Lehtinen 2003: 175), and it is this, more than any single factor, that leads to the student dislike of statistics described in Chapter 1. If it is crucial that *all* researchers are taught about significance tests in their basic training, then perhaps all we can do is find better ways of teaching them. However, such efforts may be also unnecessary. It is perfectly possible to learn a great deal about, and to use in practice, a variety of quantitative techniques without ever needing to conduct a significance test.

To what extent can traditional statistical analysis help us to overcome the problems of errors as illustrated above? The classical form of statistical testing in common use today was derived from agricultural studies (Porter 1986). The tests were developed for one-off use, in situations where the measurement error was negligible, in order to allow researchers to estimate the probability that two random samples drawn from the same population would have divergent measurements. In a roundabout way, this probability is then used to help decide whether the two samples actually come from two different populations. Vegetative reproduction can be used to create two colonies of what is effectively the same plant. One colony could be given an agricultural treatment, and the results (in terms of survival rates perhaps) compared between the two colonies. Statistical analysis helps us to estimate the probability that a sample of the results from each colony would diverge by the amount we actually observe, under the artificial assumption that the agricultural treatment had been ineffective and, therefore, that all variation comes from the sampling. If this probability is very small, we might conclude that the treatment appeared to have an effect. That is what significance tests are, and what they can do for us.

In the light of current practice, it is also important to emphasize what significance tests are *not*, and cannot do for us. Most simply, they cannot make a decision for us. The probabilities they generate are only estimates, and they are, after all, only probabilities. Standard limits for retaining or rejecting our null hypothesis of no difference between the two colonies, such as 5 per cent, have no mathematical or empirical relevance. They are arbitrary thresholds for decision-making. A host of factors might affect our confidence in the probability estimate, or the dangers of deciding wrongly in one way or another, including whether the study is likely to be replicated (Wainer and Robinson 2003). Therefore there can, and should, be no universal standard. Each case must be judged on its merits. However, it is also often the case that we do not need a significance test to help us decide this. In the agricultural example, if all of the treated plants died and all of the others survived (or vice versa) then we do not need a significance test to tell us that there is a very low probability that the treatment had no effect. If there were 1000 plants in the sample for each colony, and one survived in the treated group, and one died in the other group, then again a significance test would be superfluous (and so on). All that the test is doing is formalizing the estimates of relative probability that we make perfectly adequately in everyday situations. Formal tests are really only needed when the decision is not clear-cut (e.g. where 600/1000 survived in the treated group but only 550/1000 survived in the control), and since they do not make the decision *for* us, they are of limited practical use even then. Above all, significance tests only estimate a specific kind of sampling error, but give no idea about the real practical importance of the difference we observe. A large enough sample can be used to reject almost any null hypothesis on the basis of a very small difference, or even a totally spurious one (Matthews 1998a).

It is also important to re-emphasize that the probabilities generated by significance tests are based on probability samples (Skinner *et al.* 1989). They tell us the probability of a difference as large as we found, assuming that the *only* source of the difference between the two groups was the random nature of the sample. Fisher (who pioneered many of today's tests) was adamant that a random sample was required for such tests (Wainer and Robinson 2003). 'In non-probability sampling, since elements are chosen arbitrarily, there is no way to estimate the probability of any one element being included in the sample . . . making it impossible either to estimate sampling variability or to identify possible bias' (Statistics Canada 2003: 1). If the researcher does not use a random sample then traditional statistics are of no use since the probabilities then become meaningless. Even the calculation of a reliability figure is predicated on a random sample. Researchers using significance tests with convenience, quota or snowball samples, for example, are making a key category mistake. And commentators defending the use of probability-based tests on non-probability samples (such as Plewis and Fielding 2003) are impeding the progress of social science. Similarly, researchers using significance tests on populations (from official statistics perhaps) are generating meaningless probabilities. All of these researchers are relying on the false rhetoric of apparently precise probabilities, while abdicating their responsibility for making judgements about the value of their results.

Added to this is the problem that social scientists are not generally dealing with variables, such as plant survival rates, with minimal measurement error. In fact, many studies are based on latent variables of whose existence we cannot even be certain, let alone how to measure them (e.g. underlying attitudes). In agronomy (the science of soil management and crop production) there is often little difference between the substantive theory of interest and the statistical hypothesis (Meehl 1998), but in wider science, including social science, a statistical result is many steps away from a substantive result. Added to this are the problems of non-response and participant dropout in social investigations, that also do not occur in the same way in agricultural applications. All of this means that the variation in observed measurements due to the chance factor of sampling (which is *all* that significance tests estimate) is generally far less than the potential variation due to other factors, such as measurement error. The probability from a test contains the unwritten proviso that the sample is random with full response, no dropout and no measurement error. The number of social science studies meeting this proviso is very small indeed. To this must be added the caution that probabilities interact, and that most analyses in the computer age are no longer one-off. Analysts have been observed to conduct hundreds of tests, or try hundreds of models, with the same dataset. Most analysts also start each probability calculation as though nothing prior is known, whereas it may be more realistic and cumulative (and more efficient use of research funding) to build the results of previous work into new calculations (see Chapter 3). Statistics is not, and should not be, reduced to a set of mechanical dichotomous decisions around a 'sacred' value such as 5 per cent.

As shown at the start of this section, the computational basis of significance testing is that we are interested in estimating the probability of observing what we actually observed, assuming that the artificial null hypothesis is correct. However, when explaining our findings there is a very strong temptation to imply that the resultant probability is actually an estimate of the likelihood of the null hypothesis being true given the data we observed (Wright 1999). Of course, the two values are very different, although it is possible to convert the former into the latter using Bayes' Theorem (which is presented in Chapter 3). Unfortunately, this conversion of the 'probability of the data given the null hypothesis' into the more useful 'probability of the null hypothesis given the data', requires us to use an estimate of the probability of the null hypothesis being true irrespective of (or prior to) the data. In other words, Bayes' Theorem provides a way of adjusting our prior belief in the null hypothesis on the basis of new evidence. But doing so entails recognition that our belief in the null hypothesis, however well-informed, is a subjective judgement.

In summary, therefore, significance tests are based on unrealistic assumptions, giving them limited applicability in practice. They relate only to the assessment of the role of chance (explanation one in the introduction), tell us nothing about the impact of errors, and do not help decide whether any plausible substantive explanation is true. Even so, they require considerable judgement to use, and involve decisions that need to be explained and justified to any audience. By putting off new researchers from using numbers routinely they may also be a considerable obstacle to the relatively uncomplicated combination of quantitative and qualitative data. Some alternatives are considered here. A more radical alternative that allows the relatively simple combination of quantitative and qualitative data is described in Chapter 3.

What are the alternatives?

The American Psychological Society and the American Psychological Association, among other concerned bodies, have suggested the use of effect sizes, confidence intervals, standard errors, meta-analyses, parameter estimation, and a greater use of graphical approaches for examining data. These could be complements to significance testing, but there has also been the suggestion that reporting significance tests should be banned from journals to encourage the growth of useful alternatives (Thompson 2002).

All of these ideas are welcome, but none is a panacea for the problems outlined so far – chiefly the problem of estimating the relative size of the error component. Most actually address the somewhat simpler but less realistic issue of estimating the variation due to random sampling. Confidence intervals and standard errors are based on the same artificial foundation as significance tests in assuming a probability-based sample with full response and no measurement error, and an ideal distribution of the data (de Vaus 2002). They are still inappropriate for use both with populations and non-random samples. Even for random samples, minor deviations from the ideal distribution of the data affect the confidence intervals derived from them in ways that have nothing to do with random error (Wright 2003). In addition, the cut-off points for confidence intervals are just as arbitrary as a 5 per cent threshold used in significance tests (Wainer and Robinson 2003). In no way do they overcome the need for judgement or replication.

Whereas a significance test is used to reject a null hypothesis, an 'effect size' is an estimate of the scale of divergence from the null hypothesis. The larger the effect size, the more important the result (Fitz-Gibbon 1985). For example, a standard effect size from a simple experiment might be calculated as the difference between the mean scores of the treatment and control groups, proportional to the standard deviation for that score among the population. This sounds fine in principle, but in practice we will not know the population standard deviation. If we had the population figures then we would probably not be doing this kind of calculation in the first place. We *could* estimate the population standard deviation by using the standard deviation for one or both of the two groups, but this introduces a new source of error, and the cost may therefore override the benefit.

Above all, the use of effect sizes requires considerable caution. Several commentators have suggested that in standardizing them they become comparable across different studies, and so we see papers setting out scales describing the range of effect sizes that are substantial and those that are not. They therefore return us to the same position of dealing with arbitrary cut-off points as do confidence intervals and significance tests. Wainer and Robinson (2003) present an example of the difficulty of such scales. Table 2.4 summarizes the results of a large trial of the impact of regular doses of aspirin on the incidence of heart attacks. A significance test such as chi-squared would suggest a significant difference between these two groups. But the effect (in this case R-squared) is of the order of magnitude 0.001, which is far too small to be of practical value, according to scales describing the meaning of effect sizes. On the other hand, there were 85 fewer deaths in the treatment group, which is impressive because of what they represent. The traditional odds ratio of the diagonals is over 1.8, reinforcing the idea that the effect size is misleading in this case.

Table 2.4 'Effect' of aspirin on heart attacks in two groups

Condition	No heart attack	Heart attack	Total
Aspirin	10933	104	11037
Placebo	10845	189	11034
Total	21778	293	22071

In fact, of course 'there is no wisdom whatsoever in attempting to associate regions of the effect-size metric with descriptive adjectives such as "small", "moderate", "large", and the like' (Glass *et al.* 1981: 104). Whether an effect is large enough to be worth bothering with depends on a variety of interlocking factors, such as context, cost-benefit, scale and variability. It also depends on the relative size of the error component because, like all of the attempted technical solutions above, effect sizes do nothing to overcome errors. An effect size of 0.1 might be very large if the variability, the costs and the errors in producing it are low, while the benefits are high. Again, we are left only with our judgements and our ability to convey the reasons for our judgments as best we can.

Therefore, while these moves to extend the statistical repertoire are welcome, the lack of agreement about the alternatives, the absence of textbooks dealing with them (Curtis and Araki 2002), and their need for even greater skill and judgement means that they may not represent very solid progress (Howard *et al.* 2000). In fact, the alternatives to null hypothesis significance tests are doing little to assist scientific progress

(Harlow *et al.* 1997). They do nothing to help us overcome the major error component in our findings which, as we saw above, is not due to pure chance. Unfortunately the vagaries of pure chance are the *only* things that classical statistical analyses allow us to estimate.

Is there a school mix effect?

The relevance of the points made so far is illustrated through a more extended example that should be familiar to most researchers in education, but which meets the definition of pathological science by Park (2000). It concerns a phenomenon, rather like the parapsychology with which the last section started, which is at the limit of detectability. It is hard to pin down precisely because it is small relative to the 'noise' in the system, and we do not seem able to reduce that noise (as one would when having trouble hearing someone speak over background noise by moving closer to the source). Researchers working in this field prefer using post hoc statistical analysis to search for the phenomenon, rather than conduct any form of definitive test. And, like parapsychology, despite numerous analyses there appears to be no progress over time. This phenomenon is the 'school mix effect', or school compositional effect, or even 'sink' and 'halo' effect.

In summary, the argument for a school mix effect is relatively simple, sounds plausible, and should be easy to test empirically. It is clear that schools differ in terms of the proportions of their students achieving specified grades in public examination outcomes. It is also clear that these differences in outcome are related to the prior attainment, cognitive ability and socioeconomic background of the students. Thus, a school with a student intake with high prior attainment, high cognitive ability and low levels of family poverty (for example) generally produces higher outcome scores than a school with an intake having low prior attainment, low cognitive ability or high levels of family poverty. If we take the nature of the student intake into account in a 'value-added' analysis, and there are still differences between schools, then we might be able to argue that the higher 'value-added' schools are more effective and vice versa. This would be a 'school effect', such that students attending a more effective school would score higher in the examination outcome than exactly equivalent students attending a less effective school.

If we then look at the characteristics of the more effective schools we might find that, even after taking their student intake into account, they were disproportionately those schools with large clusters of students with desirable characteristics (high prior attainment and so on). In contrast, the less effective schools might be disproportionately those schools with large clusters of students with undesirable characteristics (family poverty perhaps). This is the claim for a school mix effect. It means not only that there is a school effect but also that part of the reason for the school effect is the particular mix of students. Harker (2004: 2) puts it thus: 'A compositional effect is said to exist when a variable (such as SES [socioeconomic status]) as an aggregated variable at the school level makes a *significant* contribution to the explanatory model over and above the contribution of the same variable in the model at an individual level'.

In order to demonstrate the school mix effect we could set out to obtain comparable, reliable and valid outcome scores for each student. We would also need reliable and valid indicators of any individual characteristics that might influence those outcome scores, such as sex, age, ethnicity, family education, family occupation, prior attainment, cognitive ability, prior motivation, special educational needs and first language. We could use the latter to make the best possible prediction of the outcome score for each student, and then compare the predicted and actual scores in each school. If there are large and consistent differences between the predicted and actual scores for each school then we have demonstrated a plausible school effect. If, in addition, the school effect is related to the aggregated student background scores for each school then we have demonstrated a plausible school mix effect.

Unfortunately, of course, neither of the premises in the above argument is realistic (Gorard 2001a). We do not have comparable, reliable and valid outcome scores for students (Nuttall 1987, 1979; Newton 1997a, 1997b; Tymms 2003a). Nor, therefore, do we have comparable, reliable and valid prior attainment scores. We do not have reliable and valid indicators of even the most obvious background characteristics such as ethnicity, family education, family occupation, cognitive ability, prior motivation or special educational needs (Gorard 2001b; Lee 2003). Allocating family members to occupational class schemes, for example, requires considerable judgement (Lambert 2002), and so introduces the potential for error. And we have no way of knowing whether we have included in our model *all* individual characteristics that might influence the outcome scores. Add to this the usual measurement, transcription, computational, propagated, non-response and dropout errors prevalent in all research (see above), and we can see that any school mix effect would have to be substantial in order for us to identify it over all of that 'noise'.

It is clear that predictions of later examination scores are largely based on the preschool and non-school context (Coleman *et al.* 1966; Gray and Wilcox 1995; Gorard 2000a). Once the individual student backgrounds have been taken into account, between 70 and 100 per cent of the variation in student outcomes has usually been explained. The larger the sample used, the higher the percentage explained (Shipman 1997). So, only between 0 and 30 per cent of the student outcome scores is explicable by the school effect. The size of this residual variation is related both to the scale of the study (small studies are more variable), and to the reliability of the measures involved (unreliable indicators generate spurious school effects, Tymms 2003b). In order to argue that the school effect actually exists, we would have to argue that this residual variation is so large that it cannot be due to chance (explanation one) or to the errors outlined above (explanation two). If so, we would need an alternative explanation and we could argue that the school effect is the best available alternative. On the other hand, we could argue that each student achieved pretty much as they would have done in any school, with any differences easily dwarfed by the likely error components. Which position we select is a matter of judgement, and must be based on a close examination of the many sources of error and an estimate of their impact relative to the residual variation (see below).

The view that performance at school is largely unrelated to any characteristics of the school other than the 'quality' of its students is quite widespread (Robertson and Symons 2004). Of course it is not possible to decide whether a student has progressed more or less in differing circumstances, because an individual cannot live two lives. Therefore, we cannot tell whether any school is more or less effective with the same students. And, therefore, we cannot tell whether the difference between our best prediction and the final outcome stems from a fault in the prediction or is a real 'effect'. Knowing, as we do, how the assessment system works it is hard to see the residual variation as a convincing demonstration that the school effect exists but the point is, at least, debatable. What about the school mix effect?

The school mix effect may *also* be simply an indication that we have not made sufficient allowance for one or more variables in our modelling of student progress. The primary-school league tables in England for 2003, for example, were intended to be value-added. However, most of the best-performing schools also had high raw-score attainment (and were sited in areas of relative advantage). Is this a fair result, or simply evidence that the value-added model was deficient, bearing in mind that 'school' performance was being judged on the progress of only around 30 to 60 students per school in terms of their 'expected' levels of attainment across different subjects, with all of the usual measurement and non-response bias? In fact, a spurious effect for the school mix is much more likely than for the overall school effect because of their relative sizes – the school mix effect is even smaller than the school effect.

The school mix effect is usually derived from studies using multi-level modelling. Prior attainment and socioeconomic context variables are used at an individual level to predict the outcome score for each student, and this level generally explains the vast majority of the variation in outcomes that can be explained. Then the same variables are used at an aggregated level along with other school-level variables to look for a school effect. If overall school-level scores for the prior attainment and socioeconomic context of students explain any additional variation in outcomes then this is reported as a demonstration of the school mix effect. This effect is, necessarily, identified statistically when individual level variables have been taken into account, but the school averages of the variables for context or attainment are still important. Concentrations of either 'desirable' or 'undesirable' students appear to have a 'Gestalt' effect on the results of all students, and if this is a real phenomenon then several reasonable explanations can be suggested for it. For example, schools with high levels of undesirable students may also have poorer discipline, or weaker teachers.

However, there are many other equally plausible explanations for such a multi-level model result because the technique itself is imperfectly conceptualized (Nash 2003). The effect could be an artefact of the statistical procedure used to uncover it, because its very existence does seem to be very sensitive to the precise method of analysis used (a common characteristic of pathological science). Many studies find no such effect, including many of the largest and best regarded (see above). The effect in any case disappears when non-cognitive dispositions, such as learner identities already possessed on entry to school, are included in the analysis (Gorard and Smith 2004). Many of the studies that *do* report a school mix effect are poorly done or poorly reported (such as Lauder *et al.* 1999, according to Nash 2003). The remainder would have to convince readers that the school mix effect is a superior explanation than any other, including those explanations based on error or omitted variables.

There are two obvious alternatives. The fact that context and prior attainment are still important at the school level could simply suggest that these have been imperfectly modelled at the individual level, or that insufficient account has been taken of them at that level. For example, the standard analysis is based on an assumption that the relationship between all predictors and outcomes is linear. If, however, the linear relationship within schools is imperfect then the *line* of best fit at the individual level is not totally efficient. If the linear relationship is better at the aggregate between-school level, then a spurious mix effect appears, stemming only from an unrealistic assumption at a lower level (but one which is imposed on the analyst by the techniques in fashion). Also, there will be measurement errors in the context and prior attainment scores that lead to a less efficient model at the individual level. However, these errors may be less important at the aggregate level, where unbiased errors tend to cancel each other out. So, again, a spurious mix effect appears, based on the propagation of errors (see above).

A second major alternative is that while the context and prior attainment variables might be perfectly good, there may be important within-variable variation that is completely unmeasured. Thus, if the school mix effect appears it could be the result of the limited nature of our explanatory variables. Measures based on concepts like 'non-cognitive disposition' or 'high aspiration' are only very weakly related to socio-economic context, for example (Nash 2003). So it is possible for two schools to have very different intakes in terms of these measures even where their gross characteristics, such as parental occupations, are identical. The UK PISA (Programme for International Student Assessment) data shows that students with low socioeconomic status in schools with similarly low status are no more likely to express negative attitudes to school than students with low socioeconomic status in schools with a high socioeconomic status. This does not support the school mix theory. On the other hand, the proportion of students with low socioeconomic status with few books at home is much higher in generally low-status schools (Nash 2003). This provides some evidence for the idea of important variation *within* the indicators usually employed in demonstrating a purported school mix effect. In summary, even the employment of a sophisticated and complex method such as multi-level modelling does not overcome the need for judgement, scepticism and conceptual clarity.

Discussion

If the above points are accepted it can be seen that merely producing a result, such as 51 per cent of heads, is not sufficient to convince a sceptical reader that the results are of any importance. In addition to explaining the methods of sampling, data collection and analysis (as relevant), authors need also to lay out a clear, logical warrant (Gorard 2002c). A key issue here is clarity of expression in the overt argument that leads from the results to the conclusions (Phillips 1999). At present, too much social science research seems to make a virtue of being obscure but impressive-sounding – whether it is the undemocratic way in which complex statistical models are presented in journals, or the use of neologisms that are more complex than the concepts they have been, ostensibly, created to describe. Jargon-laden reports go into considerable mathematical detail without providing basic scientific information (Wright and Williams 2003). Clarity, on the other hand, exposes our judgements to criticism, and our warrant stems from that exposure of the judgement. Transparency does not, in itself, make a conclusion true or even believable, but it forces the analyst to admit the subjectivity of their analysis and allows others to follow their logic as far as it leads them.

Phillips (1999) reminds us that, despite their superficial similarity, falsification is very different to the null-hypothesis testing of traditional statisticians. The first approach involves putting our cherished ideas 'on the line', deliberately exposing them to the likelihood of failure. It involves considerable creativity in the production of predictions and ways of testing them. The second involves a formulaic set of rules (mis)used to try and eliminate the null hypothesis (Gorard 2003b), and so embrace the cherished alternative hypothesis. As such, it is only a very weak test of the alternative hypothesis. Perhaps, the apparent and soothing 'rigour' of traditional statistics has satisfied both researchers and research users, and so inhibited the search for more truly rigorous ways of testing our ideas. One obvious example of this is the preference among UK social science funders for increasingly complex methods of statistical analysis (the post hoc dredging of sullen datasets), over a greater use of quasi-experimental designs (Gorard 2003c, 2003d, 2004a). For 'despite the trapping of modeling, the analysts are not modeling or estimating anything, they are merely making glorified significance tests' (Davis 1994: 190).

Complex statistical methods cannot be used post hoc to overcome design problems or deficiencies in datasets. If all of the treated plants in the agricultural example earlier in this chapter were placed on the lighter side of the greenhouse, with the control group on the other side, then the most sophisticated statistical analysis in the world could not do anything to overcome that bias. It is worth stating this precisely because of the 'capture' of funders by those pushing for more complex methods of probability-based traditional analysis, whereas of course, 'in general, the best designs require the *simplest* statistics' (Wright 2003: 130). Put another, slightly too forceful way, 'if an experiment needs *any* statistics, one simply ought to have done a better experiment' (in Schmidt 1999: 22). Therefore, a more fruitful avenue for long-term progress would be the generation of better data, open to inspection through simpler and more transparent methods of accounting. Without adequate empirical information 'to attempt to calculate chances is to convert mere ignorance into dangerous error by clothing it in the garb of knowledge' (Mills 1843, in Porter 1986: 82–3).

Because simpler techniques so often produce the same results as complex analyses, Wright (2003: 130) advises that 'the simpler techniques should be reported and if appropriate the authors may report that the more advanced techniques led to similar conclusions ... If you use advanced statistics, beyond what the typical psychology undergraduate would know, make sure that these are clearly described'. Above all, it is essential that reports make full acknowledgement of the underlying pattern of analysis which is that: data = model + error. The pattern can be made to look much more complicated than this by the use of complex techniques, but this should never be allowed to mislead readers into thinking that any technique eliminates, or even addresses, the error component.

Perhaps one reason why research is not typically taught as an exercise in judgement is that judgement seems 'subjective' whereas computation is ostensibly 'objective'. This distinction is often used by commentators to try and reinforce the distinction between a 'qualitative' and a 'quantitative' mode of reasoning and researching. But, in fact, we all combine subjective estimates and objective calculations routinely and unproblematically. Imagine preparing for a catered party, such as a wedding reception. We may know how many invitations we will send, and this is an objective number. We may know how much the catering will cost per plate, and this is another objective number. To calculate the cost of the party, we have to use the number invited to help us estimate the number who will attend, and this is a subjective judgement, even when it is based on past experience of similar situations. We then multiply our estimate by the cost per plate to form an overall cost. The fact that one of the numbers is based on a judgement with which other analysts might disagree does not make the arithmetic any different, and the fact that we arrive at a precise answer does not make the final estimate any firmer. This last point is well known, yet when they conduct research many people behave as though it were not true. 'Quantitative' researchers commonly eschew the kind of judgement at the heart of their decisions, seeking instead pseudo-technical ways of having the decisions taken out of their hands.

At present, we face a common situation in which 'qualitative' work is often amply illustrated by quotations and observations, but too often neglects to explain precisely how the patterns described were generated. On the other hand, complex statistical reports, using techniques like multi-level modelling, seldom illustrate their findings, focusing instead on the technicalities of the analysis. It should be routine for statistical reports to illustrate their model – by giving a worked example of the prediction of the results for an individual or school compared with the observed results, perhaps (see Gorard 2000b).

At present, much of science is bedevilled by 'vanishing breakthroughs', in which apparently significant results cannot be engineered into a usable policy, practice or artefact. Epidemiology, in particular, and perhaps dietary advice, cancer treatment, genetics and drug development have become infamous for these vanishing breakthroughs. The traditional guidelines for significance tests, and the apparently standardized scales for effect sizes are producing too many results that literally disappear when scaled up. When Fisher suggested the 5 per cent threshold he realized that this was quite high, but did so because he felt it was more important not to miss possible results than to save time and effort in fruitless work on spurious results. He also assumed that this was relatively safe because he envisaged a far higher level of direct replication in agricultural studies than we see in social science. However, rather than simply lowering the 5 per cent threshold this section argues for a recognition that any such threshold is only concerned with the chance explanation. Of much more concern is the relative size of the propagated error component.

We could always set out to estimate a band of error, and judge its potential impact. This would give us a far more realistic idea of the 'confidence' we can place in our results than any confidence interval. For example, imagine a survey that sets out to include 2000 people. It receives 1000 responses, for a 50 per cent response rate, of which 50 per cent are from men and 50 per cent from women. On one key question, 55 per cent of men respond in a particular way, but only 45 per cent of women do. This is clearly a statistically 'significant' result, and it leads to medium-sized 'effect size'. Therefore, traditional approaches lead us to the conclusion that men and women differ in their response to this question. But neither of these measures, nor any of the other alternatives discussed, take into account the response rate. Since 275 of the men and 225 of the women respond in this particular way, we would need only 50 more of the 500 women non-respondents than the men non-respondents to have responded in a particular way (if they could have been made to respond) for there to be no difference. Put another way, if most non-responders had responded in the same proportions as the actual responders, then we need only assume that 5 per cent of all non-responders would have responded differently for the difference between men and women to disappear. In this case, the difference we observe seems very small in comparison to the non-response. As we add in the potential errors caused at each stage of our survey (e.g. measurement and transcription errors), we may conclude that the difference is not worth investing further effort in because studies of the implementation of research findings show that the signal to noise ratio gets even weaker as the results are rolled out into policy and practice.

As a rule of thumb, we could say that we need to be sure that the effect sizes we continue to work with are substantial enough to be worth it. Clearly, this judgement depends on the variability of the phenomenon, its scale, and its relative costs and benefits (although, unfortunately, programme evaluation currently tends to focus on *efficacy* alone, rather than in tandem with *efficiency*, Schmidt 1999). It also depends on the acknowledged ratio of effect to potential error. Therefore, an effect size that is worth working with will usually be clear and obvious from a fairly simple inspection of the data. If we have to dredge deeply for any effect, such as the school mix effect, then it is probably 'pathological' to believe that anything useful will come out of it. We cannot specify a minimum size needed for an effect, but we can say with some conviction that, in our present state of knowledge in social science, the harder it is to find the effect the harder it will be to find a use for the knowledge so generated. It is probably unethical to continue to use public money pursuing some of the more 'pathological' findings of social science.

Probably, the best 'alternative' to many of the problems outlined so far in contemporary statistical work is a renewed emphasis on judgements of *the worth of results* (Altman *et al.* 2000). The use of open, plain but ultimately subjective judgement is probably also the best solution to many of the problems in other forms of current research, such as how to judge the quality of in-depth data analysis or how to link theory and empirical work more closely (Spencer *et al.* 2003). If this course were adopted it would also have the effect of making it easier for new researchers to adopt mixed-methods approaches as routine, without having to worry about which forms of data require a judgement-based analysis rather than a technical one. *They all do.*

Part of what this section has tried to do is show that standard approaches to significance testing, currently the cornerstone of many 'quantitative' methods courses, should no longer have automatic pride of place. Conventional statistics is based on frequently unwarranted assumptions regarding randomness and representativeness (among other things): 'Consequently, there is considerable abuse and misunderstanding of statistical methods; the resulting ethical as well as professional level is very low' (Shvyrkov 1997: 155). There is a pressing need for more general awareness of the relatively simple role of numbers in those common social scientific situations for which sampling probabilities are not relevant. Another common problem with using quantitative methods in isolation is their intrinsic shallowness in describing processes and their inability, in the absence of experimental control, to explain underlying causes. This is part of what qualitative work can provide, when used appropriately and in combination.

Simple qualitative approaches

'Qualitative' researchers are usually exhorted to welcome subjectivity, and this leads many of them to ignore totally the computations that are at the heart of their patterns, trends and narratives. Whenever one talks of things being 'rare', 'typical', 'great' or 'related' this is a statistical claim, and can only be so substantiated, whether expressed verbally or in figures (Meehl 1998). In fact, a consideration of how social science research is actually done, rather than how methodologists often claim it should be done, suggests that nearly all studies proceed in the same way (Eisenhart and Towne 2003). Practical research is defined by a set of guiding principles which are the same whatever method is used. The need to test our ideas by seeking their falsification obviously applies not only to the statistical analysis of passive data but also to data generated by 'qualitative' methods, such as observation (Phillips 1999). It is easy to find apparent 'confirmations' for any explanation if one looks for them. What is harder to find is an explanation that can stand the test of seeking refutations instead. We can, for example, apparently verify the theory that the world is flat by citing some confirmations (it looks flat, balls placed on the flat ground do not roll away, and so forth), but nevertheless the theory is wrong. This example also illustrates that consensual validation is not really validation at all. There are many examples of widely-held beliefs, such as that the world is flat, that have turned out to be wrong and so inter-researcher agreement about an explanation tells us nothing about its value. Immediate peer approval is not a test. Longer-term acceptance of findings tends to be based on their *practical* success. Similarly, the process of falsification shows us that mere coherence, plausibility, checking a theory with the participants in the study, and even triangulation are all weak or ineffectual as criteria for establishing the quality of qualitative inquiry. Qualitative work, no less than quantitative work, requires judgement laid open to inspection by others.

If quantitative approaches simply involve working with numbers as data, and do not necessarily involve 'buying into' or believing traditional statistical theory, what are the equivalent qualitative approaches? These are methods involving the collection and analysis of textual (and visual and auditory) data. As with quantitative work, using this data does not have to involve the researcher in any of the complex sets of beliefs purportedly associated with such data. There are similar problems and debates to those discussed above facing qualitative researchers, stemming largely from the notion of methods identities based on the traditional theories associated with this form of work (see Chapter 9). Content analysis does not *have* to be interpretive or constructivist, for example, any more than measurement is intrinsically positivist or realist (Bryman 2001). Many of the studies described in the remainder of this book are based on the premise that observational and textual data are very valuable in helping to understand education and social science phenomena. But what is the role of qualitative work by itself, and how can we judge its quality?

Is the purpose of qualitative work conducted in isolation to discover something new, or is it to illustrate and 'flesh out' something already known? If the latter, then it is, by implication, only part of a larger combined methods approach in which the original discovery is made using other methods. For example, if we discover via an analysis of public examination results that girls are achieving better qualifications at school than boys then we may use qualitative approaches to try and find out why or how this is happening. But to use qualitative approaches to try and establish the differential attainment in the first place would be inappropriate, since the issue is so clearly a numeric one. This is similar to the argument for the 'new political arithmetic' approach covered in

Chapter 4, where it is discussed further. What is interesting about this example, and many others, is that much qualitative evidence about how increasing boys' underachievement at school takes place matches so well with the original numeric analysis. Note that this is so, even though the original numeric analysis appears to have been in error (Gorard 2000a). Would a different numeric starting point have led the qualitative researchers to a different understanding, or would the results have been discordant? Ironically, the weakness of qualitative work conducted in isolation may be glimpsed in the fact that such work is so seldom dissonant with what it sets out to explain, and so often successful in producing plausible-sounding explanations.

Qualitative work in isolation, therefore, appears to set out to provide new ways of looking at things or to create plausible new theories and explanations of observed phenomena. Presumably the data is important to this (i.e. it is as evidence-based as quantitative work purports to be), for if the data is only used as a kind of Rorschach stimulus to the imagination, then presumably less expensive alternatives could be found (not involving lengthy fieldwork). But any finite dataset is capable of supporting an infinite number of equally logical explanations – just as quantitative data is said to under-determine theory. It is regrettable, then, that qualitative work does not typically offer a multitude of alternative explanations. Why is it common practice for theories to be used as lenses (starting points or even articles of faith) rather than being tested to destruction? Why do we not see appeals to simplicity as a way of establishing the superiority of one theoretical explanation over another (i.e. why should Occam's razor not apply here)? For some reason, qualitative and quantitative work have developed separate indicators of quality. Quantitative work should be concerned with simplicity, warranted conclusions, bias and so on. Good research is seen to be germane to the issue under investigation, the research design minimizes bias, and it has external validity (Slavin 1986). Qualitative work, on the other hand, has only the outlines for a tentatively agreed set of quality criteria (Spencer *et al.* 2003). Researchers are rightly resistant to the notion that standards can be neatly summarized in checklists. Quality for them is not about technical proficiency, procedural uniformity or the collection of hard facts (Pawson 2003).

Perhaps this is partly why it is qualitative work in the UK that has come in for particular criticism over its quality (e.g. Tooley and Darby 1998), and also why qualitative work is in danger of being neglected in research syntheses (see Chapter 3). What could be the quality marks for qualitative work? The most commonly agreed starting point is transparency – making the data collection and analysis process clear to the reader, and providing a coherent logical argument from the findings to the conclusion (Anfara *et al.* 2002). But even this basic minimum is probably more breached than observed (Gorard 2003a). Many research reports dealing with qualitative work still do not report the sampling procedures or even the size and nature of the sample.

Much has been written about publication bias in relation to the synthesis of quantitative work. Bias comes largely from the continued non-publication of *non*-significant results. For example, imagine 20 researchers independently conducting the same experiment. Of these, 19 find no significant effect size from their experimental intervention, and so decide not to publish their results. Only one researcher finds a difference between the treated and untreated groups that is significant at the 5 per cent level, and publishes the result. Future syntheses of research may find only this result and will not place it in the context of the 95 per cent of unpublished experiments that failed. Techniques have evolved to detect this problem and deal with it in systematic reviews (see Chapter 3).

What is the equivalent for qualitative work? Put another way, what are the qualitative studies not published? Are they the ones that merely confirm previous work, or are they the ones that seek to contradict it? Are they merely the ones that are unimportant or uninteresting? How could one tell whether a contentious conclusion was warranted if its purpose was only to suggest an alternative view? There are prerequisites for publication, such as stating the number of cases. And lack of these should be grounds for revision of a paper, but are hardly grounds for rejection. When is a paper rejected? Perhaps when it is not persuasive. But this would be the same for a 'quantitative' paper, and the overall logic should be similar for both.

Unlike work with numbers, in which we can check the figures, the sampling, the modelling and so on, advocates of the use of qualitative work in isolation from other approaches offer much weaker ways of judging its quality. Perhaps the weakest set of criteria, more artistic than scientific, for judging the quality of a piece of work has been advocated by Eisner (1981, 1988). The warrants for the validity of a piece of qualitative work are believability, credibility, consensus and coherence (note that this is preferred to stronger notions such as accuracy or practical value). But, according to Feldman (2003), the findings need to be *more* than believable, for we must have good reason to trust them whenever research is intended to generate understanding that is to be shared or used by others. What we require are explicit, transparent methods, a clear description of what counts as data and a detailed account of how a representation is constructed from the data. We need to consider and present alternative representations, and explain why our conclusion is the preferred one, and we need to provide evidence of the efficacy of our conclusion (its practical import). At present, however, mono-method qualitative researchers in the UK generally come nowhere near these stronger but perfectly reasonable criteria for quality. What both qualitative and quantitative (and, of course, combined) research have in common is that they should present their findings in such a way as to convince a sceptic (rather than playing to a gallery of existing believers). This issue, known as 'warranting', is discussed further in Chapter 10.

The problems for qualitative work conducted in isolation include those of generalization and warrant. Perhaps combination with quantitative methods can help solve these problems? A problem for quantitative work is that it is often portrayed as *so* complex. As suggested above, if we use simpler approaches we may encourage more users, and so more combined methods researchers. Simple quantitative work can supply the 'what' and the 'how many', while basic qualitative work can illustrate 'how' and 'why'. One irony might be that the pressure to combine methods leads to the simplification and therefore the improvement of both qualitative and quantitative work conducted in isolation as well.

3

Triangulation and combining methods across studies

In this chapter we describe two of what are probably the most common ways in which data derived from different methods are combined – triangulation between methods in one study, and the combination of results across a number of studies using different methods. The previous chapter provided a brief consideration of qualitative and quantitative approaches in isolation. This chapter now considers the triangulation of these two approaches, because this pattern follows what tends to happen to combined methods research in practice (Erzberger and Prein 1997). Research designs tend to split the two into exclusive parts (often conducted by different individuals), and then try to relate the results to each other at the end. In later chapters we consider more sophisticated and iterative designs.

The combination of evidence between studies using different methods is important because of current demands to synthesize the evidence on practical topics within education and social science, to 'engineer' our findings as a community into a useable product for practitioners or policy-makers. This is a difficult issue because there is no universally agreed way of doing it. Most protocols for systematic reviews, for example, have tended to privilege numeric data since this is purportedly easier to accumulate, average or meta-analyse across studies. The results of each study can be converted into an effect size, and these can be averaged across all studies, and weighted in terms of the size of each study. However, even where appropriate protocols can be laid down for textual or visual data, these do not apply easily to numeric data as well. Trying to find methods to integrate different types of data, or finding different methods of analysis to use with the same data, also poses considerable problems of scale (Erzberger and Prein 1997). In general, there is a trade-off between the number of cases to be studied and the number and depth of the attributes that can be studied for each case. While not providing in any way a total solution to this problem, this chapter develops the notion of Bayesian approaches to analysis introduced in Chapter 2, and illustrates how these can help meld both qualitative and quantitative data into at least one kind of synthesis.

What is triangulation?

Triangulation between the evidence produced by different research methods is thought to be a simple and common form of combining methods. Various reasons have been advanced for the use of combined methods triangulation, including increasing the concurrent, convergent and construct validity of research, the ability to enhance the trustworthiness of an analysis by a fuller, more rounded account, reducing bias, compensating for the weakness of one method through the strength of another, and in testing hypotheses (Perlesz and Lindsay 2003). This section considers this metaphor/analogy of triangulation in social science research. In particular we are concerned with triangulation in mixed-methods approaches, such as those involving both traditionally quantitative and qualitative techniques. 'Quantitative' work, here, refers to counts and measures of things, but not only work based on traditional statistical theory or the standard 'frequentist' approach. 'Qualitative' work predominantly uses words as data, but is not necessarily 'interpretive' (see Chapter 2). As the types of data involved differ between the two approaches, so the appropriate kinds of analysis often differ as well. We do not consider here the notion of research 'paradigms' as a barrier either to mixed methods work or to the triangulation of results (but see Chapter 9).

The concept of triangulation between datasets is explained in introductory textbooks, and will be familiar to most readers. The two or more different methods involved could both have been generated within one study, which is triangulation at its simplest, or they could be combined across two or more different studies (see below). However, the term 'triangulation' is also generally the source of considerable confusion (Kelle 2001). For example, we have heard one respected source explain that triangulation involves the collection of data from *three* vantage points, or the collection of three different kinds of data, in order to determine something about a fourth phenomenon lying within the notional triangle formed by these three points (or perhaps where the triangle is itself the metaphorical phenomenon to be investigated by multiple methods). Most sources explain, rather, that triangulation involves only a minimum of *two* vantage points or datasets to tell us something about a *third* phenomenon. It is also typically explained using a metaphor derived from an analogous trigonometric process during land surveying.

In land surveying, we could determine the position of a third point C if we know the positions of points A and B, and we also know the interior angles (X and Y) at any two points of the triangle thus formed by A, B and C (see Figure 3.1). In this case, C is the phenomenon we are trying to investigate (the unknown), while A and B are our two observations (or two different methods when we are combining both qualitative and quantitative evidence).

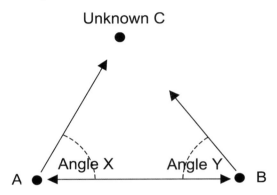

Figure 3.1 Two points provide triangulation

Alternatively, we can imagine the metaphor in terms of perspectives (see Figure 3.2). C is still the phenomenon to be investigated. A and B are our two perspectives (observation points or methods). Each isolated view of C may produce a two-dimensional picture (such as a circle or a rectangle), but when put together with 'binocular' (triangulated) vision they produce a three-dimensional image (such as a cylinder, with the 'circle' as its face and the 'rectangle' as its side).

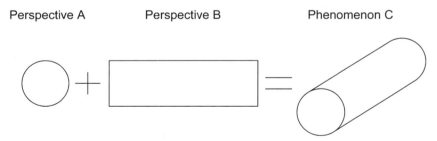

Figure 3.2 Two perspectives provide triangulation

If either of these are close to the analogy for social science triangulation, then several important conclusions can be drawn. First, the whole process assumes that there is a relatively stable, genuine observable phenomenon to be investigated. Therefore, the process explicitly rules out both positivism (the belief that the existence of objects stems solely from their measurement, Cook and Payne 2002) and relativism (the belief that objects do not have an external reality, and that there can, therefore, be genuine multiple 'realities', Sale *et al.* 2002).

Second, and again using the metaphor as it is usually constructed, and against popular practice (at least in writing about it), triangulation cannot be used as a form of mutual confirmation or validation of the two observations (or methods). In trigonometry, in surveying, and in the differing perspectives model of triangulation, the whole process depends on *all* of the observations taken being accurate. If, for example, we are trying to find a position for point C from the positions of, and interior angles at, points A and B, then any error in our information about A or B will lead to an error for C. Similarly, then, in social science two different sets of observations (whether collected by the same or different methods) cannot be used both to check up on each other *and* for triangulation. We can, of course, replicate our previous research, and even attempt near-replication with different methods (what Erzberger and Prein 1997 refer to as 'convergence'). If the two components of the replication lead us to an identical result, then there is no problem and triangulation simply becomes another term for such replication. But if the two components lead to substantially different results (such that we would conclude that we have not produced replication), then we cannot use the two components to fix a third because we do not know which of the two, if any, is in error. And even if we did know which was in error, we would then end up with only one set of valid measurements for the position of a point, and the analogy of 'trigonometry' cannot help us.

Third, therefore, if triangulation means anything in social science terms it is about complementarity, and nothing at all to do with mutual validation. The two observations or methods must be directed at different aspects of the wider phenomenon to be investigated. One of the methods might be indirect or reductionist in nature (a very valuable approach in science, Verschuren 2001), and the other direct or holistic. In this case, we will obviously expect that the results of the two observations will differ from each other (and will not be used for mutual confirmation). If we are using two different methods then the results have to be genuinely combined if something new is to result (as in the analogy of seeing a cylinder through binocular vision). Perhaps, therefore, the explanation of perspectives is easier to follow. When we view an object from two perspectives, or study a social phenomenon using two methods, then we expect to find something new as a result – whether that is point C, the binocular vision of a cylinder, a 'Gestalt', or simply a more well-rounded theory of the wider phenomenon being investigated. This kind of combination reverts back to the true meaning of the triangulation metaphor.

We cannot use two or more methods to check up on each other in a simple way. The methods should be complementary, producing different aspects of the reality under investigation and then put together. Or they could be designed to generate dissonance as a stimulus to progress. As Perlesz and Lindsay (2003) report, little attention has been paid to resolving this problem of dissonant data, perhaps because combined approaches are still so rare: 'We find it curious that there are not more reports of data divergence in the literature' (p. 38).

For the present, consider Figure 3.3. If we assume that neither quantitative nor qualitative approaches give us a complete picture of our object of study, that both will be valuable, and that both can give us a differing partial picture, then the situation is as depicted. Some of the 'object of study' may be hidden to both perspectives. A qualitative approach gives us the evidence available in sector A + C, whereas a quantitative approach gives us the evidence in sector B + C. Note that the intersect C may be empty but that, in so far as it exists, it represents the traditional view of triangulation – an overlap or confirmation between methods or perspectives. Of course, C may represent the entire object of study (i.e. there would be nothing more to find out about the given phenomenon). In this case all other findings using these two perspectives are external to the object of study, i.e. they are erroneous, noise, or about a different phenomenon (and both A and B would be empty). The research may thus generate findings unrelated to the object of study (the unshaded areas). These may be errors, or they may be examples of those valuable serendipitous findings we all encounter when in the field. However, Figure 3.3 also implies that each perspective provides further unique evidence about the object of study (sectors A and B in isolation). We assume that segments A and B are valuable parts of the object of study only available for inspection via one method. Using the results in A, B and C as *all* valuable increases the amount and range of evidence available to us. This is the power of combining methods.

Once familiar with this complementary notion of triangulation, we can use it to test our explanatory theories. For example, it may be possible to draw predictions from our initial theory not only about the likely contents of C, but also about what each approach will generate separately (i.e. the contents of A and B). Our logic would be the standard one for warranting conclusions (Gorard 2002c). If our theory is correct then we expect to find a set of listed attributes in A, B and C. If we do not find these attributes in any one sector, then this should lead us to modify our theory.

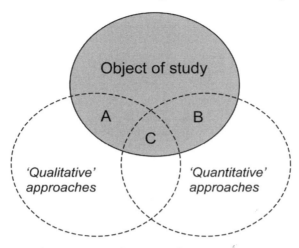

Figure 3.3 A complementary combination of approaches

The literature review

Probably the most common approach for combining evidence from several studies using different methods is the traditional literature review (Cooper 1998). The process of research generally involves some consideration of previous work in the same field. When conducting a literature review, as is normal at the start of any new project, reviewers use all and any forms of evidence relevant to their topic. All researchers read and use the research of others. They may use peer-reviewed papers, books, 'grey' literature such as websites, previous reviews and personal communication with experts. They may read sources involving theory, practice, method and evidence of all sorts. They would not, presumably, ignore or reject any source simply because of the form of evidence it provides, and this should be reflected in the final result (e.g. Gorard 1999). The balanced literature review is a very common example of combining data from different methods, requiring, in general, a working knowledge of both qualitative and quantitative techniques to allow the reviewer to be appropriately critical. All researchers require a 'mode of interrogation' for reading and using research results (Brown and Dowling 1998). If we had no sympathy for qualitative approaches, then we would tend to ignore, and therefore waste, potentially useful evidence derived from these. If we do not have any understanding of research techniques involving numbers, for example, then we have no clear way of judging the quality and relevance of work involving numbers.

These standard literature reviews, based solely on narrative accounts of prior work, are the subject of considerable criticism because, in a sense, they are so easy to do poorly. They seldom discuss their search strategy, nor describe what they sought but did *not* find in the literature, so leaving them open to the charge of selectivity. The two key issues for criticism involve quality and balance. In a standard literature review, the conclusions of prior researchers are often presented somewhat uncritically. The emphasis of the review is usually on the conclusions, not the design, method used or the warrant from the evidence to the findings (see Chapter 10). The problem of 'combining' evidence of different sorts is, therefore, largely invisible since the review may not distinguish between large- and small-scale evidence, for example. Where the conclusions of two pieces for review are dissonant there is often no consideration of the scale at all. One of the authors recently read a review for a Ph.D. in which the findings of 100 semi-structured interviews from a convenience sample were used, quite unproblematically, to contradict the numeric findings of an annual census involving a population of millions. Reviewers usually also ignore issues of quality, assuming perhaps that the 'kite mark' of publication in a peer-reviewed journal is sufficient for their purposes. This issue becomes more important as an increasing proportion of the literature comes from web-based searches and is correspondingly 'greyer' in nature. Issues of quality have come to prominence for those considering methods for reviewing evidence across many studies (Spencer *et al.* 2003). Although this is the subject of considerable debate at the time of writing, it appears to the authors that what is needed is a more systematic way of reviewing past results that takes both scale and quality into account. Note that this does not mean we advocate any particular protocol, nor does it mean that we deny the potential for the traditional literature review, done well, to succeed where what are apparently more rigorous approaches might fail.

Systematic reviews

A somewhat less common example of combining methods arises when the findings of more than one study are systematically combined in synthesis, review or meta-analysis (Glass *et al.* 1981). This alternative to narrative literature reviews is the basis for establishing 'evidence-based' practice where pedagogical and other decisions are guided by nationally agreed 'protocols' (as also attempted in the field of medicine, Department of Health 1997). The Cochrane/Campbell collaboration and the setting up of evidence-based centres for educational research are based on this notion of research syntheses (an idea with many merits and some problems, Gorard 2002d). Syntheses of what are considered by reviewers, based on standard protocols, to be high-quality studies are used to produce the findings, which are then 'engineered' into practice. The assumption, therefore, is that good evidence *has* been provided by a considerable body of previous work, but that it is difficult to see a pattern from this without systematic evaluation, and impossible for it to have an impact on policy and practice without some form of re-engineering (see e.g. the work of the Centre for the Wider Benefits of Learning, www.learningdirect.net). Simply publishing results is not enough. The beauty of this solution is that it apparently addresses issues of both relevance and quality, and it can be justified on solid practical grounds.

For example, as a result of a review of administering albumin (a protein in blood plasma) to humans, Roberts (2000: 235) concludes that it 'provides a strong argument for preparing scientifically defensible syntheses of the evidence from randomised controlled trials in medicine, as well as in other important areas of social policy, such as education'. The significance of this is that if albumin administration had ceased in the UK when doubts were first raised, this synthesis suggests that around 10,000 patients who died may have been saved. Relying on theory and craft knowledge, rather than heeding the warnings from a series of trials, led to needless loss of life. Although education is more concerned with life chances than with life or death, similar comments could presumably apply to wasted evidence from education and social science research. This approach sees large-scale randomized controlled trials as the ideal form of evidence, which a systematic review further improves by minimizing bias through selection and omission, leading to safe and reliable results (Badger *et al.* 2000).

However, while plausible, this systematic approach faces some technical difficulties that are not always highlighted by its advocates. Steering research in the direction of experimental trials (Evans and Benefield 2001) means that 'qualitative' evidence is largely ignored, which is particularly wasteful, and this is in addition to the majority of studies which are in any case rejected because of poor design or lack of published details. Systematic reviews can therefore be misleading by hiding details, and privileging trials even where considerable evidence of other forms contradicts them. This has led to false conclusions that may be just as important, in reverse, as those claimed for the evidence-based approach (Speller *et al.* 1997). Even in medicine, which receives a lot more funding than educational research, the approach is therefore being criticized (at least according to Hammersley 2001). Meta-analysis, or synthesis, of experimental evidence may show what works but it cannot uncover detailed causal mechanisms (Morrison 2001): 'It is unclear how an RCT [randomized controlled trial] can untangle this' (p. 74), nor how it can pick up multiple (side) effects. As discussed in Chapter 6, more detailed data collected in conjunction with the trials may, however, be able to remedy these deficits. But how can we combine these two forms of data within a research synthesis?

An introduction to Bayesian approaches

One answer to the last question involves a prior consideration of what are termed 'Bayesian approaches' to combining probabilities. Once we see how probabilities should be combined we can begin to build a procedure for combining evidence of *different* sorts. In Chapter 2 we showed that traditional approaches to quantitative methods have several limitations. It is important to realize that there are many viable alternative traditions, and one of these is attributed to Bayes. Here we describe two components of this 'Bayesian' approach. First, we explain Bayes' theorem for calculating conditional probabilities. Second, we question the assumptions in traditional statistics that calculations can be objective and that they must always appear to start from an unrealistic position of the total absence of preceding evidence. Putting these alternatives together provides at least one coherent, and already successful, way of reviewing bodies of evidence based on both numeric and non-numeric information (see below for examples).

Bayes' Theorem

Imagine being faced with the following realistic problem. Around 1 per cent of children have a particular specific educational need. If a child has such a need, then they have a 90 per cent probability of obtaining a positive result from a diagnostic test. Those without such a specific need have only a 10 per cent probability of obtaining a (false) positive result from the diagnostic test. Therefore, the test is 90 per cent accurate either way. If all children are tested, and a child you know has just obtained a positive result from the test, then what is the probability that they have that specific need? Faced with problems such as these, most people are unable to calculate a valid estimate of the risk. This inability applies to relevant professionals such as physicians, teachers and counsellors, as well as researchers (Gigerenzer 2002). Yet such a calculation is fundamental to the assessment of risk/gain in a multiplicity of real-life situations. Many people who do offer a solution claim that the probability is around 90 per cent, and the most common justification for this is that the test is '90 per cent accurate'. These people have confused the conditional probability of someone having the need *given* a positive test result with the conditional probability of a positive test given that someone has the need. The two values are completely different.

Looked at another way, of 1000 children chosen at random, on average 10 will have a specific educational need (1 per cent). Of these 10 children with the need, around 9 will obtain a positive result in a diagnostic test (90 per cent). Of the 990 without the need, around 99 will also obtain a positive test result (10 per cent). If all 1000 children are tested, and a child you know is one of the 108 obtaining a positive result, what is the probability that they have this need? This is the same problem, with the same information as above. But by expressing it in frequencies for an imaginary 1000 children we find that much of the computation has already been done for us (see Table 3.1). Many more people will now be able to see that the probability of having the need given a positive test result is nothing like 90 per cent. Rather, it is 9/108, or around 8 per cent. Re-expressing the problem has not, presumably, changed the computational ability of readers, but has, we hope, changed the capability of many readers to see the solution, and the need to take the base rate of the specific need into account.

Table 3.1 Probability of special educational need (SEN) having tested positive

	Test positive	Test negative	Total
SEN	9	1	10
Not SEN	99	891	990
Total	108	892	1000

This problem relies for its more general solution on Bayes' Theorem, which describes how to calculate conditional probabilities correctly. It states that the probability of an event A, given the occurrence of event B, is equal to:

the probability of A, times the probability of B given the occurrence of A, divided by

the probability of A, times the probability of B given the occurrence of A, plus the probability of not A, times the probability of B given the occurrence of not A.

Or in more formal terms (where 'p' signifies the probability of, '|' signifies given, the '.' means multiplied by, and ‾ represents the opposite of or not) we can say that $p(A|B) =$

$$\frac{p(A).p(B|A)}{p(A).p(B|A)+p(A').p(B|A')}$$

If we substitute actually having a specific learning need for A and testing positive for it for B, then we could calculate the probability of having the need given a positive result in the test, and so reproduce the table above for any probabilities. In our example, $p(A|B)$ is the probability of having the specific need given a positive diagnostic test result. This is what we were attempting to calculate. The $p(A)$, or the chance of any child having the specific need, is 1 per cent. The $p(B|A)$, or probability of testing positive for a child with the specific need, is 90 per cent. So the nominator in the equation, p(A).p(B|A), is 0.9 per cent, or 1 per cent of 90 per cent. The p(A'), or probability of not having the specific need for any child, is 99 per cent. The p(B|A'), or probability of testing positive when not having the specific need is 10 per cent. So p(A').p(B|A') is 10 per cent of 99 per cent, or 9.9 per cent. The denominator (p(A).p(B|A)+p(A').p(B|A') is 10.8 per cent, or 0.9 per cent + 9.9 per cent. Finally, 0.9 per cent (the nominator) over 10.8 per cent (the denominator) is around 8 per cent (i.e. the same as 9/108 in Table 3.1).

Bayes' Theorem helps in our quest for systematic reviews because it gives us a clear rule for learning from experience that can be used to synthesize evidence expressed numerically. For further clarifying examples, see Gorard (2003b). To see how this also helps more generally with combining methods we need also to continue from Chapter 2 our reconsideration of the notion that while qualitative work is subjective in nature, quantitative work is objective.

Are numbers objective?

The standard ('frequentist') view of probability, as used in nearly all statistics you will encounter (see Chapter 2), is based on several premises, at least two of which can be challenged. Probabilities are assumed to be susceptible to objective measurement, and to have been calculated from scratch for each new problem as though nothing previous was known. Both assumptions are suspect. The first is almost certainly wrong in relation to social science, rather than games of chance. The second is also often wrong in practice, and clearly wasteful.

An alternative ('Bayesian') approach to probability is based on an acceptance that all 'knowledge' is subjective, and that all judgements of probability are therefore made on the basis of combining prior beliefs with new evidence (Roberts 2002). This is actually a return to the origin of modern statistical thinking in the seventeenth century. It was only in the twentieth century that statisticians, after Fisher, believed that probabilities were truly objective, and that 'significance testing' should proceed from the starting point of feigned total ignorance on any question. Our decision whether to play in the UK National Lottery, for example, is not based on the odds of winning alone (1 in 14 million), otherwise *no one* would play. Rather, we might take into account the more qualitative nature of the possible consequences (a loss of £1 compared to totally transforming your life). Similar factors affect the decision to give a child an MMR (measles/mumps/rubella) injection or not (Matthews 2002). Bayesian probability is about how a person should decide, or bet (Hartigan 1983), and it shows that expected utility is subjective – the value of a bet can be subject to market forces, for example (Gorard 1997).

'People are usually seen as trying vaguely to be rational but failing frequently to appreciate normatively appropriate strategies' (Eiser and van der Plight 1988: 76), and in practice they tend to ignore prior probabilities in favour of 'convincing' new evidence (Glymour *et al.* 1987). For example, any reduction in the probability of an outcome from 100 per cent certainty produces a greater loss of its perceived attractiveness than an equivalent drop in probability from an originally lower figure, so that perception of probability is not a straight-line function. Paradoxically, low probabilities are often greatly overweighted in decisions, such as insuring for fire damage, or entering a lottery, but they can also be neglected entirely. One reason for this may be that risks from easily pictured causes, such as plane crashes, are more likely to be in the media than more common risks, such as diabetes, and so are exaggerated in subjective estimates. Decisions also depend on the phrasing of the problem and the frame of reference of the subject. For example, losses loom much larger than gains, so that most people prefer to make £100 than to have a 50 per cent chance of gaining £200, but the same people would prefer a 50 per cent chance of losing £200 to definitely losing £100 (see also French and Smith 1997).

At present it is not possible to apply probability theory easily to assess the credibility of anyone's testimony (Godfrey 2004) and this proviso also applies to calculating the value of qualitative results. However, subjective informal judgements can take into account a range of relevant factors that standard approaches to probability have to ignore. For example, if an author has an interest in the matter they are presenting, then this tends to increase our subjective probability that the testimony may be false. Put another way, evidence is more convincing when put forward by someone who has nothing to gain from that evidence being accepted.

Evidence about a phenomenon does not exist in a vacuum and its likely impact on an observer will depend to some extent on that observer's prior beliefs about the topic (West and Harrison 1997). Put another way, any observer will have some prior knowledge of the probability/ uncertainty about any phenomenon. New evidence about a phenomenon provides a new likelihood that will *modify*, rather than completely override, that prior probability, leading to a modified posterior probability. Therefore, the same evidence does not lead to precisely the same posterior probability/uncertainty for all observers. When all observers then agree, whatever their prior position, this shows the convincing power of the new evidence. What Bayes and others have produced, and technological advances have now made feasible, is a method for calculating the posterior distribution, making it proportional to the new likelihood multiplied by the prior distribution (French and Smith 1997). Bayes' Theorem offers us a prescription of how to learn, collectively, from evidence (Bernado and Smith 1994). One way forward, therefore, is to use qualitative evidence to help create the prior probability for a Bayesian model, which can then be adjusted via Bayes' Theorem using the quantitative evidence in an otherwise normal synthesis. In fact, the prior probability can also be based on expert knowledge (the notion that some people intuitively know 'what works' under certain conditions) and on the results of prior meta-analyses. Successful syntheses have been conducted using this approach (Roberts *et al.* 2002). Whether they have a future in helping to heal the wasteful schism between 'quantitative' and 'qualitative' forms of evidence remains to be seen.

A technique for systematic learning from experience

In medicine, as in education, qualitative evidence has been a traditional precursor to other research, such as aiding the design of questionnaires or the selection of an intervention or outcome measure (Dixon-Woods *et al.* 1999). It has been particularly valuable in helping to challenge the tendency for research to reflect the clinicians' and not the patients' perspective. It has also been used to help explain quantitative results (see Chapters 4 and 5), especially in explaining why an experimental trial does not work or will not generalize. It has not, until recently, been used in syntheses for a variety of reasons. Researchers are concerned that it may signal a return to haphazard reviews. Qualitative work appears to have less clear criteria for judging suitability for admission to the synthesis, and discussion of the issue tends to flounder on philosophical and epistemological problems rather than moving on to practicalities (see Chapter 2). One, very simple, solution is clearly to treat qualitative work as small-scale quantitative work, and convert it to numeric form by frequency counting, but this clearly still wastes some of the information available. Another possibility is meta-ethnography, but while promising, no actual examples of this have emerged as yet.

Another more promising solution to the problem of combining different forms of evidence in syntheses is based on Bayesian analyses. This starts with the very credible assumptions that evidence about a phenomenon does not exist in a vacuum. Synthesis of data is actually a decision-making process, and should include what we know about the nature of decision-making. There are many possible models of this process, and we present here a very simple one to make the point about feasibility.

Imagine we are setting out on a systematic review of the available evidence on the viability of a particular approach to teaching the understanding of fractions in secondary-school mathematics. We would set out to assemble as much of the literature as possible of relevance to the question. We would, as standard, include 'grey' literature obtained from conferences and the internet as well as peer-reviewed articles in case the latter contained a bias towards positive results (either due to optimism bias or because journals are less likely to publish the results of trials that do not find an effective intervention). We could divide all of these results into those susceptible to conversion for a meta-analysis of effect sizes (mostly the quantitative ones) and those which were more impressionistic (mostly the qualitative ones). The former we could assess in terms of relatively standard quality checks, such as sample size, respondent refusal or dropout, measurement error and so on.

The latter, qualitative pieces, we would present to a mixed panel of education and research experts for detailed reading. We would ask them to use their prior knowledge and experience, coupled with what they have learnt from reading the qualitative evidence to rate, in an overtly subjective way, the likelihood that this approach to teaching is effective. We can then either continue with each subjective probability separately (the better but more complex method) or find their overall mean. This figure(s) becomes the prior probability for a Bayesian calculation using successive quantitative studies in sequence as new likelihoods. In the example earlier in this chapter, the prior is the probability of a child having a specific educational need, and the posterior is the probability of testing positive in the diagnostic test. In the same way as in the example, Bayes' Theorem allows us to adjust the subjective judgements of the experts, based to a large extent on qualitative studies, using the additional information generated in quantitative studies.

For example, the expert opinion based on classroom experience and qualitative observations may be that this approach to teaching fractions is reasonably effective. A meta-analysis of the trials and other quantitative studies may show no discernible effect from using this technique compared to a control. In current procedures, the meta-analysis results would be published in isolation and used to argue that this approach to teaching is ineffective. The expertise and the qualitative studies would be largely ignored in officially published results, while some practitioners might then ignore the important results of the synthesis because it does not accord with their own experience. In this version, everybody loses. What a Bayesian analysis does, more properly, is to weigh the two versions of the evidence in terms of the common 'currency' of subjective probabilities. It asks – is the posterior evidence so strong that it should substantially change the minds of the experts? This is, quite deliberately, a much tougher proposition for the evidence than the more usual frequentist question – is the result 'significant' (see Chapter 2)?

Suppose, using a deliberately simple example, that our experts conclude after reading the qualitative evidence that the approach to teaching in question is about 70 per cent effective (or, rather, they rate the likelihood of this teaching technique being effective as around 70 per cent, or even that 70 per cent rated it as effective). This gives the qualitative work primacy, and allows the experts to blend what they learnt from the research with their predisposition to believe in the efficacy of the technique or not. The result is a subjective, but informed and considered, judgement of a prior probability of 70 per cent. Suppose we now wish to adjust this estimate for a much larger-scale quantitative study. We could use the probability of finding the data observed in that larger study, as generated by a statistical test under the 'null' assumption that the teaching technique was ineffective. If this new likelihood is 50 per cent, then Bayes' Theorem (where A is the proposition that the teaching technique is effective, and B is the data we observed) shows that the modified posterior probability is:

$$\frac{0.7 \times 0.5}{0.7 \times 0.5 + 0.3 \times 0.5}$$

This is, of course, still 70 per cent. The large-scale study has not affected our initial judgement of efficacy. If, on the other hand, the new likelihood generated by a large study is 10 per cent, then Bayes' Theorem shows the posterior probability as:

$$\frac{0.7 \times 0.9}{0.7 \times 0.9 + 0.3 \times 0.1}$$

This is just over 95 per cent. So the new 10 per cent figure has led to a modification of our prior judgement, rather than ignoring it as would be the case in traditional statistical analysis.

One of the main advantages of this method of synthesis is that, as well as including all of the qualitative results, it means that we do not need to make arbitrary decisions about the 'significance' of quantitative results. There is no threshold, such as 5 per cent, below which the probabilities can be used. A probability of 90 per cent for the data given the null hypothesis could be used to 'strengthen' our prior judgement, while a probability as high as 40 per cent could be used to weaken our prior estimate very slightly. Of course, this makes it all the more important that all studies are available for synthesis, and not only those that might be deemed 'significant' in the traditional way. If this method of synthesis seems to give the new likelihoods too much weight, then we could make a more conservative posterior probability by dampening the impact of new evidence (e.g. by scaling before calculation). If this method seems rather insensitive to the actual size of new studies, seemingly given similar weight to the probabilities generated by a study of 1000 and a study of 10,000, then this scale can also be factored in directly. Effect sizes can be used instead of significance probabilities.

Equivalent syntheses *have* been published, most particularly in medicine (e.g. Roberts *et al.* 2002). Roberts *et al.* attempted to decide which were the most important factors determining the uptake or not of the MMR vaccine by parents. Each expert reviewer first listed and ranked the factors that they believed would affect the uptake of childhood vaccines (such as parents' belief about their efficacy). They were then asked to read a series of 11 relevant studies not susceptible to numeric analysis (qualitative) in a randomized order, and to adjust their initial lists of factors and their ranking accordingly. In the process, of course, they had also to agree to standard descriptors for each identifiable factor. The final lists were then combined to yield a probability for each factor being responsible for vaccine uptake or not. These probabilities were scaled in order to sum to one. Then, for each factor its probability of being involved was updated in a Bayesian analysis (the initial subjective probability being the 'given') using those quantitative studies from a set of 32 in which that factor was studied.

The results showed that inclusion of the prior probabilities makes a considerable difference, and that excluding qualitative work and expert opinion from reviews runs the risk of losing valuable evidence for evidence-based practices (in this case, structural issues about delivery of the vaccine). Similarly, using the qualitative studies alone would have led to the neglect of potentially important factors in the uptake of immunization (in this case, the relevance of the child's health). A Bayesian approach also has the advantage of not exaggerating the substantive significance of results, a regrettable tendency in 'classical' approaches that leads to what Matthews (1998b) refers to as 'vanishing breakthroughs' wherein published scientific results are found to have no practical value (such as the frequently promised 'cures' for cancer that need only 'another year or so' to be on the market!). The implications for reviews of evidence about teaching and learning, for example, appear obvious to us. It would be absurd to endanger this practical progress by claiming, as many existing researchers do, that we cannot combine qualitative and quantitative approaches because they emerge from different paradigms which are 'incommensurable'.

However, in our opinion, there remain several issues to be resolved here. One of the most obvious is the problem of what to do with new qualitative evidence as it emerges. Do we have to start the whole synthesis again, or can we simply make a subjective adjustment to the current probability value? Second, as with all of the more traditional alternatives to significance testing, this approach still does nothing to overcome the problems caused by the error components in our figures. The new likelihoods are still based on the assumptions of random sampling, full response and no measurement error. A much more complex model would have to be devised to cater for situations where even one of those assumptions was not true.

4

The 'new' political arithmetic: a policy case study

This chapter considers one form of the sequential combination of methods within a study, in which the scale moves in the opposite direction to Chapter 2. Here we are concerned with work that starts with a large-scale numeric dataset, and then focuses on in-depth data using a subset of cases selected from the first phase – an approach termed here 'the new political arithmetic' (but also termed 'explanatory' two-phase research, Cresswell 2003). This chapter differs from the previous chapters in presenting a more detailed example of our actual research involving combined methods.

Context is everything

Whatever your choice of primary method, there is a good chance that your research will involve numbers, at least at the outset. You may wish, for example, to document the educational experiences of the growing number of homeless people. Whatever approach you intend to use (participant observation, focus groups and so on) you would start from a quantitative basis. In order to direct your search you would use as much information as is available to you from the outset. You would establish, as far as possible, how many homeless people there are, where they have been reported, how the socioeconomic and ethnic patterns of these groups are thought to change over time and space, and so on. Such figures, termed 'secondary data', already exist, and therefore a preliminary analysis of them is the best place to start any study. Only then can you sensibly select a smaller group for more detailed study. Existing figures, whatever their limitations, provide a context for any new study which is as important as the 'literature review' and the 'theoretical background' (Gorard 2002e). With increasing access to large-scale datasets, researchers are now strongly encouraged by funders to preface their studies routinely with an analysis of the relevant population figures (Rendall 2003), before moving on to work with in-depth data or case studies.

One of the most frequently used ways of combining research findings is what is termed here the 'new political arithmetic' (NPA) model. Statistics as used in social science derive from the idea of political arithmetic in the 1660s (Porter 1986). Its purpose was to promote sound, well-informed state policy (applying therefore to the 'body politic' rather than the 'body natural' of the natural sciences), and its aims included raising life expectancy and population figures, and reforming health, education and crime (usually in opposition to religious groups, see Chapter 9). NPA is a development of this approach, adding a stage of using in-depth data to help explain the patterns in the body politic. In its simplest form it involves a two-stage research design. In the first stage, a problem (trend, pattern, or situation) is defined by a relatively large-scale analysis of relevant numeric data. In the second stage, this problem (trend, pattern, or situation) is examined in more depth using recognized 'qualitative' techniques with a subset of cases selected from the first stage.

The method starts from a consideration of the importance of pattern rather than probability, ignores the usual complex statistical approach (see Chapter 2) to the prior political arithmetic tradition (Mortimore 2000) and adds other appropriate methods of data collection and analysis in subsequent phases. In this way, researchers tend to avoid what Brown (1992) calls the 'Bartlett' effect of producing plausible but false results when basing an analysis solely on qualitative data, and they also avoid the simplistic answers often gained from numeric analysis alone. This approach clearly differs from attempting to both describe and explain the phenomena under investigation using complex statistical techniques on the same dataset (e.g. as is common in school effectiveness research and econometrics). In NPA the numeric techniques are simple, and largely descriptive, but they are linked to a second dataset (consisting of the more in-depth data). The two datasets are used together in a complementary way, as suggested in Chapter 3. The approach also clearly differs from attempting to both describe and explain the phenomena under investigation using only in-depth approaches which are, of necessity, smaller in scale and harder to generalize. In NPA the explanatory phase collects new in-depth data, but in a focused attempt to elucidate the more general findings from the descriptive phase. Each type of data has a different purpose for which it may best be suited.

This model has been used quite widely with some success, although it is rather limited to the simple survey-then-case-study combination (Suter and Frechtling 2000). For example, Spillane and Zeuli (1999) started with a large-scale survey of teachers from the Third International

Maths and Science Study (TIMSS), and used the results to select cases of interest for further exploration. Schorr and Firestone (2001) conducted a survey of teachers, from which they selected extreme cases for further case study. In practice, a completed model is likely to be more complex than this. There may be different forms of data within each phase, more than two phases, or iteration between phases. On the other hand, it can be very simple and within the budget of time and effort for a single researcher such as a Ph.D. student. For example, a single researcher could start a project through a re-examination of existing large-scale datasets, such as the population census, the annual schools census, University and Colleges Admissions Service (UCAS) records, the Labour Force Survey, the ESRC data archive, and so on (see sources in Gorard 2001b, 2003a). This phase can be done quickly and cheaply, using simple arithmetic. Then the researcher could spend rather more time conducting fieldwork on case studies selected to be representative of patterns found in the first phase.

For example, our recent NPA study started with an analysis of the social composition of the student body in all secondary schools in England and Wales over 13 years (Gorard 2000a). The results were used to select a subset of around half of all local education authorities (LEAs) for documentary analysis of the admission procedures to their schools (White *et al.* 2001). The results of this analysis were used to select a smaller number of adjacent LEAs in which to conduct interviews with admission officers (Fitz *et al.* 2002). On the basis of these interviews a subset of schools was selected in which to conduct interviews with headteachers within these LEAs. The use of large-scale secondary and documentary evidence supports the belief that the patterns investigated in later phases are genuine ones, and also enables reasonably general conclusions to be drawn from the interview data. The remainder of this chapter describes this project and its summary findings in some detail, as a complete case study of successful NPA.

The measuring markets project

The purpose of the project used as a case study here was to examine the extent to which the introduction of educational markets gave rise to changes in the social composition of secondary schools in England and Wales. Using official statistics for this purpose, from the introduction of the Education Reform Act 1988 (ERA88) onwards, we measured changes over time in the tendency for pupils with particular socioeconomic characteristics to cluster in particular schools (termed 'segregation'). We considered a variety of reasons for the changes over time and the regional differences in segregation that we encountered, and also began to relate these to changes in school output figures (i.e. public examination results). The project therefore moved from description and measurement to exploration and explanation. It also raised unforeseen methodological and research-capacity issues (Gorard *et al.* 2003a).

The research was distinctive at that time because the focus of this study was on the *outcomes* of a choice programme and not the process of choice itself. It also related schools to the changes in wider social structure evidenced by the indicators which point to a rise in poverty in England and Wales since 1988 and an equivalent rise in the proportion of cases being taken to appeal in the school allocation process, in ways which had not been attempted before. We describe the methods in some detail, as is appropriate in a book concerning methods.

Sample

Our sample is a complex one, yet structured to explore macro- and micro-scale patterns and processes and how these all may interconnect. The sample is composed of three levels. It begins from a national perspective and then works down in scale to *particular* schools, headteachers and LEA admission officers. Furthermore, the sample at each level is selected during the course of the study, dependent upon data collection and analysis at earlier stages of the research process. Level 1 comprises all state secondary schools in England and Wales, Level 2 consists of 41 selected LEAs, and Level 3 is a selection of secondary schools (21 in total) in nine of these LEAs chosen as the sites for more intensive fieldwork.

At Level 1, school-level and LEA-level data was collected for all primary and secondary schools in England and Wales, although for this project we analysed only secondary-school data in detail. To provide a clear picture of what has happened to between-school segregation we analysed the social composition of schools from 1989 to 2001 at five levels of analysis: England and Wales combined; England and Wales separately; by LEA; by school district or competition space (where available); and by school.

At Level 2, 41 LEAs from Wales and England were selected for further in-depth study. These LEAs were chosen to be as diverse as possible on the basis of the results of the first stage, within the limits set by the successful negotiation of access and the constraints imposed by travel. The variation was geographic (north/south, England/Wales, urban/rural, political control, ethnic diversity), educational (selective/non-selective), and based on segregation (high/low, increasing/decreasing/static). These LEAs provided brochures on their school admission and allocation procedures for as many years as these had been retained. Where possible, we also conducted an in-depth taped interview with one or more people in each LEA responsible for the annual admissions process. In some LEAs (usually urban) this involved a team including the director of education (a post abolished in most LEAs during the period of the study), in others (usually rural) this involved only one officer, and admissions represented only a small part of their duties (since admissions were seen as such a simple task).

Level 3 was based on more detailed consideration of three contrasting LEA clusters emerging from Level 2. Each cluster consisted of several contiguous LEAs with cross-flows of pupils (nine LEAs in total). One was in west inner- and outer-London, one incorporated two counties to the south-west of London, and one was in west Wales. Our earlier interviews had suggested which schools in these clusters were in 'competition' with each other, and we interviewed the headteacher (or other school manager responsible for Year 7 entry) in 21 of these schools.

Data collection

The study collected a range of secondary data on all schools in England and Wales, including pupil numbers and years, sex, take-up of and eligibility for free school meals, statements of special needs, ethnicity, stages of English, unauthorized absences and examination performance. This national data was obtained, with relative ease, via the respective governments in England and Wales from the annual census by the Department for Education and Science via Form 7, and the Welsh Assembly Government via Stats 1. The national datasets were used to identify patterns and trends in the changing composition of secondary-school intakes.

These were supplemented by local area statistics based on the population censuses of 1981 and 1991. In addition, within selected LEAs, more detailed data were collected on admission procedures and the background and prior attainment of school intakes, including parental occupation and performance at Key Stages 1 and 2. These were complemented by the views of LEA officials and school administrators. Taped, open-ended, interviews were held with the officers responsible for admissions from each LEA, and with the heads from each school. The interviews were semi-structured based on an interview schedule appropriate to the findings from the first stage of the study for LEAs, and from the LEA interviews for subsequent interviews with heads. Data were also collected in the form of fieldnotes and observations throughout the investigation, from negotiation of access to feedback of results to end-users. A content analysis was carried out of LEA and school admission brochures.

The interview data were transcribed, coded and analysed in the light of the national and regional findings. The narratives from interview and other on-the-ground observations, and the details of admissions procedures in place in each LEA, were employed to help explain the changes and local variations in the above measures. We see these second stage interviews, then, as vital to our further understanding of the processes by which local institutional arrangements mediate the impact of national policies. This is the essence of NPA.

Measuring socioeconomic composition

In the absence of unique student identifiers and related social class data for school populations in England and Wales, we employed the number of students entitled to free school meals as a means to examine changes in the social composition of schools over time. Free school meals are available to school students from very low-income families (defined during the period of this study as eligible for state-funded Family Income Support). They are a widely used indicator of poverty in the UK. Overall, about 18 per cent of the student population fall into this group, although they are unevenly distributed geographically and by institution. There are a few problems in the recording and use of this indicator, the solutions to which have been discussed elsewhere (Gorard 2000a). In general, the method of analysis, the number of triangulating indicators and the sheer scale of the evidence overcomes the problems encountered. We use *eligibility* for free school meals, rather than take-up, wherever possible, and accept that there will be some cases of pupils from families on income support unknown to the schools. Nevertheless, several schools and LEAs, while admitting that there was no way of knowing for sure how many 'eligibles' they were unaware of, believed the annual census to be reasonably accurate, especially since school funding and the category for a 'value-added' assessment of results could rest on it. An officer in a London LEA, for example, said: 'Some of the Church schools, for instance, decided that they wanted to push families to let them know they were on income support, even if they didn't want to take up the free school meals, so that they could be included in the funding'. An officer in a rural LEA felt that even this was unnecessary: 'In rural primary schools, where everybody knows everybody else, the secretary usually knows who is on income support. There may be a few each year who are not claiming [but even these are asked to do so in order to complete the Form 7]'.

The biggest limitation of these figures of disadvantage is therefore that they apply only to a minority of the school population. However, in previous debates about the impact of markets it has not generally been the potential struggle between the middle-class and the super-rich that has concerned commentators. Rather, the focus has been on precisely the disadvantaged fraction of the population that free school meals attempts to measure. It is not perfect, but it is available with complete coverage for

13 years, based on an unchanging legal definition leading to a binary classification (free school meals or not) which is more robust and reliable than an occupational categorization.

To examine and explain changes in the proportion of disadvantaged pupils in and between schools we devised a segregation index (Gorard and Fitz 1998). This gives a proportionate measure of level of social stratification in the school compared to its surrounding schools. It is defined as the proportion of disadvantaged students who would have to change schools for there to be an even spread of disadvantage between schools within the area used for analysis (i.e. it is the strict exchange proportion). This is needed because, as Taeuber and James (1982: 134) point out in relation to racial segregation, it 'does not depend upon the relative proportions of blacks and whites in the system, but only upon the relative distributions of students among schools'. We have also analysed the same data using a variety of other indices, and also used alternative indicators of disadvantage, partly for comparison, and partly because no one index can fully describe the patterns uncovered. All proportionate indices of unevenness we have used show the same basic pattern over time (i.e. the changes we describe below are sufficiently large to appear whatever method one uses). The problems we have encountered with many other recognized indices have been described elsewhere (Gorard and Taylor 2002). It should be noted that while the issues of measurement involved in this project are sophisticated and they, quite rightly, occupied considerable attention, the analysis itself is very simple. It requires only primary-school arithmetic and is not based on probability or sampling theory (which have both been shown to be off-putting to reluctant 'quantitative' analysts, see Chapter 2).

Changes in segregation

The evidence from studies on the process of choice is quite clear (Gorard 1999). Public choice theory does not provide a good description of the process of choice according to the reports of those involved. The most commonly reported source of information about schools is word of mouth; schools have a widely-held local reputation, which explicit marketing is slow to change. Families consider very few alternatives on average (fewer than two schools). Parents and children do not generally emphasize academic and school performance factors when selecting a school; rather, they are primarily concerned with safety and happiness. Parents of a 4-year-old are generally thinking about the security of their child, and the convenience of the school. Parents of a 10-year-old (the oldest cohort in primary schools which are commonly 100–300 students in size) looking for a secondary school (where their child will be in the youngest cohort in a school which is 1000–3000 students in size) will naturally be concerned with issues such as bullying, rather than academic outcomes in six or seven years' time. The children themselves generally want to go to school with their friends. Many families therefore select their nearest school, and most of the rest obtain their expressed preference. Just about everyone who does not get their preference then appeals against their placement as a matter of course (Gorard *et al.* 2003a). One would not, under these circumstances, expect the introduction of choice to have made a marked and sustained difference in patterns of school use. Indeed, this is what our study found.

Figure 4.1 shows the level of between-school segregation in all state-funded secondary schools in England from 1989 (the last year before open enrolment) and 2001. The first thing to note is that schools in England were, and remain, socially segregated. In any year, around one third of students would have had to change schools in order for there to be an even spread of 'poor' children between schools. The period before open enrolment was not, therefore, some golden age of equity. Some commentators have commenced their analysis as though the education system was somehow less stratified before 1988 in England and Wales. What this research confirms is that, prior to the introduction of market-

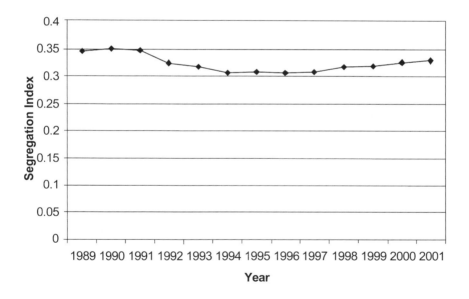

Figure 4.1 Change in segregation by poverty over time in England

Note: the points in this graph show the proportion of children from families in poverty who would have to exchange schools for there to be a precisely even spread of poverty between schools.

driven policies, secondary schools in England were already socially stratified. It appears, though, that whatever the stratifying effects of market forces may be, the effects of pre-existing catchment areas and 'selection by mortgage' may have been worse. In fact, the segregation index for 1989/90 is the highest for the years for which complete school census data still exist.

From 1990 to 1994, segregation in England broadly declined from a high of above 35 per cent to around 30 per cent. The national change in figures for all primary schools is almost identical to that for secondary schools. Segregation between all schools in terms of families in poverty decreased after 1989/90. Where other indicators are available, segregation by ethnic group, first language and additional educational need has also declined. These changes over time represent important and long-term shifts in the socioeconomic composition of schools. There is no evidence, on the figures presented here, to link education markets with increasing segregation. Such polices are not necessarily associated with increasing concentrations of disadvantaged children in some schools and their absence in others – rather the reverse. In 1995, 1996 and 1997, segregation in England stayed at around 30 per cent. This suggests that the imposition of school choice on a system with the level of segregation found in 1989 led to progressively less segregated schools (in general) as successive cohorts moved from primary to secondary school. Once all of the students in secondary schools had entered since 1989, this trend ceased and the position stabilized. In essence, the impact of choice policies (if that is what it is) was limited and relatively short-lived. Subsequently, from 1998 to 2001, segregation in England increased every year to around 33 per cent, after a change of government in the UK in 1997, and the introduction of the School Standards and Framework Act 1998.

According to the PISA study conducted for the Organization for Economic Cooperation and Development (OECD), by 2001 the UK still had lower than average between-school segregation on *all* relevant indicators of social disadvantage and attainment (see Table 4.1). It was, with Luxembourg, the only country to be in that position. Unlike Luxembourg, however, the UK also had less than average polarization of results (e.g. by family wealth). This polarization, or segregation by outcome, is strongly associated with the degree of selection in any national school system. After 12 years of public choice, the UK still has one of the fairest school systems in the European Union (EU).

The overall pattern of reduced segregation between schools between 1989 and 1994 also appears in *every* economic region in England, and in Wales. Schools in Wales were more mixed in socioeconomic terms than their counterparts in England, and segregation there continued to decline to 2001. Similar trends have emerged from Scotland (Paterson 2001).

Table 4.1 Segregation index (S) for lowest 10% score on parental occupation scale, lowest 10% score on PISA index of family wealth, and proportion of students born outside country of residence

Country	Parental occupation	Family wealth	Country of origin	Reading score
All EU	33	28	48	49
Austria	36 (+.04)	24 (−.08)	49 (+.01)	62 (+.12)
Belgium	36 (+.04)	26 (−.04)	45 (−.03)	66 (+.15)
Denmark	33	28	42 (−.07)	39 (−.11)
Finland	36 (+.04)	21 (−.14)	55 (+.07)	27 (−.29)
France	31 (−.03)	31 (+.05)	47 (−.01)	56 (+.07)
Germany	36 (+.04)	33 (+.08)	41 (−.08)	61 (+.11)
Greece	43 (+.13)	26 (−.04)	48	58 (+.08)
Ireland	29 (−.06)	30 (+.03)	45 (−.03)	39 (−.11)
Italy	30 (−.05)	27 (−.02)	55 (+.07)	58 (+.08)
Luxembourg	24 (−.16)	23 (−.10)	24 (−.33)	41 (−.09)
Netherlands	30 (−.05)	23 (−.10)	41 (−.08)	66 (+.15)
Portugal	40 (+.10)	36 (+.13)	35 (−.16)	48 (−.01)
Spain	32 (−.02)	28	57 (+.09)	40 (−.10)
Sweden	27 (−.10)	29 (+.02)	40 (−.07)	29 (−.26)
UK	31 (−.03)	26 (−.04)	46 (−.02)	43 (−.07)

Note: these figures are for segregation, representing the proportion of students with that characteristic (e.g. lowest 10% reading score) who would have to exchange schools for there to be no segregation. The figures in brackets are the proportionate difference between the first figure and the EU average.

The greatest proportionate decreases were in the South East and Outer London. These differences between the home nations and the variation in trends over time within England would suggest that there are several factors affecting between-school segregation. In accounting for the patterns observed in school segregation over time, both demographic and socioeconomic changes have to be factored into the analysis alongside changes in policy. One should not simply attribute any and all changes in segregation to the introduction of choice and competition in the state-funded education system, as other researchers have done (e.g. Gewirtz *et al.* 1995).

The findings also suggest no strong connection between markets and the changing rates of school closures, nor schools going into 'spirals of decline'. The number of children per secondary school in England has generally been increasing since 1947 (the earliest figures available). This is partly due to population growth and urbanization, partly due to successive raising of the school-leaving age, and more recently due to planned school closures. In the period of our investigation, 1989–2001, the number of students per school dropped slightly in the first year after the 1988 reforms, but has grown steadily since. This would lead us to expect that schools in 'spirals of decline' would be rare, since even 'unsuccessful' schools might be expected to grow in numbers (or at least maintain their size). In addition, the closure of schools leads to mixing students from previously distinct catchments, and could lead directly to less socioeconomic segregation. Economic growth (in this case of numbers of schools) tends to lead to segregation, while declining numbers leads to desegregation (Kacapyr 1996).

Over the period 1990 to 1994, therefore, when segregation between schools was declining, the number of state schools was also falling, and so the school population was divided into fewer units. At the same time, fewer students from higher income families attended fee-paying schools and fewer students with special needs attended separate schools. Only a 'super class', plus some professionals, use private schools and thus opt out of the state system altogether (according to Adonis and Pollard 1998). The remainder of the more privileged classes have always had access to the most desirable schools because of the link between school reputation and the cost of local housing, and because their children gain access to selective education in disproportionate numbers. Between these factors, all of which may or may not be related to market forces, we are able to explain much of the drop in segregation.

This analysis of national and international datasets has been used to illustrate the changing composition of secondary-school intakes. Trends in segregation between schools at national, regional and local scales have been used to indicate the impact of open enrolment on admissions. Furthermore, this data has begun to provide possible explanations for such trends. Of course some researchers may end their investigation there. However, many questions (and hence empirical and theoretical gaps in our understanding) still remain. Analysing the data from different perspectives, in this case at different scales (national, regional and local) and using different units of analysis as the foci (LEAs and schools), helps us establish further detailed questions and, therefore, how we need to refine our sample in subsequent stages of the research process. The subsequent exploratory phase of our project was based on a combination of documentary analysis, primary interview data and multivariate analysis of the statistical data. Not only does this complement the previous stage in the research (i.e. measuring segregation between schools), it also uses the data and findings in direct combination with other forms of data and methods.

In this second key phase of the research we attempted to explain both the differences in socioeconomic segregation between different areas, and the changes in these patterns over time. The more detailed 'qualitative' data, derived from admission brochures, interviews and unstructured observations guided our explanations or helped corroborate explanations derived from our more 'quantitative' large-scale datasets. As a result, we developed a relatively robust explanation of both phenomena. In general terms our explanatory model has three elements – local social geography, school organization and admission arrangements – and these are discussed later in descending order of importance, and in temporal order as determinants of segregation.

These three key explanations were based upon the combination of data and analysis employed in the study. For example, the role of residence in explaining school segregation came from a spatial analysis of school intakes alongside other residential or neighbourhood data (obtained from the national census). Furthermore, many LEA admission officers and school headteachers referred to the housing market when describing their school intakes and when discussing the (limited) impact of open enrolment on admissions. The second key element – the role of school organization – emerged from analysis of the national datasets at different local scales, descriptions of school provision in different locales (from a combination of national data, LEA websites, admission brochures and interviews transcripts) and discussions with LEA admission officers and headteachers from different types of school. The third main explanation – admission arrangements – was largely a result of relating the intake characteristics of different schools with their respective admission procedures and oversubscription criteria. The admission arrangements were themselves derived from a number of sources, including the LEA admission brochures, interviews with LEA admission officers and interviews with school headteachers.

The role of residence

Segregation declined in most LEAs (and the same is true at the district and school level). Areas with a sizeable proportion of residents living in poverty are more likely to have even distributions of poverty than areas where only a small proportion of the population are living in poverty. As overall levels of poverty rise, the population in poverty are likely to be more evenly distributed. Conversely, as overall levels of poverty fall the population 'left' in poverty are likely to be more concentrated in space, at least in the short term. There is extreme bifurcation of income in some LEAs which lose a large proportion of their population to fee-paying schools. One LEA had 44 per cent of students leave the borough to attend faith-based and foundation schools elsewhere. Thus, the LEA has a very large proportion of free school meals in its schools, and very little LEA-level segregation – 'equality of poverty'. Where the population is not bifurcated, segregation can still be lower because of this very uniformity. Segregation is generally lower in the North East and Wales where the population is less variable in terms of class structure, income and other socioeconomic indicators. The suggestion here is that segregation depends on the local variability of potential school users as much as their method of allocation to schools.

In England and Wales different social classes have long been substantially segregated from each other by residence, which has made any attempt to create a good social mix in local comprehensive schools very difficult, and the situation does not seem to be improving. In fact, residential segregation may itself be reinforced by the rising cost of property in desirable catchment areas, leading to selection by postcode and the continuance of educational 'ghettoization' (Association of Teachers and Lecturers 2000). Leech and Campos (2000) reported that in Coventry there is an estimated premium of 15 to 19 per cent for neighbourhoods surrounding popular schools. This is more significant given that Coventry LEA operated a 'designated' area policy for oversubscribed schools. Advocates of increased school choice have suggested choice as a partial antidote to this self-sustaining cycle of residential segregation, and there is some, albeit limited, evidence that this is possible. There has been a progressive rise in the use of schools further away from home since 1980 (Stillman 1990), and out-of-catchment schools have been chosen by more children from 'struggling' neighbourhoods than 'prosperous' ones, and this is likely to reflect a greater dissatisfaction with their local school among those living in poorer areas (Parsons *et al.* 2000).

Benn and Chitty (1996) report that at the peak of the comprehensive process (1968 perhaps), 62 per cent of comprehensive schools drew children mainly from council housing estates or areas of mixed housing with a substandard element. By 1994 this had fallen to 31 per cent of comprehensive schools. So, if the geographical link between home and school was weakened, even slightly, during the 1990s by a programme of school choice, then perhaps residential segregation has also declined over time by creating a circle of integrating forces? This is what Taeuber *et al.* (1981) described as the 'Belfast' model, when they found some evidence that residential segregation by ethnicity declined in Kentucky following the increasing integration of schools. UK policies to produce mixed housing schemes providing enough affordable houses in each area are popular with those, such as Demos and IPPR, who wish to extend choice to the socially excluded (Sutcliffe 2000). A similar phenomenon was hypothesized by Goldhaber (2000) who suggested that, paradoxically, by increasing choice in urban areas, one can actually reduce white flight (residential segregation) as parents no longer need to move away from city centres in order to use suburban schools. It is certainly the case for a variety of reasons (the nature of travel etc.) that geographical location is the key to understanding the impact of choice on the school system (Taylor and Gorard 2001).

The largest single factor determining the level of segregation in schools is the pattern of local housing, since even in a system of choice most children attend a school near their home. As one of our rural LEA respondents puts it, whatever system of allocation is used, 'it has always been preferable to live closer rather than further even before the 1988 Education Reform Act'. Many officers in rural areas would probably agree with one who said: 'We haven't really got a problem with admissions'. Some of these rural LEAs only have a part-time school admissions officer, who can tidy up the few remaining cases in an afternoon. Several said that they had never had an appeal (against placement) and hoped never to have one. Even where things are more complicated: 'It's always a major headache at transfer time fitting all the children in ... but come September it goes away somehow'.

What was clear from our rural respondents was that the whole issue of choice in the ERA88 and the subsequent School Standards and Framework Act was not intended for them. It was seen as a London-based solution to a perceived London problem. One LEA officer commented: 'It does seem a lot of it is aimed at solving problems in London that don't exist in other parts of Britain'.

Rural LEAs have always cooperated with each other. Now, because of the need for admissions forums, this officer has to formally consult with 13 authorities and all of them simply say 'no comment, no comment, no comment': 'Just because there is a problem with four London boroughs with different types of schools ... why impose nationally a system to deal with that? It has been a total and utter waste of money'.

Where richer and poorer families live 'cheek by jowl', usually in densely populated areas such as London, then residential segregation is lower, meaning that school segregation is also low. Because the price of local houses affects schools intakes, and the perceived desirability of schools can also affect the price of nearby houses, some developments are attempting to overcome this, and related problems, using a mixed housing model. As the head of a foundation school in a new unitary authority explains: 'They are going to put 95 houses here ... they have had to agree to a certain proportion of it being social housing or starter homes and not entirely five-bedroom luxury at £300,000 plus which is what most of the houses round here are'.

When such geographical factors change, through the provision of new housing estates or the closure of local industry, the levels of segregation in local schools are affected. Where these changes involve opening or closing schools, then the impact on local patterns of segregation can be very great. An officer from a London LEA near Heathrow explains: 'We've had a huge influx of refugees over the last five or more years from Somalia, Kosovo, Albania, and also way back this was a huge area for new Commonwealth settlements ... We had a huge rising population in [LEA] and we are looking at having to build another school in the north'. Due to population changes this LEA has ended up with areas where there are plenty of nearby school places but not enough residents to use them, and other areas where there are enough nearby residents but the local schools are seen by some as undesirable.

The role of school organization

The next most important factor after local geography is the nature of local schooling. One key indicator here is a change in the number of schools. When schools are closed or merged then local segregation tends to decrease (as happened in several areas in the early 1990s), and when new schools are opened then segregation tends to rise, at least temporarily (as happened in the later 1990s). An unpopular 11–16 school in a new unitary authority had to merge with a similar school as it was losing numbers, and took the opportunity to add a sixth form: 'Many parents of the brighter children in particular were taking the decision at the end of Year 6 – let's go straight to schools with a sixth form – which is why eventually the decision was made to close the two schools and open up ... as an 11–18 school'.

Another important indicator is the diversity of schooling. Areas with elements of selection have higher levels of segregation, and show less change over time. The same is true of areas with higher proportions of voluntary aided, voluntary controlled, foundation, Welsh-medium and independent schools (and more recently specialist schools appear to have a similar impact). One inner London LEA officer complains: 'All bar two of our secondary schools became grant-maintained ... which meant that for admission purposes we had no control whatsoever and still don't ... I forgot to mention that there is quite an outflow into the grammar schools [in adjacent LEA] which is really upsetting for schools'.

A rural LEA officer explains how foundation schools using apparently the same admissions criteria as the community schools can lead to segregation: 'I picked three or four at random and they're all remarkably similar to [county admissions procedures]. I think where the problems arise is that they can, for example, annexe a larger bit of catchment that didn't belong to them before and we have no power to say they can't do that'.

The same thing happens with faith-based schools, according to the officer at another London LEA: 'Because we've got predominantly voluntary-aided schools so they take from the diocese rather than locally ... across Central London'.

Thus, only around 50 per cent of local children attend a state school in this borough. The remainder go to nearby LEAs (usually faith-based schools) or to fee-paying schools, meaning that this wealthy borough appears to have a very high proportion of children in poverty (and, of course, little LEA-level segregation). As with many LEAs, having multiple admission authorities within one LEA makes it almost impossible for officers to be certain about first preferences. This was seen in an adjacent LEA as a problem for particular schools: 'I think it [growth of faith-based schools] will polarize more if we're not very careful. ... That was the issue with most of the other heads that the Church schools were interviewing because they're looking at religious affiliation ... but seem to be interviewing for other criteria as well'.

And on specialist schools: 'One is a language college and therefore highly sought after because if you're doing languages you're going to be bright and if you're bright it's going to be a good school and if it's a good school you're going to go there'.

Similar impacts on local levels of segregation, for different reasons, seems to occur when families have a choice of medium of instruction. The head of a rural English medium community school in Wales points out how the traditionally 'privileged' Welsh speakers go to *ysgolion Cymraeg* in adjacent LEAs (and these schools, like foundation and faith-based schools, do not have local catchments), and that even the English-speaking 'incomers' cannot compensate for the relative poverty of those remaining:

> The Welsh families from this area go to [school] and you can imagine the converse, you have the English medium kids from [LEA] coming here ... They are basically very English people who have moved to the area and don't like the Welsh element ... and you know the medium of communication here is mostly English ... The parents perhaps are a little bit more alternative than the usual ... more towards the hippy end. It is not always professionals, some come down from [English city] and claim dole here basically.

Areas with only LEA-controlled comprehensives have less segregation, and tend to reduce that segregation over time. We separate, analytically, school organization factors from the impact of admissions arrangements since ERA88, because factors such as diversity of schooling predate 1988. Limited 'choice' has always been available, but previously dependent only on income, aptitude or family religion. Perhaps the problem is not so much to do with diversity of schools, as with the different forms of intake they are allowed to attract (Gorard and Taylor 2001). Welsh LEAs will only pay for travel to the *nearest* school if the child is to be educated in English, but will pay for travel to a more distant Welsh medium school, for example.

The role of admissions

The vast proportion of variation in levels of segregation and changes over time is accounted for by the kind of factors already outlined. Given that geography and school organization precede school allocation procedures in historical terms, this means that the impact of increased market forces, if there is any, is likely to be confined to the margins of change. Policy changes at the Westminster parliament, the action of the adjudicator, and even the growing number of appeals are not statistically related to substantial changes in socioeconomic segregation in schools. This interpretation is confirmed by our interviews. Most families get their first preference school (as expressed), and most of these use a nearby traditional or catchment school. Most of the remaining families would probably not have used these local schools even if the policy had been different. Increasing parental choice has not reduced, long-term, the proportion of pupils in fee-paying or in faith-based schools, which have never used their LEA school allocation procedures. Oversubscription criteria are only relevant to schools with more applicants than places, but it is important to recall that several schools are: 'just taking what we can get. We are fighting for as many as we can'.

Even where schools are oversubscribed, most schools and LEAs get around the problem of making decisions by simply expanding. The planned admission numbers (PANs) are usually somewhat artificial in any case. In Wales, the Popular Schools Initiative has allowed some schools to expand due to oversubscription, but even in England the same thing happens, but less publicly and less formally (at least at the time of writing). Whether they agreed with this 'policy' or not, most LEA, and all of the school, interviews reported popular schools expanding to meet demand. One rural LEA has a school with a planned admission number of 370 which is now taking 490 per year. A popular community school in a new unitary authority regularly negotiates an increase every year:

> With [pre-unitary authority] the phone call would have been – 'this is the number and can you take an extra thirty?' No, we need two new classrooms – and it would be done ... With [new unitary authority] we applied to increase our number and the LEA opposed it. After that we went to the Secretary of State and ... they caved in at the end. We then changed our admission number to 227 ... Because we were continually increasing our standard number, I would say that ... everyone who applied got in.

A foundation school said: 'We have been expanding a lot ... we have just had a basic need bid that is extra funding from the DfEE to expand the school still further'.

A rural county LEA admitted:

> It is very difficult if you have got a 1233 school to say you can't take 1234 or 5, so unless we have strong case i.e. health and safety ... we don't go to appeal because the school down the road has got places ... We don't necessarily publish admission numbers as the standard

number. We consult with the governors each year ... if we have exceeded it we have exceeded it. We are now trying to get a PAN which reflects reality.

The same kind of thing happens in London LEAs: 'The members wanted to respond to this public feeling ... and what they wanted for their children ... and they expanded [school] just like that – 25 extra places'.

However, both LEA and school-level admission procedures do play a small part in producing our explanatory model. For example, LEAs that have retained some element of banding (mostly ex-Inner London Education Authority) have levels of segregation in their schools running at half what would be expected *ceteris paribus*. LEAs that use catchment areas as their main method of allocating places have levels of segregation around 20 per cent higher than would be expected otherwise, and, as explained above, LEAs where a large proportion of schools are their own admissions authorities also have above average segregation. Catchment areas can be amended to counter the problems of segregation, notably the creation of unpopular schools, as observed by the head of one of these in a new unitary authority: 'But since they shifted some of the boundaries around ... there were very few if any problems like that this year. The change to catchment areas that affected this current year group has actually smoothed things over slightly'.

However, it is generally very hard to change catchment boundaries because of public resistance and, ironically, the possibility of damage to the unpopular school:

> We are often pushed to change the catchment area particularly by the school and we have found that can be very counter-productive because any changes ... generate quite a high level of emotion, but what it usually ends up in is a lot of negative press for that school. So therefore you start off with doing something to support the school ... and you actually just drag it through the dirt.

Historical catchment areas therefore generally remain as they were even though residential and economic changes make them inappropriate (and LEAs try to help unpopular schools with image-building and extra funding instead). This helps to explain why some catchment area LEAs move towards a more segregated local school system, and the situation is worsened when a rigid catchment system exists alongside the few schools with the ability to set their own geographical boundaries.

Choice policies do not appear to entail the dangers of segregation their opponents feared, and it is clear that they are generally popular with parents, and also with many LEAs and schools. Other than this, in many areas there is considerable doubt that they have made any difference, except symbolically, at all. A rural LEA officer believes that choice has been minimal because of travel limitations, that nearly everyone gets their expressed preference, and that it has become increasingly used by families from a wider range of socioeconomic backgrounds:

> Unless you live in an urban area, maybe with two or three schools in your general community, you don't particularly have a choice ... because we haven't extended our transport policy ... I come at that from the opposite end which is the number of parents who do go on to appeal is probably 1 per cent and by definition 99 per cent are not totally unhappy about it. A majority of parents certainly get their first choice ... I think parental preference initially was something which was taken advantage of by relatively few people, more informed maybe. There is greater awareness now I would say.

An officer from another rural LEA agrees with all of these points. Families do not have much choice in reality, and since 95 per cent or more choose their traditional catchment schools it is relatively easy to accommodate everyone, but the remaining 5 per cent represent a range of backgrounds:

> When the government started talking about parental choice ... I think parents got misled into thinking they'd got choice when in fact there's very little ... This only led to more appeals, with no chance of them winning unless we have made a mistake ... I would have to say that a lot of our appeals are from people who are not particularly articulate. We get terribly scrappy notes with bad punctuation, not very well written, so it's not necessarily the most articulate middle class who are submitting appeals.

Her counterpart in a London LEA has been in post for a long time and also sees no real change since 1988: 'I am not sure if there was any difference in the admittance to schools. I think the schools that are popular have always been popular and vice versa. [On the other hand] when it changed [from selection] in 1976 ... those schools remained oversubscribed because they were ex-grammar schools and that's continued [and had an effect on local house prices]'.

Conclusion

What we have shown is that the determinants of school segregation are various. The most important ones are geographical, including population density, the nature of local housing, the diversity of the local population and local levels of residential segregation. Once geographical and economic determinants are accounted for there is little variance left in our model, and most that remains is accounted for by school organization factors, such as the nature and number of local schools. There is almost nothing left for the marketization of admissions to explain, and it is accordingly very difficult to attribute school-level changes to policy changes over time. The local variation in the implementation of national policy, and the lack of diversity or even alternative schools in some regions, show a simple and universal model of market outcomes to be invalid (e.g. it depends on the *status ante*, see also Narodowski and Nores 2002). What choice policies may do is change the rules by which segregation takes place, but without markedly increasing or eliminating levels of segregation that are largely shaped by structural factors. The policy implications of these findings are described in Gorard *et al.* (2003a).

There has been a great deal of interest in our research in the Pacific Rim, US and the UK although we detect some differences in its reception arising from differences in the research cultures and traditions on either side of the Atlantic. It is fair to say that UK researchers in the area of school choice have found the research challenging – not least because it has run against an established orthodoxy of suggested findings emanating from predominantly small-scale, fieldwork-intensive studies of the process of choosing schools. US researchers, and indeed researchers in other disciplines, have generally been more familiar with the scale of the research, the techniques and instruments employed and the means by which conclusions have been drawn.

We feel that our methods and the findings form an important step towards the further development of a 'new' political arithmetic – a concept widely talked about until now but little in evidence – in which complex situations can be examined by relatively simple arithmetic techniques in combination with other forms of data. We have also successfully combined educational data with geographical information systems. But this again has led us into conflict with those who would prefer more complex (but less appropriate) probability approaches. At present the kind of research we have undertaken here, using complete national datasets, is well understood within the mainstream of social sciences but is relatively new in the arena of educational policy analysis. The danger, as we found, is that even simple combined methods approaches such as this face opposition from researchers wedded to a particular research tradition. This is especially so when, as here, the results from this new approach were found by many to be politically and ideologically inconvenient.

The next chapter also examines a study that uses this progressive focusing method, but one in which the mix of data and the techniques for data analysis are more complex.

5

Understanding life histories by varying the scale

This chapter provides a summary of another combined methods research project, and one that, like the project described in Chapter 4, moves from larger to smaller-scale work using a detailed case study. It differs from that simpler study in the range of methods and data sources used, and most notably because the larger-scale work involves more complex statistical analysis. Combining such analysis with in-depth data is rarer than the NPA approach, perhaps because statistical models are routinely used both to describe and explain the phenomena of investigation (i.e. they perform the tasks performed by the two methods in the NPA model). In saying this, we do not suggest that it is a desirable situation. In fact, both modelling and then testing the model on the *same* dataset should be actively discouraged. The work described in this chapter is also different because it concerns the life course of individuals. For such longitudinal or retrospective work, it is recommended that we use quantitative data concerning the structure of the life course, and qualitative data to interpret the experiences during the life course (Erzberger and Prein 1997).

The study described here concerns people's interaction with lifelong learning opportunities, seeking the determinants of participation and non-participation and, therefore, improved policies to widen participation. For this study, we selected research sites using the national population census, the Labour Force Survey, and local economic histories. We conducted a large-scale household survey, collecting learning and training biographies from families in three selected sites (Gorard and Rees 2002). We conducted a second sweep of the survey to contact children of families from the first sweep. We undertook open-ended interviews with 10 per cent of the families, selected to represent the variation in the surveys, and supplemented these with interviews with teachers and trainers in each site, and with archived oral family histories from the same areas. Again, the advantage was that the in-depth datasets were easily examined for ways in which they could, and could not, explain the patterns derived from the secondary sources and the survey biographies (Gorard *et al.* 2001a).

Patterns of participation project

Understanding the determinants of participation in lifelong learning involves tracing out the interactions between the social relations which are specific to particular places, patterns of historical change and the experiences which constitute individual biographies. In what follows, we explore some of these issues by reference to the results of an empirical study of patterns of participation in lifelong learning in industrial South Wales over the past 100 years. Focusing on one region has allowed a detailed reconstruction of the changes which have taken place in patterns of lifelong learning and how these are related to shifts in the economic structure, as well as transformations in social relations more widely. Industrial South Wales provides a context in which changes of this kind have been especially marked and rapid.

Methods

There were three principal methods of data collection: a questionnaire survey, semi-structured interviews and archival analysis. The study was regionally focused to allow the researchers to gain clear descriptions of the changing structures of objective opportunities for participation over 100 years, and this was achieved primarily by analysis of taped oral histories of families dating back to 1890 from the South Wales Coalfield Archive, by interviews with key participants with long experience in local training, by secondary analysis of official statistics, and through the experiences of the researchers in previous locally-based studies. The taped transcripts of oral history interviews held in the archive, although carried out originally with different objectives in mind, provided a primary source of data on the nature and determinants of participation in education and training during the first half of the twentieth century.

Within the focus area, a systematic stratified sample of 1104 education and training histories were collected from respondents aged 15 to 65, originally identified from the electoral register. The second wave interviewed 200 of the children of those in the first wave. The questionnaire was designed to collect data of four principal kinds: the social/demographic characteristics of individual respondents; detailed histories of respondents' post-compulsory educational and training careers; simplified histories of respondents' employment careers; and simplified histories of the educational and training careers of respondents' children. Information on individual histories was collected on a modified 'sequential start-to-finish date-of-event basis' (Gallie 1994: 340).

A 10 per cent sub-sample, representing the characteristics of the main sample, provided the basis for 105 extended, semi-structured interviews. The interviews were tape-recorded and transcribed. These interviews again focused on the respondent's recollections of how his or her education and training career unfolded. However, here it was the ways in which this is understood by respondents which provided the focus. Although respondents were encouraged to speak freely on these issues, interviewers followed an *aide-mémoire* to direct the discussion to a predetermined analytical agenda.

The structured interviews attempted to capture all and any episodes of formal learning including one-off health and safety training, leisure reading and evening classes as well as the more usually reported induction training, and further and higher education. The patterns of participation of all individuals in the survey were encapsulated in four classes of learning trajectories. A learning 'trajectory' is an overall lifetime pattern of participation which is predictable to a large degree from the educational and socioeconomic background of the respondent (Gorard *et al.* 1999a). The 'non-participants' are those who reported no extension of their education immediately after ending compulsory schooling, no continuing education in adult life, no participation in government training schemes and no substantive work-based training. The 'transitional learners' reported only the continuation of full-time education or a period of initial work-based training immediately after completing compulsory schooling. Those on the 'delayed trajectory' had a gap in participation between leaving school and at least 21 years of age, but followed by a minimum of one substantive episode of education or training. The 'lifelong learners' reported both transitional participation and later episodes of education and training – albeit of varying kinds – as well.

Logistic regression analysis with backward stepwise entry of predictor variables was used to predict these lifelong patterns of participation. The dependent variable is the trajectory and the independent variables were entered in batches in the order that they occur in the individual's life. At birth these variables include sex, year, place, and parental occupational and educational background. By the end of initial schooling these variables include details of siblings, type of schools attended, and so on. In this way, the variables entered at each step can only be used to explain the variance left unexplained by previous steps.

Our comparison of patterns of trajectories *within* families was based on an established genre of work which relates occupational categories across generations in the same family (e.g. Blau and Duncan 1967; Goldthorpe *et al.* 1987). Using standard forms of odds calculations, it is possible to measure changes over class from one generation to the next in a form that takes into account the changes over time in the frequency of occupational classes (Marshall *et al.* 1997). A similar approach was used here, but replacing the analysis of occupational class with patterns of lifelong participation in learning.

Patterns of lifelong learning

For a substantial minority of respondents (32 per cent), their experience of formal lifelong learning ended with initial schooling (see Table 5.1). A further 21 per cent reported no formal learning as an adult after the age of 21 (of course, as we show below, informal learning continues for many of these). This confirms other accounts of the size of the task confronting policy-makers seeking to promote lifelong learning (e.g. Beinart and Smith 1998; Gorard 2003e; Gorard *et al.* 2003b).

Table 5.1 Frequencies of the lifelong learning trajectories

Trajectory	Percentage
Non-participant	32
Transitional	21
Delayed	14
Lifelong	33

The pattern of typical trajectories has changed very substantially over time. The archival research, for example, shows that, during the early decades of the twentieth century in South Wales, the dominant forms of formal, post-school learning were employment-based and largely restricted to men. Within coalmining, the pervasive method of acquiring knowledge and skills was through working under the tutelage of an experienced worker, usually an older family member. This came to be supplemented by organized evening classes, which enabled individuals to acquire the technical qualifications which became necessary for career advancement in the industry (and which were consolidated during the period after nationalization in 1947). However, with the intensification of conflict between miners and owners during the inter-war years, the nature of participation was transformed through the rise of 'workers' education', aimed at raising political awareness.

Although the nature of the evidence is different, the pattern of trajectories revealed by the survey also changed significantly in the period following the Second World War. Disaggregating the total sample into age cohorts shows that there has been a clear trend away from non-participation over the period since the oldest respondents left school. The proportion of each cohort reporting no formal adult learning has therefore decreased (despite the greater number of years in which participation was possible for the older groups). However, the increase in post-school participation which this implies is mainly due to the substantial rise in the proportion of 'transitional learners', primarily reflecting increased investment in initial schooling. Indeed, later participation in learning has actually decreased in overall frequency, duration and the proportion funded by employers (Gorard *et al.* 1999a).

Moreover, when these changes are analysed separately for men and women, distinctive patterns emerge. For men, the increase in post-school participation took place chiefly for those completing initial education during the 1950s and 1960s; while for women, it occurred a decade later, for those finishing school during the 1970s and 1980s. The increase in participation for men is attributable to the growth of 'lifelong learners', although only up until the 1980s. For women, in contrast, the increase is the result of more 'transitional learners'. Hence, sex remains a significant determinant of participation in lifelong learning, even where it has been eliminated as a determinant of extended initial education.

The determinants of learning trajectories

To begin to explain this changing pattern of participation in lifelong learning, logistic regression analysis can be used to identify those characteristics of respondents which enable good predictions of the trajectory they later follow. These characteristics are tentatively identified as social determinants of patterns of participation.

Time

When respondents were born determines their relationship to changing opportunities for learning and their social expectations. For example, a number of older respondents reported having experienced quite radical changes of job, with no training provided to equip them to cope with their new position. This was something which was believed to be much less likely today. As one of them put it: 'Nobody worried about things like that then. It's quite a new thing, isn't it?' Similarly, the salience of educational qualifications was widely perceived to have increased as a consequence of shifts in the nature of employment. One father, for example, contrasted his own experiences with those of his son 'so they kept me back from my 11-plus ... I didn't go to school that day ... As soon as I was old enough to work, they wanted me to work ... [But] he's not coming out of school until he's 18, you know. It's as simple as that, because we know how important it is, especially today'.

It is significant that respondents with similar social backgrounds from different birth cohorts exhibit different tendencies to participate in education and training.

Place
Where respondents were born and brought up shapes their access to specifically local opportunities to participate and influences social expectations. Those who have lived in the most economically dis-advantaged areas are least likely to participate in lifelong learning. This reflects both sharp inequalities in the availability of learning opportu-nities between different localities, as well as differences in values and attitudes. However, those who have moved between regions are even more likely to participate than those living in the more advantaged localities. It is not too much of a simplification to say that those who are geographically mobile tend to be participants in lifelong learning (of some kind), while those who remain in one area tend to be non-parti-cipants. One of our respondents, for example, had left school at 15 to enter employment in the local colliery, along with all his friends: 'but that was closed then, in 1969. I had an accident just before it shut and it was while I was out that Llanilleth shut'. He was clear that none of the local jobs now required any special skills or qualifications, and that there was little point in his seeking out alternative employment elsewhere, even though the opportunities may have been better. As he put it: 'I'm not brainy enough, I suppose. Well, I never looked to be honest'.

Sex
Men consistently report more formal learning than women. Although the situation is changing, these changes are different for each gender. Women are still less likely to participate in lifelong learning, but are now more likely to be 'transitional learners'. Staying on in education after 16 and undertaking some form of initial training (including apprenticeships) is now relatively evenly distributed between young men and women. However, participation in learning later in life is *increasingly* the preserve of males (Gorard *et al.* 1999a).

Women's participation in lifelong learning is often constrained by the expectations placed upon them by their parents and by their husbands and children. And this seems to have changed rather little over the 100 years or so covered by our study. A particularly vivid example of the contemporary salience of these factors is provided by a respondent who had succeeded in gaining the first ever formal qualification in her family: 'Well, I found work then [as a management trainee]. We moved away to Birmingham, up there. But Steve [her husband] didn't like it up there. And he was promised a job here, so we came back. But it fell through and then the kids came along'. Her husband has been unemployed ever since. Our respondent now works as a packer, helps with a local playgroup, is learning Welsh and taking further qualifications in childcare. She still looks\after the children.

Many older women describe the ways in which the learning opportunities available to them were limited by local employment, social expectations as to what was appropriate or by a 'forced altruism' with respect to family commitments (themes which are reproduced for the even earlier periods in the archival analysis). Even the younger women respondents frequently provide similar accounts, confirming the points made earlier about the very partial nature of changes in women's trajectories over time. Moreover, for a number of those – women and men – who *had* participated actively in post-school learning (albeit mainly in the form of conventional further and higher education), this was seen as a product of what was normatively prescribed within the family or, less frequently, the wider community, rather than their own active choice. Certainly, it is clear that, to make sense of individuals' learning histories, it is necessary to understand the ways in which learning opportunities were understood when decisions over participation were being made. Moreover, there is strong evidence that these 'social constructions' of opportunities, in turn, are shaped by a range of contextual influences. The most important of these is the early family.

Family
The sample included 200 respondents whose parents were also part of the sample, so it is possible to compare the relationship of trajectories within these 200 families. Table 5.2 examines these trajectories in a collapsed form. All trajectories involving *any* participation after initial schooling are grouped together (as participants), and contrasted with those cases reporting no formal learning episodes (non-participants). From this table it can be calculated that the odds of participation if one's parent also participated in any post-compulsory education and training are $(77 \times 20)/(45 \times 13)$ or 2.63. At this level of analysis, reproduction of patterns of participation within families is strong, but it should be noted that due to the increase in transitional, front-loaded participation, the majority of children of non-participants are themselves participants of some sort.

Table 5.2 Participation of parent and child

Origin\destination	Participant	Non-participant
Participant	77	13
Non-participant	45	20

Note: the total is less than 200 here since some of the children were too young to be classified as adult learners.

When the same analysis is applied to lifelong learning, supposedly the target of much post-war government policy, the lack of overall progress is also apparent (see Table 5.3). Here all trajectories other than lifelong learner have been grouped as a contrast. The odds of being classed as a lifelong learner if one's parent were is $(24 \times 76)/(28 \times 27)$ or 2.41. A clear majority of people are not lifelong learners, but even more so if their parents are not lifelong learners.

Table 5.3 Lifelong learning of parent and child

Origin\destination	Lifelong learner	Not lifelong learner
Lifelong learner	24	27
Not lifelong learner	28	76

Those who become lifelong learners without a parent of a similar trajectory are generally younger than the others in the table (so the differences cannot be attributed to their necessarily incomplete life histories), with no children of their own, and living in the coalfields north of Cardiff. They are more likely to be males, from atheist or non-conformist religious backgrounds. All took some qualifications at age 16, and most gained the equivalent of five or more GCSEs at grade C and above. On the other hand, those with lifelong learner parents who have not become so themselves are likely to be slightly older, often with several children, with the first child coming as early as age 18 or earlier, and living in the former steel region of Neath Port Talbot. They are more commonly female, from Anglican families. None have five or more GCSEs at C and above. Thus, as well as being trajectory determinants for individuals, factors such as age, sex, area of residence, initial education and having children are all also correlates of those who are 'mobile' in terms of trajectories within families.

Parents' social class, educational experience and family religion are perhaps the most important determinants of participation in lifelong learning. Family background is influential in a number of ways, most obviously in material terms, but also in terms of what are understood to be the 'natural' forms of participation (as is indicated by the importance of family religion, Gorard *et al.* 1999b). As one respondent explained: 'My mother and father would have been devastated if I hadn't passed [the 11-plus], totally devastated. My father was a collier, but the attitude in our house was if you don't learn, you won't get on, and you'll go down the colliery'.

As shown in the overall survey analysis, there is clearly a gendered pattern in family attitudes to lifelong learning. 'Reproduction' is used here to refer to the influences producing identical learning trajectories for both parent and child in the same family. Such reproduction is nearly always gendered. In one family, the 62-year-old father had a succession of varied jobs after leaving the Parachute Regiment, including several such as draughtsman for which he had no qualifications, before returning to higher education much later. He says of his transition to the workforce at age 15: 'The headmaster told us on our last day there that if we could add up our wages, check our wages, he thought our education had been sufficient in so many words ... Well at that time in that area there was loads of work around ... I didn't see anything except working in one of the local factories or on the buildings like my father'. His wife had stayed on in full-time education much longer, eventually leaving to become a housewife and mother. Perhaps partly due to her influence, and what are described as her 'thwarted' ambitions, he later took a degree intending to be a science teacher. His sons now have low-skill manual jobs and no qualifications, while his daughter has taken an Open University degree during her pregnancy. Even in the previous generation, the respondent's father had left school to get a job, while his mother had tried to continue her education with a place at a 'posh' school. So for three generations of this family, the women have a more extended education than the men, but in the first two generations, so far, the men have had greater opportunity for work-related training.

A similar picture emerges from the family of a 53-year-old woman. Her mother and father had no qualifications, her mother never had a job, while her father was a fitter. She has had many low-wage jobs with no training, although she had gained A levels before leaving full-time education. In her own account she and her husband were not very supportive of their own daughter. She would have liked her daughter to continue to higher education, but: 'My husband says "Well if they don't want to learn just leave them alone. They'll learn the long way"'. The daughter, who is still only 17, has dropped out of her A level and says of her parents: 'Well, once I had a job they were all right'.

A 21-year-old man acknowledges the influence his parents, among others, have had on his educational choices, and explains how he ended up in the same career as his father. On taking A levels: 'Yeah, that's the natural progression – I didn't really want to go into employment at that age ... That's always been instilled into me to get an education first ... by my parents ... very few of my friends went into employment at that age'. As a result he started a teaching degree: 'Well, my mother was a teacher, that was a big factor like, but saying that I've always ... my mother used to come home and tell me stories about the satisfaction when a pupil got something right ... and I was listening one night and thought it sounds a worthwhile job'. But he dropped out of that to become a policeman like his father: 'I think I've been a little naive. I've never really thought and planned. Like my choices, I've never really ventured outside my parents

... My father used to talk to me about his job and that seemed fun as well'.

Another man of similar age was asked what options he would have had if he had left school at 16: 'Leave school? Get beaten up by my dad for starters ... No, I wasn't brought up to know about any other options. I just expected to do A levels ...'. Explaining why he has chosen medicine as a career: 'It's just that I've lived with this all my life. My dad's a doctor and I've been to his surgery ... I just always enjoyed seeing what my dad did and the work he was doing'. However, in many ways he suggests that it is his mother, who also has postgraduate qualifications, who has been the biggest direct influence on his trajectory. In relation to subject choices, he states:

> She's the one that really kind of steers me. She's the one who said – like my dad was more laid back. He like said if there was something else I wanted to do he'd go along with it and let me make my own mistakes. Whereas my mum was always there to stop me making silly mistakes. She's always set her heart on me being a doctor ... She's kept me on the straight and narrow ... I'd get these strange ideas in my head like I wanted to be an architect or something ... When I told my Mum she just pointed out that these were just little fads ... Medicine is the right choice I guess.

A man of 48 explained how his father had helped him into printing college: 'I knew what my trade was going to be basically from the age of 5 because you see it ran in the family. My grandfather and father was a printer in the arts like'.

'Reproduction' also takes the form of non-participation in education. A 44-year-old woman had left school as soon as possible in order to leave home: 'There were 13 of us and we all left home at 16. Our dad was ... we never got on with our father'. Her daughter also left education at 16. Both mother and daughter now work in the same factory. Her son is currently unemployed, and although he originally went to a further education college, he dropped out to work as an untrained mechanic: 'My old man's a bus driver and I've always been involved with cars and buses and stuff like that'.

In some cases, both generations of the family are illiterate. In one example, both son and father attended the same literacy class, to no apparent effect. Not only are many jobs not open to this pair, all other learning opportunities they have sought (and the son in particular is ambitious to be a care assistant) have rejected them. A woman of 37 was illiterate until very recently, because of her parents in her opinion. She learned to read with her current partner, and proved it by reading the *Mirror* newspaper to the interviewer. Of her parents:

Interviewer: Did they encourage you at school?
Respondent: No. It was never the thing then was it?
Interviewer: Why do you think that was?
Respondent: I don't know. I suppose it was the way my parents were bought up.
Interviewer: Did they not think it was important?
Respondent: Not in those days it wasn't was it?

Three overall patterns of parental reproduction of trajectories have emerged from these second and longer interviews. First, there are the parents who would not countenance an education of the sort they never had, whatever the intervening societal changes. For example, a man of 56 recalls how his father made all the major decisions about transition from school at 15.

> School trips, I could never go on ... He organized the job for me and took me out of school before I could try ... I wanted to stay in school ... to try my O levels ... but you couldn't get an apprenticeship over 17 so ... he said I've got a job for you in W H Watts ... I was there about three months and I went home one day and he said I've got you a job at Ivan Waters ... It'll save you the bus fare from Bridgend. He wants you to start next Monday.

Second, there are the parents who cannot imagine an education other than the one they had. A woman of 30 recalls how her parents had met at university and the influence that had on her choices:

> I think they thought it would be a better school ... it was a religious school as well, a convent school. My mother went to a convent school herself and she felt quite strongly that she wanted us to have the same experience ... I think they really expected us to go to university. They expected it and we were really forced into it, and it was always held out as a really enticing prospect. You know, if you do well you will be able to go to university and going to university is great.

Third, there are families where everything can be provided for a formal education that the parents never had, except the necessary finance. The ensuing reproduction is clearly unintentional. A woman of 40 followed the route of informal learning, when the economic situation meant that her early educational promise was not fulfilled:

> My family, especially my grandfather, very big ... no he was more than a socialist, he was actually a communist. He was an activist for the Communist Party in the Rhondda. He did quite a lot for education in the you know ... very, very staunch union ... I spent most of my very young years with my grandfather. I mean I could read

when I was 3 . . . Yeah my mother had to stop buying the *News of the World* because I could read it . . . I was not allowed to read comics. If I wanted to read it had to be a book.

If I'd worked harder I think that I could have got . . . you know I've got 4 O levels, I could have got a lot more but it was just at the time really, uh, all living at home with mum. Mum was a single parent. She was widowed at 27 . . . My dad died when I was eight, and there's my sister and brother . . . quite a difficult time then . . . and when I was going through my O levels and things like that my grandmother came to live with us because she was ill . . . you know we all took shares in sort of helping . . . and my mother also looked after, well cared for the housework, with her brother who was a bachelor who lived with my grandmother just a few hundred yards away.

Further examples, including several where children broke away from this 'reproductive' cycle of families, appear in Gorard *et al.* (1999b).

Initial schooling
Experience of initial schooling is crucial in shaping long-term orientations towards learning; and in providing the qualifications necessary to access many forms of further and higher education, as well as continuing education and training later in life. There are important 'age effects' here, however, relating especially to the reorganization of secondary schooling in the maintained sector. For the older age groups, the 11-plus was a clear watershed. Those who did not sit the examination, as well as those who failed it, were especially affected. 'Success' or 'failure' at school lays the foundation for what appears to be an enduring 'learner identity'. It is striking, for example, how numerous respondents who had experienced the 11-plus examination testified without prompting to its major and often long-term effects. For example, a respondent explained that he had left school at the earliest opportunity to be a coalminer; only passing the 11-plus would have offered an alternative: 'It's just the normal thing, I think, around here, unless I went to a grammar school or whatever'.

For respondents too young to have gone through the tripartite system, although 'success' and 'failure' are less starkly defined, it remains the case that they identify positive experiences of schooling as crucial determinants of enduring attitudes towards subsequent learning. For many individuals, then, the significance attached to 'doing well' at school within families and even the wider community has long-term consequences. In particular, while 'passing' the 11-plus is certainly not a sufficient condition for becoming a 'lifelong learner', a number of respondents do attribute their post-school education and training to the influence of their adolescent experiences of the traditional grammar school, especially in the wider context of the South Wales coalfield, where the conventional non-conformist emphasis upon the intrinsic value of education continued to be influential. As one respondent recalled, for example:

> When I was in school, we won the Urdd Eisteddfod play ten years on the trot ... Mind you, look at the people we had there ... We had debating societies every Monday and we had to prepare a speech ... You were influenced by your peers as well, not just your parents ... And I think it held you in good stead later on ... you were never afraid to stand in front of an audience.

In contrast, those who 'failed' at school often come to see post-school learning of all kinds as irrelevant to their needs and capacities. Hence, not only is participation in further, higher and continuing education not perceived to be a realistic possibility, but also work-based learning is viewed as unnecessary. There is, thus, a marked tendency to devalue formal training and to attribute effective performance in a job to 'common sense' and experience. While this is certainly not confined to those whose school careers were less 'successful' in conventional terms, it is a view almost universally held among this group of respondents. For example, one of our respondents had left school at 14 and gone straight into a successful career in British Steel Tinplate, despite having no formal qualifications or even training: 'You learn as you get along ... You got to train yourself and you use your hands and ears. No one came along and said "you mustn't do this" or "you mustn't do that" ... I mean common sense will tell you not to do certain things ... I can pick up most things purely by watching someone else doing it ...'.

In reality, of course, it is difficult to interpret the implications of these findings. Reluctance to acknowledge a significant role for formal training may not impair an individual's ability to do a job, especially where the requirements are minimal. Conversely, there is considerable evidence from the semi-structured interviews that many people are able to acquire substantial knowledge and skills – both inside and outside of employment – *without* formal training (Gorard *et al.* 1999c). The evidence from one of our respondents is used as an example.

> I haven't got a GCE or a BSc or whatever they're called these days ... but as I say you don't have to be academic to be able to do things ... It's the same with the French polishing, you see. I used to do it as a favour. I got a book from the library. I had a blind chappie who was a pianist, like, and he used to tune pianos and do them up. He asked me if I knew anything about polishing and I said "not the foggiest". So I went to the library, got a book on it. We got the French polish and promptly went into business. It was just a sideline when I was working for the printers.

Conclusion

It is important to note that all of the factors described above reflect characteristics of respondents which are determined relatively early during the life course. This can be expressed more formally, as the variables were entered into the logistic regression function in the order in which they occur in real life. Hence, those characteristics which are set very early in an individual's life, such as age, sex and family background, predict later lifelong learning trajectories with 75 per cent accuracy. Adding the variables representing initial schooling increases the accuracy of prediction to 86 per cent. And this rises to 89 per cent and 90 per cent respectively, as the variables associated with early adult life and with respondents' present circumstances are included.

Therefore, not only is there a clear pattern of typical trajectories which effectively encapsulates the complexity of individual education and training biographies, but also *which* trajectory an individual takes can be accurately predicted on the basis of characteristics which are known by the time an individual reaches school leaving age. This does not imply, of course, that people do not have choices, or that life crises have little impact, but rather that, to a large extent, these choices and crises occur within a framework of opportunities, influences and social expectations that is determined independently. At this level of analysis, it is the latter which appear most influential. For a discussion of the implications of these findings for policy, see Gorard and Rees (2002).

In using archive, local history, secondary data, a survey with complex statistical modelling and family interviews this case study is a more complex example of the progressive focusing technique represented by the NPA than that in Chapter 4. In this model, the in-depth data in the second phase is coded for analysis using codes generated by the analysis of the more clearly generalizable data from the first phase. The first phase provides the patterning, and the second phase provides the explanation of those patterns. However, the model also allows the grounded coding of data for analysis in the second phase. In this way, the new ideas that emerge can then be used to re-analyse the data from the first phase. This is not so much a two-phase design as a fully iterative one. Although it is not possible to do justice to this project in one chapter, we hope that the examples given demonstrate again that the mixing of numeric and textual information is relatively simple and trouble-free. Or to put it another way, the difficulties in conducting this study arose from factors such as the difficulty of contacting non-participants, not from the fact that many different data sources were available for combination in analysis and interpretation.

6

The interplay of scale and type: complex interventions

Several commentators have suggested that progress in education and social policy depends upon a more widespread adoption of research designs based on experiments, as has also been happening in medical research (Torgerson and Torgerson 2001). This is a view with which we have some sympathy, for it is often only by using an experimental design that we can tell whether a particular approach works or not (Gorard 2003a). We may conclude as a result of a trial that a drug is effective as a treatment for a specific problem, or whether a new way of teaching fractions leads to greater understanding. However, the standard experimental approach also has limitations. It does not address the issue of why an intervention works and, more crucially, of why an intervention does not work. In this chapter we describe a model for complex interventions that overcomes these deficiencies by using in-depth study as the basis for a classic experiment, and we conclude with a summary of a recent successful piece of social science research using this model.

Combining methods in experiments

Governments, particularly those in the US and UK, have become increasingly interested in the quality of evidence regarding the effectiveness of alternative practices, programmes and policies. The US Congress's Committee on Education and the Work Force, for example, has been 'concerned about the wide dissemination of flawed, untested educational initiatives that can be detrimental to children' (Boruch and Mosteller 2002: 1). History suggests that this concern is not misplaced, since there are many examples of education interventions that have been widely disseminated on the basis that they are driven by good intentions, seem plausible and are unlikely to do any harm, yet when they have been rigorously evaluated have been found to be ineffective or positively harmful. Such interventions include the 'Scared Straight' programme, which aimed to deter delinquent children from a life of crime, was well received and widely implemented, yet in seven good-quality trials was found to increase delinquency rates (Petrosino *et al.* 2000); and the 'Bike-Ed' training programme to reduce bicycle accidents among children, which was actually found to increase the risk of injury (Carlin *et al.* 1998). And, of course, there have been much larger national interventions that have never been tested properly (in education these could include the introduction of the 11-plus examination, and more recently the creation of specialist schools).

In clinical medicine, the randomized controlled trial (RCT) is well established as the best way of identifying the relative impact of alternative interventions on predetermined outcomes. The salience of this research design is largely due to the random allocation of participants to the alternative treatments in relatively controlled conditions, such that any difference in outcomes between the groups is due either to chance, the likelihood of which can be quantified, or due to the treatment difference. The RCT is most easily applied to the measurement of the efficacy of simple, well-defined interventions, delivered in an ideal research setting, and where there is a short-term impact on an objectively measured outcome. The classic application of the RCT design in clinical medicine is the drug trial where, for example, the relative efficacy of two alternative antihypertensive drugs can be established by recruiting a sample of hypertensive patients, randomly allocating half to receive drug A and half to receive drug B, and then measuring the blood pressure of the patients at some predetermined follow-up point(s). The difference in their mean blood pressure at follow-up should be an unbiased estimate of the difference in treatment efficacy of the two drugs, and appropriate statistical methods can be used to determine how likely it is that this observed difference is due to chance.

In education, this approach to research is almost certainly underused, but valuable (Fitz-Gibbon 2001). Goodson (1999) randomized Year 2 pupils to undergo either formal or informal testing, and found that the pupils performed better when tested in the informal normal working environment, rather than formal test conditions. Butler (1988) randomized students to three groups, which after testing received either just their numerical grade, or a more detailed comment on their performance, or both of these. Those receiving just comments performed better in subsequent tests, particularly among the subgroup of lower achievers. These studies have provided clear answers to important questions, and are examples of where RCTs can be used as the most effective method in empirically driven knowledge development. The fact that the results have not been allowed to affect national policies on assessment (at the time of writing) looks curious in the light of current government demands for just this kind of evidence of what works, to form the basis of evidence-based policy-making.

However, it can be argued that because many health promotion and educational interventions are so dependent on how they are implemented, and upon the context (environment, policy etc.) within which they are delivered, RCTs are not suited to their evaluation. The RCT design does have the advantage that the randomization process ensures that systematic differences in external influences between groups do not occur, and that an unbiased estimate of the average effect of the intervention is obtained. Even so, randomized trials can be expensive both in monetary terms, and more particularly in terms of their demands on research subjects and researchers. It is, therefore, morally dubious to conduct a trial until there is a reasonable basis on which to believe that the intervention is likely to be effective (and also perhaps morally dubious to deny the treatment to the control group once that basis has been established!). In the context of drug trials, basic pre-clinical science and further applied pharmacological research precedes small-scale trials. Only a minority of potential new treatments emerge as being of sufficient promise (and safety) to warrant definitive testing in a large-scale clinical trial.

The application of the experimental design remains problematic, therefore, both in the evaluation of complex health services interventions and in the field of education (Hakuta 2000). There are important differences between education and the models of research and development used in industry and biomedicine (the inability to legislate for teacher classroom behaviour being one), and it has been argued that outcome measures in medical matters are generally less problematic than in education (Hammersley 2001). The measurement of 'life span' may be less ambiguous than that of 'standards', for example. Experimental designs should therefore be combined with, not replacements for, other recognized modes of research such as secondary analysis and detailed case studies.

The Medical Research Council (MRC 2000) model for complex health education interventions suggests that interventions are most likely to be successful if they are based on sound theoretical concepts (Campbell *et al.* 2000). In this model, which has phases like the NPA model used in Chapter 4, the first phase would involve the initial design of an intervention based on current theoretical understanding, with an explicit underlying causal explanation for its proposed effect (see Figure 6.1). The second phase involves the formative evaluation of that intervention, using qualitative approaches such as interviews, focus groups, observation and case studies to identify how the intervention is working, the barriers to its implementation, and how it may be improved. The third phase is a feasibility study of the intervention, or full pilot study, involving both measurement and in-depth feedback. This phase also sees the main development of the alternative treatments or controls. The fourth phase is the trial itself, and the fifth might be the scaling up and 'marketing' of the results.

Preclinical phase: theory

> Explore relevant theory to ensure best choice of intervention and hypothesis, and to predict major confounders and strategic design issues.

Phase I: modelling

> Identify the components of the intervention and the underlying mechanisms by which they will influence outcomes to provide evidence that you can predict how they relate to and interact with each other.

Phase II: exploratory trial

> Describe the constant and variable components of a replicable intervention and a feasible protocol for comparing the intervention with an appropriate alternative.

Phase III: definitive randomized controlled trial

> Compare a fully defined intervention with an appropriate alternative using a protocol that is theoretically defensible, reproducible and adequately controlled in a study with appropriate statistical power.

Phase IV: long-term implementation

> Determine whether others can reliably replicate your intervention and results in uncontrolled settings over the long term.

Figure 6.1 Medical Research Council model for complex interventions

It is deemed important to conduct a comprehensive qualitative investigation within any complex RCT, so that the quality and variability of intervention delivery is monitored. If the intervention is not found to work, then the qualitative research may identify why this was the case, and if there is variation in the impact of the intervention, this may be related to the variability in implementation. Furthermore, by building into the RCT design a strong qualitative component, variability in context can be documented, and its impact on the intervention's delivery and effectiveness can be identified. In summary, 'the RCT design ensures that an unbiased estimate of the average effect of the intervention is obtained, while the qualitative research provides useful further information on the external factors that support or attenuate this effect' (Moore 2002: 5).

An example of a sex education intervention

Sex education can be a problem area in schools, for both staff and pupils. One study looked at emergency contraception and its teaching, in the light of the declining age for first intercourse and the rise in under-18 conception in the UK (Moore *et al.* 2002). Previous studies of teenagers had found relatively high levels of knowledge about protected sex in schools, and some awareness of the value of emergency contraception when sex has taken place without protection or where the planned method of protection visibly fails. However, there was relative ignorance about some of the key details of emergency contraception, such as its timing.

The study started with a questionnaire survey of the personal, social and health education (PSHE) coordinators in one region. The survey revealed gaps in the teachers' knowledge about emergency contraception, including how it worked, alternative methods, when it could be used effectively, and how and where pupils could obtain advice and access to it (Graham *et al.* 2000). Therefore, a two-hour training session was devised for the PSHE teachers themselves, to provide them with information about a planned lesson for pupils based on a standard resource. A further survey of the providers of emergency contraception in the same region provided an up-to-date guide to its availability and access, that then formed part of the same lesson. The lesson delivery was piloted in one school, and the results were evaluated by means of 'qualitative' analysis of lesson observation, and two subsequent focus group discussions. The feedback led to substantive changes in the lesson delivery (e.g. a confusing role-play element was discarded and replaced by a quiz).

Pupils' knowledge of sex and contraception changes quickly at age 14+. Therefore, it was considered not possible simply to measure changes in pupils' knowledge of emergency contraception after completing the lesson. What was needed was a comparison of the change among those receiving the lesson in addition to their existing PSHE, in contrast to the change among equivalent groups not receiving the lesson (but continuing only with their existing programme of PSHE). This simple notion of a comparison group for an intervention lies at the heart of the experimental approach.

In education research, experiments in realistic settings often require the allocation of the experimental and comparison treatments to existing groupings, such as school classes, rather than individuals. This has the side-benefit of allowing group learning. True randomization of individuals to the experimental and comparison groups, on the other hand, would mean that pupils would have to be taught separately to the rest of their class, which is an unrealistic setting. It also encourages contamination, whereby pupils from different experimental groups meet later in the same class, and may discuss what they have been doing. Instead therefore, it is the schools that are randomly allocated to one of the two experimental conditions. Each school agreeing to take part is offered a longer-term benefit for their PSHE (free training at the end), but has to accept a 50 per cent chance of being in either group for the duration of the trial. As long as there are a large number of schools, this saves the researcher from having to match the schools in terms of measurable characteristics, and from having to worry about the bias caused by asking schools to volunteer either for the experimental condition or the control. This approach is known as a 'cluster' RCT.

There were 24 volunteer schools in the PSHE study. Because this is a relatively small number of clusters (but a large number of pupils), the schools *were* balanced before the randomization process in terms of four characteristics: percentage of pupils entitled to free school meals, size of school, whether sex education was taught by a tutor or specialized team of teachers, and whether sex education was mainly taught in Year 9 or in Year 10. The outcome variable was pupils' knowledge of various key facts about the use of hormonal emergency contraception. This was elicited in a prior baseline survey, and in a follow-up survey six months later, for both groups.

It is widely assumed that RCTs require the interventions being tested to be standardized and uniformly delivered to all participants. This is the case in an efficacy trial, which seeks to identify the impact of the intervention when delivered in ideal circumstances. However, since educational interventions are so dependent on the quality of delivery, the value of efficacy trials is limited (Flay 1986). For example, smoking education interventions have been found to work well in efficacy trials, when delivered by enthusiastic teachers with ample curriculum time, yet when implemented in the real world they have not been found to be effective. In an effectiveness trial, a more pragmatic approach is taken, with the intervention delivered in the trial in the same (variable) way as would realistically be achieved in the real world (see also Chapter 7).

Therefore, in this emergency contraception trial, a number of methods were used to evaluate the process and context of the implementation of the intervention. Six teachers were sampled purposively to include both those working within a team and teachers who were class tutors, male and female teachers, and teachers with more and less confidence and experience in the area. A non-participant observer of these lessons took fieldnotes that were later transcribed. An independent researcher conducted telephone interviews with a randomly selected teacher from 9 of the 12 intervention schools. These semi-structured interviews focused on the content and delivery of the lesson that the teachers delivered themselves, and also asked about the in-service training that they had received to prepare them to deliver the lesson. In summary, a 'qualitative' pilot led to a survey, a field trial with statistical analysis of outcome scores, and a qualitative evaluation of the process.

The proportion of pupils knowing the correct time limits for hormonal emergency contraception was higher in the intervention than the control group by about 15–20 per cent for both males and females. This is so, even when it is assumed, for the sake of calculation, that *all* of the absentee pupils on any day of testing did not know the correct time limits. The process evaluation indicated that lessons generally went very well, with substantial pupil interaction by both sexes. Teachers commented very favourably on the in-service training they were given, and particularly spoke of the value of having a knowledgeable general practitioner to deliver the training. All teachers interviewed were glad that their school had participated in the trial, and stated that their school would continue to use the emergency contraception lesson package.

Conclusion

It is not easy to evaluate a complex health promotion or educational intervention using an RCT design. However, a framework has been developed within health services research that highlights the key challenges in evaluating complex interventions, and how they may be overcome. In particular, this framework emphasizes the importance of combining quantitative and qualitative methods to ensure that the intervention is well developed and tested prior to the conduct of an expensive trial, and that the trial, which may be a cluster randomized design, is a pragmatic one in which variations in delivery and context are allowed to occur but are fully documented.

This example shows that by randomizing schools, and through careful attention to the choice of a control condition, schools are willing to participate in RCTs. Using a range of research methods, including observation, interview and survey, the quality of the intervention is increased in its development and formative evaluation. Also, the factors affecting its success, such as context and delivery, can be evaluated within the trial. This is the power of combining methods in complex interventions. Experiments are not only 'quantitative'.

7

The promise of design studies

Researchers in education have long borrowed techniques from other disciplines. Some use laboratory methods derived from psychology, others use ethnography, survey methods and so on. In 1992, Ann Brown, a psychologist, looked to the field of engineering for inspiration on how to conduct experimental research in classrooms. She called her formulation – a hybrid cycle of prototyping, classroom field-testing and laboratory study – 'design experimentation'. In the past decade, that original notion of the design experiment has been transmuted. Now a diverse set of teaching interventions, educational software design projects and learning environment manipulations are loosely termed 'design experiments', 'design studies' or 'teaching experiments' (Kelly and Lesh 2000). This chapter considers the emerging method of design experimentation, and its use in education research. It considers the extent to which design experiments are different from other more established methods and the extent to which elements of established methods can be adapted for use in conjunction with them.

Design studies tend not to be very prescriptive, not having a given set of rules which the researcher should follow. In this sense they represent an *approach* to doing combined methods research. In education, this kind of research has been typically associated with the development of curricular products, teaching and learning methods or software tools (Collins 1992). At the core of such research is the development of an artefact for the purposes of improving teaching and learning, and recent years have seen a marked growth in the number of investigators associating their work with this genre of research. However, design experiments can also be used to develop other policy interventions within the education setting. For example, a design experiment could be undertaken to study and develop approaches to, and initiatives for, school admissions or the impact of grouping pupils by aptitude.

The first design experiment?

We start the chapter by using the theory of design from the engineering sciences as a useful analogy, touching on the distinction between design and artefact. Education research has been likened to engineering, as opposed to the natural sciences (Cobb *et al.* 2003). To some extent much mainstream education research *is* already engineering if what we mean by engineering is designing products and systems that solve problems of significance to society. In the field of engineering, design is considered the basis of the profession. The emphasis of the word 'design' in this context can be twofold. It relates to 'design' as the practice of engineers, and to the 'designs' as intellectual products that those practices ultimately produce. As such, in the grammar we present below, 'design' can be considered as both a verb and a noun. 'Design' (the verb) is the creative process by which designers consider a problem within their field of expertise and generate a hypothetical solution to that problem. 'Design' (the noun) constitutes that general hypothetical solution, often embodied in material form (e.g. a blueprint or physical model).

The main objective of a design experiment is to produce an artefact, intervention or initiative in the form of a workable design. The emphasis, therefore, is on a general solution that can be 'transported' to any working environment where others might determine the final product within their particular context. This emphasis also encourages theory-building and model-building as important outcomes from the research process. The strength of this is that the 'design' for an intervention, artefact or initiative can then be readily modified in different settings. Or it can be further developed by other practitioners, policy-makers, researchers or designers without having to make a 'leap of faith' in its interpretation, generalization or transformation.

Historically, design experiments have been the province of the artificial and design sciences including such disciplines as aeronautics, artificial intelligence, architecture, engineering and medicine. Whereas the natural sciences have been concerned with how things work and how they may be explained, design sciences are more concerned with producing and improving artefacts or design interventions, and establishing how they behave under different conditions (Collins *et al.* 2001). The process of designing an artefact or intervention that can be utilized independently, across a variety of settings, may begin with established theory and may provide insights that reflect on, shape or create established theory. However, this is *not* the main aim of the design science approach as it often is for the natural science approach.

The application of the methods and metaphors of the artificial or design science approach to education and social science has a fairly short history, and it is one that is bound up with a shift in the US from a traditional social science approach to experimentation in learning research, to a design experimental approach to the study of learning (Kelly 2003). Traditionally, in order to determine what strategies are effective in education, educational processes have been subjected to experiments based on made-up situations in laboratory conditions, which isolate the topic from its context and which rest on the assumption that there is a clear theoretical basis for addressing questions related to the processes being tested. Within a design science approach on the other hand, currently accepted theory is used to develop an educational artefact or intervention that is tested, modified, retested and redesigned in both the laboratory and the classroom, until a version is developed that both achieves the educational aims required for the classroom context, and allows reflection on the educational processes involved in attaining those aims (note the similarity to the model in Chapter 6). In other words, a design science approach allows the education researcher to study learning in context, while systematically designing and producing usable and effective classroom artefacts and interventions. In doing so, it seeks to learn from sister fields such as engineering product design, the diffusion of innovations and analysis of institutional change (Zaritsky *et al.* 2003).

The potential of this shift from traditional to design-based experimental approaches to educational research is illustrated in Brown's (1992) seminal piece on design experimentation. Brown's work began by addressing a theoretical question concerning the relative contributions of capacity and strategic activity in children's learning and instruction. Laboratory experimentation was used to address the question of why children fail to use appropriate strategies in their approach to learning tasks. This experimentation involved teaching children strategies for learning, and then asking them to use the strategies to memorize lists of words. Results suggested that even the most meagre form of strategic activity would increase the children's memory, but that this improvement was not maintained outside of the laboratory. The strategies were not transferred from the work with word lists as used in laboratory conditions to the coherent content children are expected to learn in complex, realistic settings.

A design experiment approach was used, therefore, to address the question of what the absolutely essential features are that must be in place to cause change in children's capacities for learning under the conditions that one can reasonably hope to exist in normal school settings. This question was addressed by designing an intervention, known as reciprocal teaching, on the basis of (impoverished) theoretical understanding. The intervention was implemented in the classroom, evaluated, allowed to modify current theoretical understanding, revised, re-evaluated and reapplied in an iterative fashion. It demonstrated feedback coupling from each stage, within an overall iterative process. Each modification to the design of the reciprocal teaching intervention was monitored and recorded, and represented a new phase in the design experiment. Testing of the design iterated between the laboratory and the classroom as an attempt was made to arrive at an optimal design for the classroom setting, while also building theoretical understanding of the mechanisms involved in learning, and generating questions for further research. Testing relied on the evaluation of each modification to the design on the basis of observational data, measurement data and current theory (just like complex interventions). The researcher and the teachers were able to make *in situ* changes to the intervention, making it possible to establish via observation which were the critical and non-critical elements of the reciprocal teaching strategy, as well as establishing *how* the strategy worked. Thus, the design experiment generated an effective classroom intervention that could be used independently by teachers in their own classrooms.

Characteristics of design experiments

Although the design experiment may be beneficial and appropriate in several areas of educational inquiry, adopting this approach is currently not a straightforward matter. Design experiments are messier than traditional experiments, because they monitor many dependent variables, characterize the situation ethnographically, revise the procedures at will, allow participants to interact, develop profiles rather than hypotheses, involve users and participants in the design, and generate copious amounts of data of various sorts. They tend to involve the following characteristics:

- design activity – focus on process and product;
- transportation – focus on design and outcome;
- academic scholarship *and* scientific enquiry;
- multiple datasets and multiple research methods;
- a central role for users (e.g. practitioners and policy-makers);
- evaluation;
- design-based model building.

Design activity is a creative process incorporating continuous modification and testing. It begins with proposing the 'form' of an artefact, intervention or initiative, which in turn drives its 'behaviour'. As a consequence of its 'behaviour' the artefact, intervention or initiative serves a particular 'function'. Subsequently both the actual 'behaviour' and 'function' of the artefact, intervention or initiative can then be compared against their desired or intended counterparts (see Figure 7.1).

Both the 'form' (proposed and at some point realized) and the desired 'behaviour' and 'function' are hypothetical entities that are linked by a theoretical model. In engineering this model is called the 'function structure'. The behaviour of the artefact, intervention or initiative constitutes observable and empirical data. An iterative design-and-test cycle is critical for the transformation of both the 'form' of the artefact, intervention or initiative and of its intended function to conform to the pragmatic demands of utility and market.

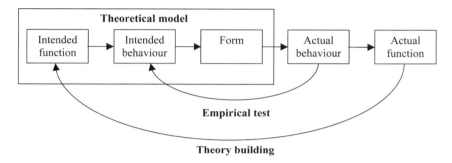

Figure 7.1 General model of design research

The resulting design is not necessarily an actual product. Rather, designs can be thought of as the *theory* that specifies the parameters of an ostensible product, and the conditions under which a product (if it embodies the design) can be successfully implemented – i.e. its 'form', 'function' and 'behaviour' (Horowitz and Maimon 1997). For example, the concept of a 'bridge', and more specifically the *design* of a bridge, are plausible solutions to the problem of getting from point A to point B across a river. The power of a design as a theory rests in the fact that a common design can be enacted across different situations. In other words, a common blueprint can guide the construction of two different bridges across two different chasms, each with different geology, elevation and other minor differences and still be recognized as the same design.

An example from education is a common curriculum. Situational demands (e.g. national and local standards, school calendar, language constraints) dictate that teachers alter the available tasks and materials to meet the needs of their students. Even so, the resulting classroom activity, obstacles, useful tools, models for teaching and subsequent achievement based on a curriculum are likely to be similar from class to class and school to school across the intended age range or key stage. In other words, though variation will exist in the outcomes of a design, the range of possible outcomes is finite, and the qualities of the outcomes will be constrained by the behaviour of the design. Whether or not that behaviour facilitates or inhibits learning and instruction is an empirical question of the degree to which the design process accounts for robustness to situational perturbations. This can be assessed in a trial or testing phase.

In the process of designing and testing, a design can be developed to better enact a chosen 'function', but it can also change the way the initial problem is perceived, or it can generate as yet unseen problems such that new 'functions' become possible. For example, the invention of Bakelite (phenol formaldehyde) in the early twentieth century was initiated by the need to coat bowling alleys with a hard lacquer-like surface (Bannan–Ritland *et al.* 2004). Once the initial problem was solved, the designed properties of Bakelite afforded 'transportation' to other problems of the day such as the mass production of billiard balls. In part due to its transportability across critical problems of the late industrial age, Bakelite became a common material for the production of everyday household products such as containers, picture frames and heat-resistant handles for cookware. Theoretically, it also stimulated the most pervasive material revolution of the twentieth century – plastics. Have there been similar advances in education which have afforded widespread adoption and adaptation, leading to equivalent revolutions? Some might claim that the invention of intelligence tests and associated aptitude and achievement instruments has generated both new elements of statistics (e.g. Item Response theory, or multi-dimensional scaling) and intricate procedures for the adaptation of test theory to the assessment of attitudes, beliefs and other indirect survey methods such as the Likert scale, or multiple choice formats. But, even so, it is not clear that there has been a direct impact on the quality of learning.

As has already been highlighted, traditional approaches to establishing the effectiveness of educational artefacts and interventions, such as laboratory-based experiments, can be unrealistic and they tend to rely on the assumption that the educational processes under study are already well theorized. Because educational processes operate in complex social situations, and are often poorly understood theoretically, design experiments may offer a more appropriate approach to many areas of educational research (National Research Council 2002). Traditional approaches, such as laboratory experiments, end when an artefact or intervention is found to be ineffective and is therefore discarded. Design experiments carry the additional benefit of using, rather than discarding, an ineffective design as the starting point for the next phase of the design process (see also Chapter 6). Whereas laboratory experiments may never indicate why a particular artefact or intervention is ineffective (only that it *is* ineffective), the changes that are necessary to move from an ineffective to an effective design in a design experiment may well illuminate the sources of the original design's failure. Additionally, design experiments provide a formal, clear and structured place for the expertise of practitioners or policy-makers to be incorporated within the production of artefacts and interventions designed for use in the classroom. Where other approaches, such as action research, also provide such a role for implementers, the design experiment does so while retaining the benefits and minimizing the drawbacks of an experimental approach to education research.

Design experiments also offer a strong emphasis on model formulation, with various objectives (summarized by Sloane and Gorard 2003: 29–30; see also Cox and Snell 1981; Gilchrist 1984):

1 To provide a parsimonious description on one or more sets of data. By parsimonious, we mean that the model should be simple, but also complex enough to describe important features of the target process and the data that purport to represent it. Design experiments can address this issue by using videotape and narrative accounts to reflect the complexity of the settings they are modelling.
2 To provide a basis for comparing several different sets of data.
3 To compare or refute a theoretical relationship suggested a priori.
4 To describe and understand the properties of the random or residual variation, often called the error component. When based on randomly drawn samples, this enables the researcher to make inferences from a sample to the corresponding population, to assess the precision of parameter estimates, and to assess the uncertainty in any conclusions.
5 To provide predictions which can act as a 'yardstick' even when the model is known not to hold for some reason.
6 To provide empirical insight into the underlying process (sometimes by perturbing the model).

A particular strength of design experiments is an idea that unifies all of engineering – the concept of 'failure'. From the simplest paper-clip to the Space Shuttle, inventions are successful only to the extent that their developers properly anticipate how a device can fail to perform as intended (Petroski 1996). The good scientist (or engineer) recognizes sources of error: errors of model formulation, of model specification and model validation (and of course errors of measurement – see Chapter 2). Design experiments must also recognize error but, more importantly, they must *understand* error or failure, build better practical theory ('humble theory' according to Cobb *et al.* 2003) and design things that work (whether these are processes or products). Unfortunately, many design experiments have been conducted by advocates of particular approaches or artefacts, and sometimes by those with a commercial interest in their success. This makes it an especial concern that so few of their reports make any mention of comparison or control groups (see

Educational Researcher 2003, 32(1)). Without these, and without working towards a definitive test, how can they persuade others that they have successfully eliminated plausible rival explanations? Is retrospective narrative analysis enough? We do not believe so.

Most engineers develop failure criteria, which they make explicit from the outset. These criteria provide limits that cannot be exceeded as the design develops. However, failure manifests itself differently in different branches of engineering. Some problems of engineering design do not lend themselves to analytic failure criteria, but rather to models of trial and error, or to build-and-measure techniques. In the design of computer programs, for example, the software is first alpha-tested by its designers and then beta-tested by real users in real settings. These users often uncover bugs that were generated in the design or its modification. Furthermore, these users also serve to show how the program might fail to perform as intended. No matter what method is used to test a design, the central underlying principle of this work is to obviate failure. This is a very different model than the one currently used by many social scientists (see Chapter 9).

Although design is a creative process, for it to constitute a design study it must conform to standards of scholarship generally recognized by the scientific and educational communities as necessary conditions for programmatic study (National Research Council 2002). Among these conditions are the provision of a coherent and explicit chain of reasoning; the attempt to yield findings that replicate and 'transport' across studies; and the disclosure of methods and analyses for critique by the broader community (Gorard 2002c). While the structure of a complex instructional tool or intervention may be considered an embodiment of a local theory, unless that structure is made explicit, and the propositional framework upon which the design rests laid bare, it does not constitute a test of that theory, and therefore contributes little to the broader body of disciplined knowledge about teaching, learning, or anything else.

The adoption of design experiments by educational researchers also rests on an acceptance of the need to collect, combine and unproblematically make use of data of different sorts (see e.g. de Corte *et al.* 2001). The design experiment has similarities with many more established methods for combining data of different sorts. It can, therefore, be rightly placed as a member of this combining methods family. The design experiment shares and draws upon several different methods more traditionally employed in educational research, such as action research. Indeed, some research studies that adopt an action research approach might also be considered as design experiments. However, the important characteristics already discussed help differentiate design experiments from these more established methods in education research. Furthermore, design experiments go beyond and could arguably be seen as an improvement on these (where they are practised in an ideal form and with a degree of rigour at least equal to these other methods).

Of course, some researchers claim to be doing design experiments by simply modifying multiple classroom interventions continuously and documenting the process (often via video recordings), but it is not clear that this behaviour is very different to the standard, purely qualitative, action research (McNiff and Whitehead 2002). In their ideal form, design experiments go beyond action research. In the original formulation, Brown (1992) assumed that work would iterate between laboratory and classroom, capturing the advantages of both. Typically, action research only takes place within the classroom or real-world setting. Other examples of methods for combining data, such as NPA and research syntheses, cannot be used to test educational interventions directly. And by allowing theory to be built alongside the design and testing of an intervention of some sort, design experiments negate the need for well-established theory stipulated by the complex intervention. As a consequence, design experiments can be used more widely. If a complex intervention fails, a researcher must go back to the drawing board, rather than being able to arrive at an optimal new design in a rigorous way. Put another way, design experiments give us a potentially superior approach to the model- and hypothesis-generating stages of research – of working towards a 'definitive' trial. At each stage, therefore, different data collection methods are more or less appropriate and complementary.

Procedural aspects of design experiments

Just as the design activity for an artefact, intervention or initiative is a creative process so too is the ensuing research process. As a result it is difficult to provide a detailed outline of the procedures one must follow to do a design experiment. What we provide below is an outline for a generic design experiment (see Figure 7.2). The specific timescale and methods used are largely determined by the objectives of this approach in meeting the characteristics discussed above. As highlighted earlier, 'fitness for purpose' and methodological freedom are essential for this purpose. A generic design experiment is articulated as involving three key phases. However, the process of a design experiment is unlikely to involve three *distinct* phases – the experiment moves between these three phases, but where they begin and end is dependent upon the particular research study. Instead we describe each of the three phases of a design experiment as a set of prerequisites and objectives. Indeed, our model proposes repeated iterations between Phase 2 and Phase 3. The number of iterations will depend upon the judgement of the researcher given the prerequisites and objectives we outline for each phase.

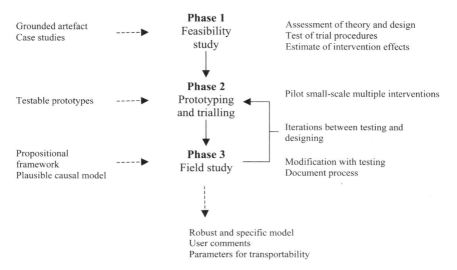

Figure 7.2 General procedure for design experiments

The first phase, a feasibility study, would start with an initial design of the intervention, ensuring that the intervention was grounded in whatever theory was available and an explicit interpretation of the proposed causal mechanism. In Brown's example above, the reciprocal teaching intervention was designed on the basis of a priori theoretical understanding. Without this the intervention may have been entirely inappropriate to the problem being addressed, and without some understanding of the theoretical underpinnings of the intervention there may be great difficulty in understanding how the intervention works and hence how to modify it or evaluate it. The early stages of the feasibility study would involve primarily qualitative methods in the formative evaluation of the intervention, using interviews, focus groups, observation and case studies to identify how the trial intervention is working, barriers and facilitators to its implementation, and provide early indications as to how it may be improved. These more 'explanatory' routes of inquiry powerfully complement any earlier use of secondary data analysis in identifying the initial research problem (see Chapter 4).

The first phase of the design experiment should, therefore, start with an intervention that has been sufficiently well developed to be tested in a feasibility study, where it can be implemented in full, and tested for acceptability to both providers (policy-makers and teachers) and the target audience (students and learners). The feasibility study is also an opportunity to test the trial procedures, such as the definition of the alternative treatment, which may be the usual care, control, or some alternative intervention, and to pilot and test the eventual outcome

measures. It may be used to provide a tentative estimate of the intervention impact, which can then be used to plan the size of the later trials.
The results of the feasibility study will help to decide whether the
intervention should proceed to the next phase, or whether it is necessary
to return to the process of identifying the research problem and developing the theoretical framework on which the intervention is originally
based. Given the pragmatic and fiscal constraints of all scientific research,
the feasibility study may suggest that the entire research process should
end at this first phase – although real-life funding structures suggest this
is unlikely to happen in practice.

The second phase (prototyping and trialling) begins a process of
iteration between the testing and further modification of the intervention. Parallel to this is the potential to iterate the process between the
laboratory (or other controlled environments) and the classroom (or real-
life environments). These iterative processes continue into the third
phase (field study). Phase 2 is characterized by piloting small-scale
multiple prototypes of the intervention (in the same way that a wind
tunnel can be used to test many variations of an aircraft wing at the same
time). As the iterations between testing and further design become more
sophisticated, and the iterations between laboratory and classroom settings become more robust, advances are made in the intervention's
prepositional framework and in outlining its plausible causal models.

It is at this point that the research sequence enters the third phase (the
field study), where it is implemented in full and tested for acceptability to
both providers and the target audience. The iterative process may continue but the design of instructional sequences becomes stronger and
stronger leading, eventually, to a robust model that aids the implementation of the intervention in many contexts. At this point the
documentation and recording of the process for implementing the
intervention should be systematic, as this develops the parameters for
future 'transportation' of the design. This field study should involve a
definitive test. In the design experiment, this definitive trial could take
the form of a randomized controlled trial, an interrupted time series
analysis (Harris and Corcoran 2002) or a concurrent quasi-experiment
(McGee *et al.* 2002). Borrowing this procedure from the complex intervention model suggests that the outcome(s) of interest for the design
experiment must be fixed first else, if this is modified as well as the
intervention, there will be no fixed point to the research. The approach
simply becomes a 'trawl' that will eventually find 'something'.

Conclusion

The notion of 'design experiments' is relatively new, and was recently the focus of a special issue of the US journal *Educational Researcher* (January 2003). This suggested that there are three key concerns related to the development and funding of design experiments: their general validity (Shavelson *et al.* 2003); how they relate to model-building (Sloane and Gorard 2003); and how they combine the disparate datasets that they generate. For a fuller discussion of all of these issues see http://gse.gmu.edu/research/de/index.htm, Gorard and Roberts (2004), or Bannan-Ritland *et al.* (2004).

In some respects the full model of design experiments, including the generation of the idea for the intervention, its refinement over successive iterations, the eventual formal testing and the scaling up, can be seen as an amalgam of several of the other approaches to research described so far in this book. Different methods are seen as complementary rather than direct alternatives, but their appropriateness changes with the phases of a research programme. Designing an intervention, for example, might justifiably use all and any approaches, including creativity. Developing the intervention may involve simple measuring and in-depth monitoring. Testing an intervention may mostly involve precise measurement. Working out how to generalize from a successful intervention, or learn from an unsuccessful one, may mostly involve analysis of the 'braided' narratives of set and setting. Some phases would appear like art or craft, and some more like science. It does not matter what they are called or what analogies and metaphors people find 'cosy' in describing the stages. Fitness for purpose is the key.

Design experiments are dependent, to some extent, upon the knowledge and understanding of the particular problem or issue to be addressed. It would, therefore, be useful to undertake prior research before embarking upon a design experiment. For example, an NPA approach (see Chapter 4) could provide a greater insight into the issue or problem that is of concern. This would highlight areas of deficit in our understanding, and identify some of the broader processes and structural factors that the design experiment will be working within. Similarly, systematic research syntheses (see Chapter 2) would ensure that the initial design of an artefact, intervention or initiative is based on a sound understanding of the relevant education processes (although we have also highlighted the advantage of design experiments where theoretical understanding is relatively weak). A weakness of design experiments is that in practice there may be no definitive test or evaluation conducted on the artefact, intervention or initiative at any time. This is inevitable given the main objective of generating a design infrastructure rather than a final product. However, it should be necessary, particularly when taking an artefact, intervention or initiative into the marketplace or to policy-makers, to undertake a full trial so as to measure its performance and effectiveness. This is something that the complex intervention does incorporate.

For example, imagine that the study starts with identification of an artefact to be progressively refined in practice. The initial idea and design for the artefact may come from prior knowledge, theory, serendipity or inspiration (Campanario 1996). In this way it is very like the pre-clinical phase to identify an intervention in the Medical Research Council model (see Chapter 6), but expressed in more traditionally 'creative' terminology. Once the artefact is being used, this use is monitored in much the same way as 'gadgets' are monitored for consumer reports. The observations will be detailed, and will naturally contain numeric and non-numeric elements. This prolonged phase is like the modelling and exploration components of the Medical Research Council model. The qualitative element is like an ethnography, but is based on an intervention rather than a naturally occurring situation. The quantitative monitoring element is like a field experiment, except that the results can be used to guide live revision of the design. A close analogy from another design field is that of an aeroplane model in a wind tunnel. In fact, many models would be tested in tandem, revised and retested. The data generated would be both observational and measurement. This analogy helps us because it is often argued that education is a complex phenomenon to research. But the same is also true of aeronautics with its competing claims for the speed, safety, comfort, efficiency and so on, in any design.

Design experiments clearly have a number of possible advantages over traditional and more established methods in education research but they also have a number of disadvantages. For example, because they draw upon the benefits of craft and creativity alongside scientific and logical inquiry they tend to involve messy and complicated methodological frameworks. This craft of research makes it difficult to provide textbook outlines and definitions for design experiments. This, in turn, makes it difficult to construct a timeframe or budget for such research, important components of most research grant applications. Furthermore, there are, currently, few obvious or agreed rules, other than generic rules for high-quality research (see Chapter 10), that can be used to evaluate the conduct of a design experiment (again, an important component for awarding research grants). Many of these factors could reduce the likelihood of this kind of research being funded by external agencies.

These methodological weaknesses may be avoided by considering the design experiment within a 'compleat' design cycle, incorporating all elements of research from the birth of an idea to the full implementation, dissemination and impact of a final artefact, intervention or initiative (Bannan-Ritland *et al.* 2004). Models of principled design are still needed to make design experiments *more* systematic and explicit (Kelly and Lesh 2002), before the educational researcher can incorporate them into existing research practice with ease.

8

What is the current prevalence of combined methods research?

Throughout this book we have highlighted some of the advantages of, and constraints facing, the combination of methods within education and social science research. Research that combines methods is relatively infrequently reported. This may be due to the substantial occurrence of single method research or because little attention is paid to the notion of combining methods when publishing research findings. For example, it may be that the drive in the UK towards relatively brief journal publications, as a result of the periodic funding-driven Research Assessment Exercise (RAE), encourages a focus that is to the detriment of writing and producing more 'in progress' working papers that describe in greater detail the methodological approaches, the data sources and the analytical techniques being used.

In this chapter we draw upon a range of empirical sources to examine in detail the current *prevalence* of combined methods research within the UK education research community. In particular, we highlight the most frequent ways in which research methods are combined and identify where combination is still limited. In describing current patterns and approaches we hope that readers will come to realize that research that combines methods is actually more common than usually reported. Additionally, we hope to illustrate the further potential for combining methods within the UK research community, both in terms of current research skills and future research topics or issues. The focus of this chapter is on research in education, because of the nature of the datasets available to us.

Our sources

In examining the current and potential uses for combining methods in education research we draw upon a range of sources of data collected while working on a project to enhance the capacity of the UK research community to undertake relevant high-quality research (see www.cf. ac.uk/socsi/capacity). These data include:

- interviews with key stakeholders from across the education field, including researchers, practitioner representatives, policy-makers and policy implementers;
- a large-scale survey of the current methodological expertise and future training needs of UK education researchers;
- detailed breakdown and analysis of the 2001 RAE submissions;
- a small systematic review of research publications.

As you will see, this 'mapping' exercise itself constitutes a case study of combining methods – drawing upon semi-structured and unstructured interviews, interviewing the 'powerful', a large-scale survey with closed and open questions, systematic coding of documentary evidence, descriptive statistics, multivariate analysis and content analysis. We therefore describe the methods in some detail.

Stakeholder interviews

We interviewed 25 key stakeholders, each representing the major constituencies of the UK education community in 2001/2. They included representatives from the following:

- national and local government – comprising elected members, policy-makers and researchers;
- research funding agencies and education research organizations such as the British Educational Research Association (BERA), the National Foundation for Educational Research (NFER), the National Educational Research Forum (NERF), the Nuffield Foundation, the Office for Standards in Education (Ofsted) and the Economic and Social Research Council (ESRC);
- higher education researchers – including ESRC Teaching and Learning Research Programme (TLRP) project leaders, non-TLRP researchers and RAE panel members;
- the teaching profession – including the General Teaching Council and the Teacher Training Agency;
- education research journal editors;
- stakeholders with an international perspective (OECD).

In most cases (15) our respondent was the official spokesperson for the body that they represented – the academic secretary, chief executive, head of research, panel chair, programme director and so on. In another six cases, the respondent was suggested by others, and the remaining cases were selected on the basis of their public response to criticism of the standard of UK education research. It is important to note in the light of the findings that none of the respondents were, or were associated with, high-profile critics of the quality of education research. We cannot provide any more information than this and still hope to provide any protection for the anonymity of respondents.

The semi-structured interviews concerned the nature of research capacity, the current capacity of the UK community, the role of the respondent's own body and ideas for capacity-building. In particular, respondents were asked about the current state of education research in the UK, why it is like this, and how education research could continue to move forward. Interviews were recorded and transcribed, and then sorted according to a variety of themes. Here the emphasis is on the methods used in research, and the reported need to improve the quality of research.

Survey of methods used

We conducted a survey of current UK education researchers, by sending a self-completion questionnaire to all researchers within the TLRP, all members of the BERA, and via the then Learning and Skills Research Network (LSRN). The questionnaire is available via www.cf.ac.uk/socsi/ capacity. We received 521 responses, including around 80 per cent of the researchers involved in the TLRP. We are unable to provide an overall response rate since bodies like the LSRN distributed the forms themselves. However, on all subsequent analyses there is no substantial difference between the results for the TLRP alone and for any other subgroup of researchers. The instrument asked respondents to summarize their knowledge and use of a range of methods for design, data collection and analysis. Nearly 300 methods were specified, and respondents could add further techniques as they wished. For each method, respondents were also asked to summarize the level of training, if any, they would like. For this chapter, all responses have been coded in binary form (have the respondents used the method or not). The classification system for methods was initially collapsed into 29 categories for the purposes of this analysis. Clearly, these 29 categories do not do full justice to the range of methods reported, and the categories could have been collapsed in a number of different ways. They also overlap (e.g. a case study probably involves interviews), and some could represent an entire approach to research rather than just a method. We started with the questionnaire structure, itself piloted with acknowledged methods experts, and its modifications in the light of self-reporting. The classifications used in the tables presented in this chapter are the product of discussion between six researchers with expertise in different methods.

RAE returns

Having experienced difficulties in assessing the quality of research returns in education for both the 1992 and 1996 RAE, a task force was established by the education panel members to suggest improvements to facilitate judgements for the forthcoming 2001 RAE. The problems stemmed largely from the scale of the enterprise, because education is routinely one of the largest submissions. Part of the attempted solution was the requirement for three additional fields of information to be submitted with each publication. These were intended to aid judgements on the scope and value of each submission by the panel. One of these fields concerned the theory/method used. The guidelines by the Higher Education Funding Council for England (HEFCE) (1999) suggested that the education panel should examine in detail 10 per cent of the output, and at least 5 per cent of each submission, making use of the theory/ method field as 'A succinct description of the theoretical and methodological approach' (p. 304).

This chapter uses the information now publicly available in these additional fields to give a general overview of the nature of research being undertaken in departments of education throughout the UK. The new 'theory/method' field, although limited to 100 characters, has provided a valuable 'snapshot' into education research, allowing analysis to be carried out on a much larger scale than has previously been possible (8726 individual returns from 2330 researchers). Information submitted from each institution was downloaded from HERO (URL:<http:// www.hero.ac.uk/rae/>), and strict guidelines were followed by the research staff involved in the coding process. The coding frame used to record the different methods employed in the research returns was based on the ESRC-funded Research Capacity Building Network consultation instrument (see above), although minor changes were made during the coding process in the light of anomalies. Five additional entries were included. Four of these represented methods that were unclear and therefore unable to be coded more precisely. The fifth additional category was the use of workbooks. These could represent tests or other textual or visual sources of primary data. However, since they were encountered frequently they have been given their own subcategory for the purposes of our analysis. Each submission was coded for type of publication (book, article etc.), journal title (where appropriate) and each of the methods specified in the field.

The theory/method field is limited to 100 characters, not allowing for a complete description of the complex methods utilized in all forms of research. There were also inaccuracies in recording, some confusion over what should be included in this composite field, and a lack of time and effort by some institutions to complete it. McNay (2003: 52) acknowledges that the new fields 'were not well used in their first time of operation. This was a positive innovation, but may need a second round of usage to get the best from it'. This is confirmed by our own discussions with individuals responsible for completing this field (Gorard *et al.* 2004).

Therefore, we start our analysis in the knowledge that these fields are limited in use and imperfectly completed. However, such a situation is not uncommon. In 1992 an audit of RAE submissions was undertaken to verify the accuracy of the RAE returns. Ten per cent of submissions were scrutinized and it was found that 'whilst the audit has not identified any cases of excessive and unacceptable opportunism, it has identified a number of misinterpretations of the data requested and data entry errors' (HEFCE 1992). An audit was also undertaken in 1996, and 'checks revealed that the submissions contained a number of minor inaccuracies, and a smaller number of quite significant errors' (HEFCE 1996: 4).

Probably the first finding from this work is that greater guidance for consistency is required in the completion of this field if it is to be used again. We need much greater consensus in the use of method terms more generally (see Sheffield and Saunders 2002), probably including the creation of standard thesauri for the searching and indexing of methods, as we already have for substantive areas of research. We found a number of errors in the information submitted. These were primarily in the information submitted for journal entries (mismatching ISSNs, misnamed journals etc.). However, since these inaccuracies were found merely by coding the information, we suspect that if the information had been checked more thoroughly with the original sources then many more inaccuracies would have been discovered.

A number of submissions were clearly based on empirical research but did not include enough information about the methods used to allow them to be represented in the coding frame. There were also a number of returns which gave *no* indication of methods, and others that displayed general lack of regard for the information required. We quote here a few examples of the 'completed' theory/method field that would give problems to any methods classification system:

- empirical investigation of visually impaired children's play and language;
- analysis of course materials;
- uses two projects to illuminate strengths and weaknesses of model;
- gender studies: analysis of experiences and attainments of academically able boys;
- research;
- cognitive development;
- empirical study of learning: comparison of approaches.

It is important, we feel, that the problems associated with re-analysis of this field are discussed, so that the findings are viewed with appropriate caveats. However, we also wish to stress that (unlike the richer data described above) this analysis enabled us to make a comparison of around 8700 research pieces – the largest such overview of methods in education research (and probably in any discipline).

We present the results of a multi-dimensional scaling, providing a graphical representation of the likelihood that different research methods are used by the same researcher. This multi-dimensional scaling is based upon a two-by-two matrix, representing the 'distance' between pairs of methods by their similarity or proximity. In our analysis, this similarity is the likelihood that our sample of education researchers has used any pair of methods. Using a stress score we determined that the most appropriate number of dimensions for our graphical representation was two (Bartholomew *et al.* 2002).

For the purposes of this brief analysis we also selected three journals, and collated the methods used in all papers for the calendar year 2002 (the most recent complete year at the time of writing). We chose for this purpose the *British Educational Research Journal* because it was, by some way, the most frequent outlet for work submitted to the 2001 RAE. We also chose the *British Journal of Educational Psychology* as a frequent outlet for work submitted to the 2001 RAE, but one that was disproportionately used by centres of assessment rated 5 or 5* (i.e. considered to be of overall 'international' standard). Finally, we chose *Educational Management and Administration* as a frequent outlet for work submitted to the 2001 RAE, but one that was disproportionately used by centres of assessment rated 1 to 4 (i.e. not considered to be of overall 'international' standard). In this way we can both triangulate and extend our other sources of data.

Wider debates about the state of education research

In so far as the criteria can be said to be the same over time, the results of the 2001 RAE record an *overall* improvement since 1992 and 1996 in research quality in universities and colleges across the UK (HEFCE 2001). In 2001, 55 per cent of all research-active staff worked in departments graded 5 or 5* compared to 31 per cent in 1996. In addition to this, research at the lower end of the scale (rated 1 or 2), previously accounting for a quarter of all research, fell to just 6 per cent (HEFCE 2001). In 1996, 43 per cent of all submissions by higher education institutions were graded with 4, 5 or 5*, and this rose to 64 per cent in 2001. Some of this improvement is due to the substantial number of persistently low ranking higher education institutions choosing not to enter for the 2001 RAE due to little or no chance of funding allocation

(The United Kingdom Parliament 2002). For 2001, of the 174 institutions that did submit, 75 per cent of the funding was allocated to just 24 institutions (McNay 2003).

The situation for education (unit of assessment 68) was very different. In 2001, only 29 per cent of submitted researchers were in 5/5* departments (compared to 55 per cent across all subjects), and only 17 per cent of submissions were rated 5/5* (compared to 39 per cent across all subjects). There has not been anything like the equivalent increase for this subject as there was for others such as sociology, psychology, geography or social policy. There may, of course, have been mis-classified submissions (in either direction) and significant education-relevant returns were made to other panels, but the scale of the difference between education and others subjects is remarkable. McNay (2003) points out disparities in the exercise concerning funding allocation, consistency of sampling and quality assessment definitions for each unit of assessment. Therefore, it is possible to argue that education has been unfairly treated by its panel, and that the quality of submitted work is actually better than these grades show. However, this is a double-edged argument since it also allows that the panel could have been overly generous to their own discipline, and that the quality of education research is actually worse than recorded. The simplest explanation overall is that the results for education suggest a relatively poor quality of research, or at least a pressing need to improve the way in which it is reported.

In fact, when these results are put together with a series of widely-publicized criticisms of UK education research, it seems there may be a case to answer. In recent years there has been mounting attention to the quality of education research both within the research community and in a wider public policy sphere (Richardson 2002). This can be partly attributed to a number of high-profile publications (Hillage *et al.* 1998; Tooley and Darby 1998; Woodhead 1998; Hargreaves 1999) which have questioned the standards of education research then being undertaken within higher education institutions nationwide. Of these commentaries, only Tooley and Darby's was based on an, albeit limited, direct study of the work itself as reported in 264 articles from four journals. It claimed, among other things, that too much research was based on a weak form of qualitative methods, and too little on quantitative methods (see also Chapter 1).

Issues of quality

When asked about the current state of education research, many of the stakeholders in our interviews began by addressing the published criticisms referred to above. These have clearly had a major impact on the stakeholders and prompted them, if they had not already done so, to reflect upon the state of education research in relation to their own experiences. Notably, while written public reaction from academics to these commentaries has tended to be defensive about the current state of education research (e.g. Hodkinson 1998), the response of *all* stakeholders was to express some agreement with the criticisms, while stressing that some research was, and always had been, extremely good (see Taylor 2002). The consensus was that the criticisms had some basis in fact. Here are some typical comments:

> I think well certainly I and other people I know actually go along with a great deal of what David Hargreaves says.
>> (Higher education researcher and UCET Executive Committee member)

> I am starting to sound like David Hargreaves. He had a point actually. The butt of jokes in education departments, who think he is terribly crass to say this, but I think some of the stuff that you look at is rubbish.
>> (Education researcher and BERA Executive Council member)

> There is a lot of stuff talking about policy, but it wasn't helping anyone. When you bring it down to the technical level very large amounts of it was technically so bad as to be embarrassing. No discussion about validity and reliability of data for example. No attempt to theorize.
>> (Higher education researcher and member of NERF)

> I mean I to be honest have been surprised sometimes with what I see as the relatively low level of sophistication in some of the research that's done.
>> (Ofsted research manager)

> Lots of low-level cottage industry stuff … As somebody that edits two journals and sits on four or five editorial boards I see a lot of the stuff which people see as their best shot. If you're submitting something for a journal you've really worked it over. Some of the stuff that I see … thank Christ somebody has brought this for somebody else to look at, never mind considered to be published.
>> (Higher education researcher)

> The people who are doing the current EPPI [evidence for policy and practice] reviews, the review groups, keep coming back and saying how shocked they are by the poor quality of the literature.
>> (Department for Education and Skills officer)

> I think the quality of the policy-oriented research has been poor.
>> (OECD researcher)

Well strangely enough I had some sympathy for some of the things Chris Woodhead said about it, because a lot of educational research frankly doesn't tell you a lot that you don't already know ... sometimes you question whether in fact it's been done very thoroughly ... I think the money we spend is not spent wisely at all. I *do* share the criticism.

(Chair of a local education authority education committee and Local Government Association executive member)

So there is considerable agreement (privately at least) that there is something amiss with the standard of UK education research. There is little support here for Hodkinson (1998) and others who seek to defend themselves from criticism by asserting that there is no problem of quality, and so no need for us to improve our research. It is not clear what the quality of education research *should* be, but the clear consensus among these powerful stakeholders is that we are not there yet. So what, according to them, could we improve about our ability to undertake research?

Problems of method

Again, there was near consensus among the respondents. While other issues such as impact were also highlighted, the core issue about quality concerned the lack of skills in key methods. A number of stakeholders referred to the lack of research 'skills' among the research community. In most cases, the deficit referred to concerned knowledge of 'quantitative' techniques:

I mean, I think the quality of some people in education is highly questionable. I can point to you, I could point to the people walking around with Ph.D.s, who demean the title, right?

(Higher education researcher)

Actually the situation is *so bad* that people don't realize they haven't got the skills they need which is even worse than having people who are struggling but aren't sure where to get the skills they need.

(Department for Education and Skills officer)

Another common criticism of research is that the conclusions drawn bear no relationship to the evidence presented (i.e. they are not warranted, see Chapter 10). In particular, the stakeholders believed that research over-generalized, largely because the majority of education research is considered small-scale and non-cumulative: 'There is a gulf between your evidential base and your conclusions, so sometimes it is like that, quality issues, but other times you cannot understand the relevance of the whole area of study. I would just say it is always a

problem about generalizing from a small sample.
(Education researcher and BERA Executive Council member)

Too little quantitative research?

There was a clear perception that there is a lack of quantitative research but, as we shall see, the issue of quality and rigour was raised equally for quantitative *and* qualitative research. The issues of causality, being able to test propositions and the process of generalization raised by many stakeholders are more complex than simply the problem of a lack of quantitative research. But nearly every stakeholder reported that there was a regrettable lack of quantitative research, and that this has straightforward consequences for the quality, range and relevance of research:

> There is a widely acknowledged absence of quantitative research of particular kinds, especially, there's a weakness, there's a relative absence and there's no mechanism for addressing that currently.
> (Higher education researcher and TLRP team leader)

> Where I think that has failed in a way is when it has not kept the proper balance, as there are plenty of questions that have to be addressed through quantitative methods.
> (Higher education researcher and RAE panel member)

> As a journal editor what worries me slightly is that you have so much qualitative stuff. It's very very unusual to get anything quantitative.
> (Higher education researcher and UCET Executive Committee member)

One consequence of this shortage is that there are simply too few researchers to pass such skills on to their peers or the next generation of researchers:

> It's a real worry in this department that you know in a department of [thousands of] students and [over 100] staff there isn't one strong quantitative lecturer.
> (Higher education researcher and Universities Council for the Education of Teachers (UCET) Executive Committee member)

> I do feel that we are short of good quantitative researchers in this country and that is a particular need.
> (Higher education researcher and TLRP team leader)

Among the researchers we interviewed, many proposed that a key weakness of education research was it was often method-driven rather than question- or problem-driven. This, they suggested, was a result of too many researchers employing singular research methods:

> So, what they do is they do the research that they can do to match the skills that they've got. So, they body-swerve around the direct way of addressing the question and they have some second best or third best take on it that they get from using the only technique or methods that they *can* use. And that's a characteristic weakness of a lot of social science and often because people have got this hang-up about quantitative work – disproportionately that's the bit they avoid.
>
> (Former head of UK research funding agency)

> What did they say about single methodology people – give a child a hammer and everything becomes a nail.
>
> (Director of non-higher education research organization)

For one, the problem was the limited ability of education researchers to be able to simply 'consume' (i.e. read, interpret and understand) existing research using alternative methods to their own:

> Certainly in terms of quantitative and qualitative, the importance is being able to interpret the claims that come, and you can only do that if you have an understanding of the methods that are used. You may not be able to use the methods, I don't expect everybody to do multi-level modelling but I do expect them to understand what it is all about, why it is important as an advance that has been made in the last 15 years.
>
> (Higher education researcher and RAE panel member)

Many stakeholders agreed that it was necessary for education researchers to develop a wider repertoire of methodological skills, both in 'consuming' other research and in their own research. Indeed, a number of stakeholders proposed that more education research should be using combined, or mixed, methods:

> I also think there's a thing about, kind of, using mixed methods and people not always knowing how to use mixed methods and there isn't, I mean, there is some mixed methods research but there's not a huge amount of it actually. There's probably more, I mean, you do see more in terms of the [ESRC] grants board but then because it's been pushed to some extent. But in terms of the RAE there isn't a huge amount of that.
>
> (Higher education researcher and former ESRC Grants Board reviewer)

There's also I think a great deal of defensiveness, politically, about evaluations of policy for the obvious reasons that they can ... as well as being positive they can be negative. I think that is tricky and that is an area where the whole area of evaluation of the policy process is in general underdeveloped and where you would be looking for combinations of both descriptive and experimental methodologies.

(OECD researcher)

This was not necessarily the view of all those we interviewed. Indeed, the majority were silent on the issue of combining methods. This may reflect how little value our research community places, or at least reports placing, on combining research methods in education. However, those interviewed frequently argued that education research needed to become more interdisciplinary, although some argued that this could also be a source of weakness:

You're going to have a group of people who are going to be the career researchers who will be addressing fundamental problems in education over the long term, on the large scale and quite possibly from an interdisciplinary perspective. So, you say how do you create not only those people, but the conditions under which those people can work and that's something to do with freeing people up from teaching, for instance, creating interdisciplinary collaborations within institutions, thinking about inter-institutional collaborations ... Rather than saying there's one model of education research and it starts at the bottom and here's the top, it's much more like a branching tree where there are different ways of doing things.

(Higher education researcher and member of NERF)

So it's quite a difficult one I think to untangle but I can't help feeling that where there is interdisciplinarity, and there is, for example, research that brings in people that might normally be thought of as sociologists, political scientists, geographers as well as people that might come from education departments, then that's probably where the concerns about lack of quantitative sophistication, or appropriate quantitative development to be effective, where those worries are best met.

(OECD researcher)

People talk about [the fact that] we must encourage interdisciplinary work. Well just walk up and down this corridor and you'll find a whole range of disciplines and that's a great strength of education, but it's also a weakness ... There isn't that kind of agreed theoretical structure, I suppose theoretical knowledge. It's because education is this mixture of disciplines.

(Higher education researcher and TLRP team leader)

Implicit in the notion of interdisciplinary research discussed here is the desire for greater theoretical and methodological *diversity*. However, the last quotation above reminds us that some structure or coherence is also needed within diversity. This is a theme that underpins this book.

Although combining research methods may not be seen by all as a 'solution' to concerns about the current state of education research, it does offer a genuine response to the further advancement of methods diversity. This is not to suggest that we encourage the combining of research methods for its own sake. After all, we would agree with the following key stakeholders when they argue that the choice of methods in any research study should be appropriate to the research problem or question being addressed:

I think on balance it's a good thing to be problem driven.
(Director of non-higher education research organization)

You go for the methods that are appropriate to the problem.
(Former chief executive of UK research funding agency)

However, as research questions become more sophisticated and attempt to uncover, disentangle and explain increasingly more intricate processes, then we will have to find increasingly more sophisticated research designs. Typically, but not always, these will include a variety and mixture of data sources and, therefore, more diverse or complex theoretical and analytical tools to analyse such data.

In the next section we examine the prevalence of combining research methods in education and begin to describe the many different ways in which research methods are already being combined in practice.

Prevalence of combining methods in UK education research

Here we start without an overall binary classification into qualitative and quantitative work, and simply consider which sets of methods have been used by the same individuals. We distinguish between research methods employed to collect data and between research methods to analyse data. In the first group of methods we then also made a distinction between the primary collection of data (i.e. where the researcher undertakes 'fieldwork' and collects their own data) and the sourcing of secondary data (i.e. where the researcher utilizes data that has been collected by others, usually for other purposes). From these we produce subcategories of research methods that bring together the many different ways in which we can collect and source data and the ways in which we can then interrogate that data further.

Our survey

The subcategories of methods for collecting and sourcing data are listed in Table 8.1. Although there is a temptation to characterize each sub-category as either 'qualitative' or 'quantitative', it is important to note that almost all of them include numeric and, for want of a better term, non-numeric types of data. For example, surveys can include closed and open questions, producing both frequencies and narratives. Such overlap also exists, although to a lesser extent, within each of the subcategories of secondary data sources. For example, many government surveys collect frequency counts (numeric) and interview-type responses (non-numeric).

Table 8.1 Categories of methods for collecting and sourcing data

Primary data collection	
Interviews	Including: structured, semi-structured, unstructured/ informal, one-to-one, group/focus group, telephone, email and internet relay
Observation	Including: participant, non-participant, observation schedules and unstructured observation
Survey	Including: one-off, repeated (same people), repeated (different people), self-completion, face-to-face, telephone, email and internet
Textual, visual or audio	Including: diaries, pictures/painting/artwork, photographs, sound recordings, video footage and maps/ mental maps
Tests	Including: written tests, attitude/personality scales, behaviour performance tests and physical/chemical tests
Secondary data sources	
Official education statistics	Including: DfES Statistics of Education (UK) and school examination results
Government surveys	Including: UK Census of Population, National Child Development Survey, Youth Cohort Study of England and Wales, British Household Panel Survey, Labour Force Survey and other numeric data sources (e.g. Family Expenditure Survey, National Crime Survey)
Textual, visual or audio	Including: textual data sources (e.g. letters, diaries, biographies, poems), visual data sources (e.g. films, video footage, paintings) and sound data sources

Where the distinction between 'quantitative' and 'qualitative' methods is more pronounced is in the theoretical approaches and analytical tools used to *analyse* data. This is because the methods employed to analyse data are largely dependent upon the *type* of data being considered, irrespective of the methods used to collect or source the data in the first instance. Survey data does not necessarily have to be analysed numerically, and so on. Table 8.2 lists the subcategories of methods that could usefully characterize data analysis. These also include the use of computer software for supporting data analysis.

Table 8.2 Categories of methods for analysing data

Analytical approaches	
Describing quantitative data	Including: means, standard deviations, frequencies, graphs and charts, cross-tabulations, handling missing values, corrective weightings, probability, set theory, indices of inequality and political arithmetic
Statistical analysis of quantitative data	Including: transforming data distributions, correlation (bivariate), regression (multivariate), comparing means (e.g. ANOVA, t-tests), comparing frequencies (e.g. Chi-squared, Mann-Whitney), principal components/factor analysis, classification/cluster analysis, multi-level modelling, log-linear modelling, time-series analyses and spatial analysis (e.g. nearest neighbour index)
Qualitative data analysis	Including: content analysis, discourse analysis, narrative analysis, textual analysis, conversational analysis, interpretative approach, grounded-theory approach, quasi-statistical approach, interactionism, ethnomethodology, semiotics and use of typologies
Computer software	
Qualitative data analysis software	Including: NUD*IST, ATLAS.ti and Ethnograph
Quantitative data analysis software	Including: SPSS, MLWiN and GLIM

Table 8.3 summarizes the overall use of these methods by respondents to our survey, taking no account of the frequency of their use by each researcher. It simply reports whether an education researcher had ever used one or more of the methods within each subcategory. Nearly all education researchers have conducted some form of interview at some time (93 per cent), for example. Many fewer have used secondary datasets, particularly government surveys (36 per cent) and secondary textual, visual and audio data (31 per cent). In terms of analysis, the largest proportion of education researchers have undertaken some form of qualitative data analysis (80 per cent), followed by the use of methods to describe quantitative data (73 per cent). Fewer researchers have used methods to conduct statistical analyses, although still over half of our respondents had used statistical analysis at some time (57 per cent).

The last column in Table 8.3 highlights the self-reported levels of 'expertise' in each subcategory of research methods. These figures are probably a better reflection of the relative frequency with which these methods are used, since to have expertise probably means they have been used regularly. Unsurprisingly, reported expertise in each method shows the same pattern as overall use, but on a reduced scale. Again, the largest proportion of education researchers considered themselves as having expertise in undertaking interviews in some form, although this is only half of the number who reported using them in their research.

Table 8.3 Summary of use and expertise by subcategory of method from survey of education researchers

Subcategory of methods	% of total respondents (n = 520)	
	Total use	Expertise
Interviews	93	48
Qualitative data analysis	80	32
Observation	80	32
Survey	75	25
Describing quantitative data	73	27
Textual, visual or audio	67	19
Statistical analysis of quantitative data	57	18
Official education statistics	57	12
Quantitative data analysis software	53	12
Tests	47	13
Government surveys	36	5
Qualitative data analysis software	33	5
Secondary textual, visual and audio	31	7

We can also ask what group or cluster of methods are typically used by each education researcher – or what does each researcher's toolbox contain? Table 8.4 is a two-by-two matrix demonstrating how frequently respondents report having used each pair of methods (whether in isolation or in combination). This shows that the most common pairing of methods among education researchers was the use of interviews *and* observations (79 per cent). This was followed closely by the pairing of interviews *and* qualitative data analysis (78 per cent) and the use of interviews *and* surveys (74 per cent). The least common pairings of methods used were qualitative data analysis computer software *and* government surveys (14 per cent), and qualitative data analysis computer software *and* secondary textual visual and audio data (14 per cent). These pairings may not be surprising given they are among the least used methods overall in any case. Perhaps more revealing are the relatively few respondents who have used surveys *and* official education statistics (18 per cent overall), secondary textual, visual or audio data *and* government surveys (15 per cent overall) and tests *and* qualitative data analysis software (18 per cent overall). The first pair, surveys *and* official education statistics, probably reflects the infrequent use among education researchers of both primary data (in this case survey-based) *and* secondary data (in this case official education statistics). Although both could be using numeric data, and may use similar methods for describing and analysing the data, these findings would suggest their combined use is probably rather lower than might be expected. Although not all of these pairs of methods, or tools, may be appropriate for combination, the overall results do indicate some considerable divergence between researchers who use numeric and non-numeric data.

However, there remains considerable potential for combining methods among our sample of education researchers. During their careers a majority of education researchers have collected data using interviews, observation *and* surveys. Whether these have been used within the same study is not known, but at least these researchers should be able to understand and critique the use of a variety of methods for collecting data. They also have the potential to use these methods together within the same study.

Perhaps a better reflection of whether these pairs of methods have actually been used in combination can be found by examining the occurrence of self-reported 'expertise' in their use. As we suggested above, to have expertise probably requires the regular use of a given method. Therefore, to have expertise in two methods gives a greater likelihood that they had been used together within a single study. Table 8.5 presents the corresponding two-by-two matrix of self-reported expertise for our sample of education researchers. In many ways the patterns of paired expertise are similar to the paired use of methods (Table 8.4). The frequency of expertise in pairs of methods was significantly lower than their overall use. For example, just under 79 per cent of respondents indicated they had used both interviews *and* observation to collect data, but only 29 per cent reported having expertise in the use of both methods. Similarly, interviews *and* qualitative data analysis had been used by just over 78 per cent of our education researchers, but only 29 per cent indicated they had expertise in both.

There are more important differences between the patterns of expertise in pairs of methods and patterns in the overall use of corresponding pairs of methods. For example, while it was quite common for those researchers who had used methods to describe quantitative data to have also collected data using interviews (69 per cent overall), those who had expertise in describing quantitative data were much less likely to also have expertise in undertaking interviews (17 per cent). Similarly, while most researchers who had undertaken observation in their research had also used surveys in order to collect data (79 per cent), a significantly lower proportion of researchers who had expertise in the use of observation reported having expertise in the use of surveys (16 per cent).

So far we have used cross-tabulations to help outline the patterns of use and expertise for pairs of research methods among our sample of education researchers. However, we are also interested in identifying more general patterns of use and expertise, involving the whole range of

Table 8.4 Paired use of research methods from survey of education researchers: % of total respondents (n = 520)

	Interviews	Observation	Survey	Textual, visual or audio	Tests	Official education statistics	Government surveys	Secondary textual, visual or audio	Describing quantitative data	Statistical analysis of quantitative data	Qualitative data analysis	Qualitative data analysis software	Quantitative data analysis software
Interviews		79	74	65	46	57	35	30	69	55	78	33	50
Observation	79		64	61	42	49	30	29	60	47	69	29	43
Survey	74	64		52	42	18	31	25	63	50	63	27	47
Textual, visual or audio	65	61	52		38	42	25	29	51	39	60	25	36
Tests	46	42	42	38		33	19	17	43	37	40	18	32
Official education statistics	56	49	18	42	33		29	22	47	38	48	24	36
Government surveys	35	30	31	25	19	29		15	30	25	31	14	23
Secondary textual, visual or audio	30	29	25	29	17	22	15		25	17	30	14	15
Describing quantitative data	69	60	63	51	43	47	30	25		56	60	28	49
Statistical analysis of quantitative data	55	47	50	39	37	38	25	17	56		48	24	44
Qualitative data analysis	78	69	63	60	40	48	31	30	60	48		30	44
Qualitative data analysis software	33	29	27	25	18	24	14	14	28	24	30		25
Quantitative data analysis software	50	43	47	36	32	36	23	15	49	44	44	25	

Table 8.5 Paired expertise of research methods from survey of education researchers: % of total respondents (n = 520)

	Interviews	Observation	Survey	Textual, visual or audio	Tests	Official education statistics	Government surveys	Secondary textual, visual or audio	Describing quantitative data	Statistical analysis of quantitative data	Qualitative data analysis	Qualitative data analysis software	Quantitative data analysis software
Interviews		29	21	18	8	9	3	7	17	10	29	4	7
Observation	29		16	16	7	6	3	6	12	8	22	3	5
Survey	21	16		9	8	8	4	3	15	10	14	3	8
Textual, visual or audio	18	16	9		4	4	2	5	8	4	14	1	3
Tests	8	7	8	4		5	2	2	10	8	5	1	5
Official education statistics	9	6	8	4	5		3	2	8	7	5	1	5
Government surveys	3	3	4	2	2	3		1	4	3	2	0	3
Secondary textual, visual or audio	7	6	3	5	2	12	1		3	2	6	1	1
Describing quantitative data	17	12	15	8	10	8	4	3		17	10	2	11
Statistical analysis of quantitative data	10	8	10	4	8	7	3	2	17		6	1	10
Qualitative data analysis	29	22	14	14	5	5	2	6	10	6		4	4
Qualitative data analysis software	4	3	3	1	1	1	0	1	2	1	4		1
Quantitative data analysis software	7	5	8	3	5	5	3	1	11	10	4	1	

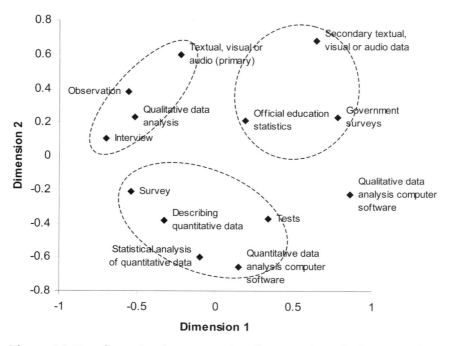

Figure 8.1 Two-dimensional representation (from a ratio multi-dimensional scaling) of research methods used, based on results from survey of education researchers

methods. We use multi-dimensional scaling to represent graphically the 'position' of each method and their relative 'distance' from one another (see Figure 8.1). In fact, there are only two dimensions. Dimension 1 is related to the context of data collection, with methods near the left-hand side being primary and more naturalistic in nature, and methods near the right-hand side being secondary and more formal in nature. Methods at the lower end of Dimension 2 are traditionally quantitative (probability, sample-based, modelling and significance tests), while those at the higher end are qualitative and non-traditionally quantitative (contextual, population-based, trends over time, descriptive). As you can see, interviews, observation, qualitative data analysis and the collection of other textual, visual or audio data are clustered together in the top left of the representation. This indicates that if any given education researcher has used one of these methods they are very much more likely to have used the other three than any other method considered. This group represents researchers who are predominantly qualitative in approach. However, note the position of surveys in relation to this set of research methods. Interviews and observation are actually located slightly closer to surveys than they are to the collection of other textual, visual or audio data. This means that education researchers who have undertaken interviews or observations to collect data are just as likely to have used surveys as they are to have collected other textual, visual or audio qualitative data.

Towards the bottom left of Figure 8.1 are methods that collect and use more clearly numeric data: starting with surveys and then, going further away from the first cluster of methods highlighted, to describing quantitative data, analysing quantitative data and quantitative data analysis computer software. Again, note the position of surveys in relation to interviews, observations, analysing quantitative data and quantitative data analysis computer software. Survey methods may be acting as a bridge between qualitative and quantitative approaches, but many education researchers who have used surveys *and* interviews or observation to collect data are less likely to have also undertaken complex statistical data analysis than those who used surveys alone. Indeed, the position of methods to collect test data, the remaining form of primary data collection, helps to differentiate purely numeric researchers further.

Three forms of secondary data are located in the top right corner of Figure 8.1. Their disparate position would suggest that they are not frequently used by the same individuals as the primary methods. The more central position of official education statistics indicates the somewhat greater use of such data with other methods, be it the first cluster of interviews, observations and other textual, visual or audio primary data, or the second main cluster of surveys, tests and other methods to describe or analyse numeric data. The use of secondary textual, visual or audio data (far right corner) is located the furthest away from methods for collecting primary data, particularly more numeric data. They are more likely to be used with other secondary data sources such as government surveys. The last research method considered here towards the bottom right corner is the use of qualitative data analysis computer software. Interestingly, this is located in almost the opposite corner to the main methods for collecting qualitative data. This may be because only a minority of education researchers who collect and analyse qualitative data use computer software to help them in the process of analysis. However, Figure 8.1 also shows that it is those education researchers who used other methods for collecting data, such as surveys, tests and other secondary sources, who are the most likely to have used computer software to help analyse qualitative data. This means that the technological skills rarely go hand-in-hand with the conceptual or theoretical skills to analyse qualitative data. This is in contrast with the close proximity of methods to analyse quantitative data with the use of computer software to support such analysis.

The use of multi-dimensional scaling has helped to 'locate' the relative use of each set of research methods against one another. If we look at the corresponding results for reported expertise among the different sets of research methods, then slight variations emerge (see Figure 8.2). The overall distribution or clusters of methods is very similar, but rotated approximately 180°, and the density of each cluster is different. Hence, expertise in interviews, observations and other textual, visual or audio data is more dispersed between individuals. A similar situation exists for expertise in the use of surveys and methods to describe and analyse quantitative data. In contrast, indications of expertise in using different sources of secondary data are much closer together, suggesting that having expertise in one of these means an education researcher is more likely to have expertise in using other secondary data than to have expertise in the use of other methods for collecting primary data. Expertise in a *range* of methods is probably limited to a small number of education researchers. It is these who are the most likely to develop expertise in combining methods. It is also clear that these researchers tend to develop expertise in methods that are currently under-utilized among our sample, such as secondary data use. In some respects these researchers can be considered as the 'pioneers' for methodological development and diversity in this field.

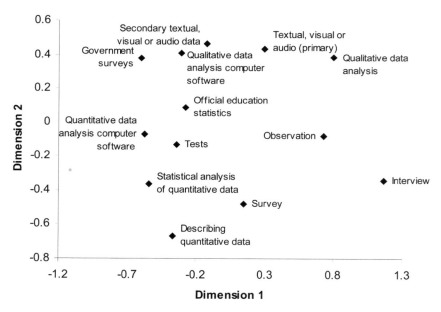

Figure 8.2 Two-dimensional representation (from a ratio multi-dimensional scaling) of expertise in the use of research methods, based on results from survey of education researchers

The findings show that some education researchers have used a variety of research methods – perhaps a greater range than expected and probably also greater than in some other fields, such as economics or psychology. This suggests that a considerable capacity already exists for education researchers to combine methods. The survey showed that many researchers had used a variety of methods for collecting primary data, had used a variety of secondary data sources, had the ability to analyse quantitative and qualitative data, and had used computer software to aid their analysis. However, the survey also highlighted a number of constraints that could prevent the further combination of methods in the future. Many researchers reported having only *analysed* quantitative or qualitative data. Less than a third had ever used data from existing large-scale government surveys, had used secondary textual, visual or audio data, or had used qualitative data analysis computer software. The pioneers are likely to be relatively few at present.

The RAE analysis

The survey of education researchers has only given us a proxy indication of the prevalence of combining methods in education research. Our figures from the 2001 RAE returns, on the other hand, are based on the actual use of combined methods in the pieces of work submitted. Of course no judgement can be made as to what these figures should *ideally* be. Indeed, we have argued, and will continue to argue throughout this book, that the use of methods, be it mono-method or in combination, should be determined by the aims and objectives of the research. Instead we use these figures to supplement the findings from the survey of education researchers and to ascertain the current prevalence of combined research methods. Both sources of data provide evidence that combined methods research exists. Both also suggest that there is a distinction in practice between research that combines methods in a simple way – for example, using appropriate qualitative data analysis approaches to examine interview data, or summarizing data from a survey using cross-tabulations and charts – and research that mixes different methods – for example, collecting data in more than one form and subsequently analysing data using more than one approach.

For all submissions to the 2001 RAE, whether journal articles or not, Table 8.6 shows the frequency of different types of research. The table represents 5513 of the 8691 submissions. The remaining 3178 submissions did not state the overall type of research they were but did identify which methods were used to either collect or analyse data (see Table 8.7). A large proportion of submissions were based on 'think pieces' with no empirical content, as self-reported (18 per cent overall). A further 10 per cent were recorded as literature reviews and 4 per cent were declared non-empirical or otherwise unclassifiable by method. This means that just over 31 per cent of all submissions to education were not chiefly empirical (according to the theory/method field). It should also be noted that non-empirical research submissions had no apparent impact on the final RAE outcomes, because a similar proportion of such submissions were submitted by departments that received an RAE grade between 1 and 4 as by departments that received an RAE grade of 5 or 5*. Of the clearly empirical research, case studies were the most common (8 per cent) followed by comparative studies (6 per cent) and policy studies/ analyses (5 per cent). It is difficult to say from these types of research whether they were predominantly 'quantitative' or 'qualitative' or whether they combined methods. The low rate of experiments (1 per cent) may be surprising given that according to the survey of education researchers discussed earlier, around 41 per cent reported having undertaken an experiment at some time. This would suggest that while many education researchers have the skills to conduct experiments they seldom actually do so.

Table 8.6 Frequency of type of education research submitted to the 2001 RAE

Types of research submitted	Of all submissions (n = 8691)	
	Number	Percentage
Think pieces	1533	18
Literature reviews	828	10
Case study	674	8
Comparative study	479	6
Policy study/analysis	465	5
Not classifiable	364	4
Historical/archive	344	4
Action research	233	3
Philosophy	191	2
Programme evaluation	131	2
Longitudinal study	121	1
Experiment	94	1
Systematic review (meta-analysis)	31	0
Intervention	25	0

Table 8.7 shows the frequency of the collapsed categories for research methods identified for submissions to the 2001 RAE, using the same subcategories of methods as in the previous section. In coding these methods it was not always possible to discern the precise methods used. Therefore, we have included four additional subcategories that do at least distinguish between 'qualitative' and 'quantitative' data analysis and primary and secondary data. Similarly, the entry 'workbook' has been included as it was used in the RAE submissions but does not easily fit any of our existing subcategories of methods.

The most common methods identifiable from the RAE submissions were interview (15 per cent), 'qualitative' data analysis (15 per cent) and survey methods (13 per cent). These were followed by general 'qualitative' data analysis (9 per cent) and general 'quantitative' data analysis (7 per cent). If we consider the figures presented in Table 8.7 at a higher level of aggregation we can see that 2067 (24 per cent) submissions clearly used 'qualitative' data and that 1424 (16 per cent) submissions clearly used 'quantitative' data. This means that on balance education research tends to use 'qualitative' data. However, the balance towards qualitative data at the expense of quantitative data is perhaps not as great as often assumed, such as in the comments presented earlier in this chapter by key stakeholders within education research. These figures confirm the findings from our survey (see above).

In terms of data analysis the figures presented in Table 8.7 suggest that 2004 (23 per cent) submissions reported having undertaken qualitative data analysis of some form, whereas only 686 (8 per cent) submissions reported having undertaken 'quantitative' data analysis (either descriptive or statistical). This balance is even greater in favour of 'qualitative' research methods. The majority of submissions reported having used primary data (3370 submissions or 39 per cent), and only a very small proportion (also) appeared to use secondary data (318 submissions or 4 per cent). This is much lower than from the survey of education researchers (of whom 65 per cent reported having used secondary datasets) and may be partly due to the kind of terms used in the theory/ method field.

Table 8.7 Frequency of education research methods submitted to the 2001 RAE

Subcategory of methods	Of all submissions (n = 8691)	
	Number	Percentage
Interviews	1305	15
Qualitative data analysis	1265	15
Survey	1109	13
General qualitative data analysis	739	9
General quantitative data analysis	574	7
Observation	473	5
Tests	242	3
Textual, visual or audio	167	2
General secondary data use	123	1
Secondary textual, visual and audio	122	1
Statistical analysis of quantitative data	100	1
General primary data use	52	1
Official education statistics	50	1
Government surveys	23	0
Workbooks	22	0
Describing quantitative data	12	0

These comparisons (primary or secondary data, 'qualitative' or 'quantitative' data, and 'qualitative' or 'quantitative' analysis) provide a framework for examining the combined use of methods in research submitted to the 2001 RAE. Table 8.8 shows the frequency of education submissions that involved (as far as it was reported) combining methods. The first column shows again the overall proportion of submitted pieces using each method. The combined methods columns are divided into the three comparisons, and show how frequently the method in each row was used in conjunction with the method in that column. The reported use of combined methods is generally very low, especially given the *potential* for combining methods described earlier. Again, this may be due to the limitations of the theory/method field (which is one reason why we look at actual publications in the next section), or it could be that researchers wish to claim a greater range of expertise in research methods than they present in their research.

Around 5 per cent of all submissions combined interviews with other more 'quantitative' data. Similarly, 5 per cent of all submissions combined the use of surveys with more 'qualitative' data. On the basis of this analysis these two classifications of combined methods research were clearly the most common. Together these two classifications (as reported in the 2001 submissions) accounted for the overwhelming majority of combined methods research.

Approximately 2 per cent of all submissions reported having used methods for analysing qualitative data and methods for analysing quantitative data together. This small proportion still constitutes the third most common classification for combining methods. The use of primary data alongside secondary data was reported in only 1 per cent of all research submitted, and Table 8.8 shows the breakdown of such research by the different methods or sources used. For example, interviews were the most commonly used primary research method alongside secondary data of any sort, followed by surveys. The secondary data most commonly used with primary data were sources of textual, visual or audio data (0.4 per cent). This may reflect a difficulty in distinguishing between whether such qualitative data is from a primary or secondary source. A similar proportion of research used methods for observation alongside secondary data sources and official education statistics alongside primary data (0.2 per cent in both cases).

Because of the nature of the RAE we are able to use this data to make some tentative judgements about quality. There is clearly some good research in education using quantitative and qualitative approaches, both in isolation and in combination (and this is reflected, within the recognized limitations of the system, in the RAE results for that work). However, we have still not satisfactorily solved the issue of judging prevalence. The theory/method field is limited, and relies on unstandardized self-reporting. So we move to a brief assessment of what is being published, both to triangulate, to some extent, our analysis here and to consider differences between journals.

Table 8.8 Frequency of combined methods across all education submissions to the 2001 RAE

Subcategory of methods	All submissions	Combined submissions (% of all submissions)					
		Secondary data	Primary data	Qualitative data	Quantitative data	Qualitative data analysis	Quantitative data analysis
Interviews	15	0.6	–	–	4.6	–	–
Observation	5	0.2	–	–	1.1	–	–
Survey	13	0.4	–	4.7	–	–	–
Textual, visual or audio	2	–	–	–	0.3	–	–
Tests	3	0.1	–	0.5	–	–	–
General primary data use	1	0.3	–	–	–	–	–
Official education statistics	1	–	0.2	0.1	–	–	–
Government surveys	0	–	0.1	–	–	–	–
Secondary textual, visual and audio	1	–	0.4	–	0.1	–	–
General secondary data use	1	–	0.6	–	–	–	–
Describing quantitative data	0	–	–	–	–	–	–
Statistical analysis of quantitative data	1	–	–	–	–	–	–
General quantitative data analysis	7	–	–	–	–	1.8	–
Qualitative data analysis	15	–	–	–	–	–	0.3
General qualitative data analysis	9	–	–	–	–	–	1.6

What is being published?

The *British Educational Research Journal* (*BERJ*) was the most widely submitted outlet for RAE 2001 papers. In 2002, the most recent complete year, the *BERJ* contained 42 articles in six issues and these showed several differences to the RAE returns more generally. The category 'unclassifiable' from the RAE analysis on the basis of the method field (3 per cent) obviously does not exist for papers in the *BERJ*, since in this case we have read the articles. Nor are any of the pieces stand-alone literature reviews (as befits a research-based journal). This means that the other categories should be larger. Only five articles (12 per cent) were apparently non-empirical think pieces compared to 18 per cent in the RAE. The most common method category was interviews, occurring in a total of 18 papers (43 per cent), much higher proportionately than in the RAE (17 per cent interviews, case studies, ethnomethodology and conversational analysis). The *BERJ* figure includes 11 pieces solely with interviews, one piece simply with interviews but related to a companion piece involving regression analysis, two combining interviews and surveys, and one each with discourse analysis, case study (with interviews but also documents and observation), interview with observation, and interview with textual analysis. Four further *BERJ* papers used texts (usually pre-existing), one was based on 'qualitative' observation, and one on autobiography.

Of the remaining papers, 13 (31 per cent) were clearly quantitative in nature, not counting a factor analysis that also appeared in one of the papers above. Another paper used factor analysis with psychometric scales, three used multi-level modelling in a school effectiveness vein, and three used regression with secondary data (but not multi-level modelling). Two papers reported a questionnaire survey with a comparison of means, one a survey with regression, and one a survey with a school-based test. There was a further paper using secondary data for simple numeric analysis, and one conducting observation leading to numeric outcomes. Thus, numbers-based papers were a significant component of *BERJ* output, and exhibited considerable sophistication and variation in technique.

The *British Journal of Educational Psychology* was also an avenue for a large number of RAE submissions, predominantly those awarded 5 or 5*. It published 28 articles in four issues during 2002. Of these, all but one (96 per cent) were clearly or largely quantitative – the odd one being a literature review. There were five experiments or quasi-experiments (18 per cent), a much higher figure than all other sources (see above). Seven of the papers were based on data collected via a questionnaire (25 per cent) and then analysed via factor analysis (3), Rasch modelling, comparison of means (2), multi-level modelling, regression or cluster analysis. Five were based on formal tests, variously with a questionnaire, a comparison of means (3) or a factor analysis. One further paper used factor analysis on pre-existing data, one used growth curves, and one each correlation, Rasch modelling and longitudinal assessment data. The prevalence, high level and variety of quantitative techniques may be a function of the disciplinary nature of this journal, but it is also notable that this outlet clearly distinguishes between high and low-medium RAE outcomes.

Educational Management and Administration (*EMA*) was also an avenue for a large number of RAE submissions, predominantly those awarded 1 or 4 grades. It published 24 articles in four issues during 2002. Of these seven (29 per cent) were think pieces with no discernible direct empirical content, and a further three (9 per cent) were literature reviews. Six were based on interviews (18 per cent), including one in conjunction with textual analysis, and another with secondary numeric data. Three papers described 'qualitative' case studies, one was comparative, one a policy analysis, and three used a questionnaire with analysis of frequencies and means. Therefore *EMA*, which was disproportionately submitted by departments gaining RAE 1–4, contained less direct empirical work overall than the other journals considered, and also considerably less quantitative work. Perhaps it is fields and journals such as these that lead commentators to the idea that there is a marked lack of quantitative skills in UK education research.

Overall, across three very different journals in 2002, 17 per cent of the articles were clearly or largely non-empirical (although this description includes literature reviews, presumably based on empirical evidence), 4 per cent were empirical pieces using a combination of 'qualitative' and 'quantitative' methods (therefore a rather rare phenomenon), 34 per cent used qualitative methods alone, and 47 per cent used quantitative methods alone. While the selection of journals used here may indeed overemphasize quantitative approaches, this simple analysis of published papers in one year confirms that at least one element of our stakeholders' view of problems in education research is incorrect. There is no particular shortage of quantitative work in relation to qualitative work, as evidenced by any of our indicators – the reports of researchers themselves, RAE returns and journal contents. There is no clear answer to the question of how much quantitative work is needed ideally, and our analysis cannot determine, therefore, whether there is enough, too much or too little. But the amount reported would probably surprise our informants.

Conclusion

If there is, indeed, more quantitative work going on in education than is usually realized by commentators, then why is there this discrepancy? There are several possible explanations. First, of course, the distinction between quantitative and qualitative work is not a clear one, and taken literally almost all work involves both textual analysis *and* counting, so our classifications and the frequencies based on them may be misleading. Second, our stakeholders generally talked about education research as an activity in higher education institutions in specialist education (largely teacher training) departments. Much research relevant to education goes on outside of these, in other disciplines (such as psychology), in governmental structures, and in outside bodies such as NERF or the National Institute for Adult and Continuing Education (NIACE). Researchers from these bodies appear in our survey and in the journals (with a considerably higher level of quantitative work), but not in the RAE analysis (where the proportion of quantitative work was lower). Perhaps the distinction is not so much within education higher education institutions, because our analysis of RAE returns shows little difference between high- and low-ranked departments in their use of methods, but between the higher education institutions (who do less quantitative work) and everyone else. Our stakeholders were not, therefore, bemoaning the lack of quantitative work in general, but in what are mainly teacher-training departments. It is these, therefore, that may be least able to increase their amount of combined methods work. What other potential barriers do they face?

9

Theory as a barrier to the combination of research methods

We have, so far, reviewed a variety of models for the successful combination of methods, from triangulation and Bayesian synthesis, through NPA to complex interventions and design studies. Conducting all of these studies presented their researchers with various practical, ethical and analytic problems, several of which have been described in this book along with their real-life solutions. But it is important to stress that conducting these studies has not presented their researchers with any great *philosophical* barriers stemming from incompatible epistemology or ontology. That is why there has been little discussion of qualitative and quantitative paradigms so far – they provide no practical assistance at all to the combined methods researcher. Now is the time to return to such issues. We will try to explain that it is not that we do not think about the logic of science when conducting research, but rather that it does not seem to make much difference. As explained in Chapter 1, empirical studies of how people conduct research suggest that everyone adopts a very similar approach in practice, whatever their public epistemological position. Again, we do not seek to persuade everyone, or indeed anyone, that we are right about this. But we would like readers to at least consider our argument that training for new researchers should no longer start with the teaching of a division of qualitative and quantitative work into theoretical 'paradigms'. This can be very damaging.

In many ways this chapter should be seen as a counterbalance to Chapter 2, which devoted most of its space to a critique of current traditional approaches to statistical analysis, because this is where some researchers seek an illusory haven of 'objectivity' in research. This chapter, on the other hand, devotes most of its space to a critique of the way in which avowedly 'qualitative' researchers use the notions of theory and paradigm to protect themselves from having to deal with a larger range of evidence. This focus is necessary because they, more than any other group, are the ones suggesting that the combination of data from different 'paradigms' is impossible. However, it should be noted that equivalent issues arise in other fields, such as economics, where the majority of researchers use only *quantitative* methods, and we have written extensive critiques of this situation elsewhere (e.g. Gorard 2003a, 2003b, 2004b). We need to leave our 'silos' in this unwinnable war of words, so that the researchers in no man's land are those who want to get on with a job of research using all and any data that can be of benefit. Grand words, big theories and untestable propositions about the nature of the social world are, too often, more of a hindrance than a help.

Of course, this does not mean that a pragmatic approach does not use theories (see Chapters 4 to 7), but these theories are of the kind that can be tested to destruction rather than artificially preserved. It also does not mean that a pragmatic approach has to ignore the philosophy of science, rather the reverse – hence this chapter. We could suggest, as others have done, that the philosophical foundation for combined methods work is 'pragmatism', but we fear that the act of labelling what is, after all, how we behave in normal life will eventually lead to the creation of a 'pragmatic paradigm'. We start with a consideration of the idea of research paradigms, especially the idea that qualitative and quantitative research represent two such paradigms.

Limitations to combining methods in education research

A key constraint on any increase in combined methods work is the limited use of specific methods, irrespective of whether they are used in combination with other methods or not. In particular, we noted in the last chapter that the use of secondary datasets in education research was limited to a minority of researchers (see Chapter 8 for a description of the datasets used here). Consequently, there will inevitably be little research that combines secondary data with other forms of data. More generally there is a perceived lack of quantitative work. We saw that nearly half of education researchers responding to our survey had never employed any statistical analysis with their data. No matter what form of data is collected or used, the capacity to analyse data using statistics will tend to constrain the possible combination of methods. As one of the key stakeholders that we interviewed pointed out when discussing the use of combined methods in education research: 'It's not easy. But it's easier if you've got the skills, at least you don't try and avoid the question' (former chief executive of UK research funding agency).

So far we have identified one key constraint in combining methods in education research: the limited use of particular methods even in isolation. There are also a number of other factors that could possibly constrain the greater use of multiple methods in education research. As the following stakeholder argued, there are possible financial constraints to undertaking research that combines methods: 'I think there have been funding problems in the large-scale quantitative studies and quantitative combined with qualitative, which tend to push people to smaller projects' (director of a research funding agency).

This is even more applicable to new research students undertaking research for their masters or their Ph.D. Both forms of research training are constrained both in terms of finance and time. Consequently, many new students will automatically opt for methodological frameworks they feel most comfortable with – i.e. what they have read and have been stimulated by, or what they think is achievable within the time constraints. This stakeholder suggests this prevents new students from undertaking large-scale quantitative studies: 'In terms of Ph.D. students doing large quantitative studies, practical problems ... tend to push people at that level to do either secondary analysis or qualitative small-scale studies' (director of a research funding agency).

A similar argument can be used to explain why few new research students combine methods in their research. This relates to the formal methodological training that new research students receive. Of course, if there are few experienced education researchers combining methods in their own research then the level of formal training in this is also going to be limited. Furthermore, although increasing in number, there are few methodological textbooks that teach new students how to combine methods. Indeed, as this stakeholder highlights, the majority of new methodological texts simply reinforce the continued use of particular methods in education research:

> I suppose that it's also ... that if you look at what's written on research methods, there's an awful lot more written on qualitative methods than quantitative methods. I mean Sage publish about, you know, ten titles a week as far as I can see, and that's just one publisher on qualitative. They don't publish as many on quantitative and they don't publish as many on mixed methods.
>
> (Higher education researcher and former ESRC grants board reviewer)

Even if we move towards a balance of research methods training, as the current ESRC's 1+3 scheme tries to promote, or a focus on how to combine methods, some would argue that there still remains some form of *resistance* to using particular methods and combining methods in general. As one of our stakeholders argues when discussing research training: 'I think one of the problems we have in capacity-building is trying to persuade, and this is a very kind of parochial little problem, but I think that it may be the core of something else, is trying to persuade

Ph.D. students to take an interest in any method apart from the one they are using themselves' (Higher education researcher and TLRP team leader).

This stakeholder went on to try and explain why this resistance may occur:

> I think there has been this huge increase in qualitative research in education over the last 10 or 15 years or whatever. I think that's basically very good, very healthy. It's provided a huge new perspective on work. But I think part of the fallout has been the drop of interest, if you like, in quantitative research . . . I think it's partly that qualitative researchers or people who promote it have actually promoted it in a way that is very very appealing to students and so on. I've sat in on, organized, been involved in, a lot of research methods courses and often, I know I'm caricaturing, it's often said 'there are two ways of seeing the world, a positivist, a scientist in a white coat and you use quantitative methods'. And students recoil from that. 'Or you can be an open and a qualitative researcher, you engage with meaning and you know you're a warm cuddly sort of person.' And students think, 'Yeah, yeah, that's me. I want to do that. That's me. I don't want to be a scientist in a white coat. I think there are two ways.' And for me I just think those images that go with the different images is a complete travesty. I think they are just different ways of doing research. Sometimes the project's appropriate to use qualitative, sometimes it's appropriate to use quantitative methods, and sometimes you want to use both. Just like sometimes you want to drink red wine and sometimes you want to drink white wine. That's it, sometimes you want to drink everything!
>
> (Higher education researcher and TLRP team leader)

Another stakeholder used very similar words when discussing the resistance of experienced education researchers to using 'other' methods:

> At the moment when I've talked to some education researchers about this, they say that what they are interested in is the quality, the qualitative area, and they don't think statistics and that kind of material has any connection at all. It may be that they can argue that strongly from an epistemological strength. My feeling is that they're arguing it from ignorance. They are actually defending . . . it's a post hoc justification for the situation they are in and I would include myself in that to a certain extent. I'm more interested in the touchy feely stuff as opposed to the number crunching.
>
> (Higher education researcher and UCET Executive Committee member)

Furthermore, it may also be the case that experienced researchers want to avoid learning new techniques and approaches. One explanation for this may be the fear of acknowledging, and then admitting, what we do not know and understand:

> I think there's this kind of fear, you know, that you don't really want people down the road to find out what you don't know. And my guess is that may also apply to research methods, that people don't necessarily like to admit what they don't know. They're happy to tell you what they do know but they don't want to kind of say, 'Well I really don't know anything about this'.
>
> (Higher education researcher and former ESRC grants board reviewer)

Apart from 'taste', desire or fear dictating the use of particular methods, there would also appear to be wider disciplinary and philosophical constraints to combining methods. The following stakeholder proposes that interdisciplinary research teams, bringing a diversity of methodological expertise to a project, are the way forward:

> But it's also about ... it is about disciplines and of course it's very difficult, it's a very tricky area to overcome long-standing intellectual snobberies and habits. I think those snobberies and habits are very real and I think that addressing them and developing horizontal teams and interdisciplinary teams rather than thinking that each discipline is better, is the way forward. I do think that inter-disciplinarity is the way forward.
>
> (OECD researcher)

Indeed, it should be common for research projects to try and address the lack of methodological diversity among individual researchers by ensuring the research team have a diversity of methodological expertise. However, it would appear that the greatest obstacle for many existing education researchers to combining methods continues to be the qualitative-quantitative divide in research. Although, as the following stakeholder discusses, methodological diversity is increasing, there still remains strong resistance:

> In some ways I think we're, we're in a healthy period, in principle. But in practice we're not realizing the potential of that healthiness ... Just to expand on that, the, what I mean is, that I think we, we're in a stage where we have got a more liberalized conception of education research methodology and there is more openness to a whole range of approaches. I would have thought we're post paradigm wars, except I know bloody well we're not ... But we've got this, we've gone past this sort of antithesis sort of stage. We've got

potentially a synthesis. We've got people like Martin Hammersley, I've a lot of respect for, in their attempts to, to sort of, get beyond the simplisms of the, so-called qualitative-quantitative divide and to deconstruct them. So, I think, in principle, we could have quite a rich, eclectic, you know, radically triangulatory type of stance. I suspect we're not quite yet there and there are still people who plump for one thing or the other. I don't think we're perhaps realizing that possibility. We, we've got more liberal but that's in a way just becoming more tolerant but without having a rationale as to why we're more liberal, that sort of thing.

(Higher education researcher and journal editor)

We therefore turn now to a discussion of the supposed philosophical basis for this qualitative-quantitative divide.

The problem with theory as paradigm

In the sociology of science the notion of a 'paradigm', as a description of the sets of socially accepted assumptions that tend to appear in 'normal science' (Kuhn 1970), has some considerable descriptive value. A paradigm is a set of accepted rules within any field for solving one or more puzzles – where a puzzle is defined as a scientific question that it is possible to find a solution to in the near future, to distinguish it from the many important and interesting questions that do not have an answer at any particular stage of progress (Davis 1994). 'Normal science' in Kuhnian terms is held together, rightly or wrongly, by the norms of reviewing and acceptance that work in that taken-for-granted theoretical framework. A paradigm shift occurs when that framework changes, perhaps through the accumulation of evidence, perhaps due to a genuinely new idea, but partly through a change in general acceptance. Often a new paradigm emerges because a procedure or set of rules has been created for converting a more general query *into* a puzzle. But, what Kuhn saw as normal science could also be simply passive and uncritical rather than genuinely cumulative in nature. It could be based on practices that differ from those stated (i.e. where there is deceit, either of the self or the audience). As Lakatos (1978: 44) points out, maintenance of the status quo in any scientific endeavour 'is [often] achieved by censorship'. Normal science may therefore give an appearance of harmony, and of fitting together, because its practitioners conceal their actual methodological divergence in practice (Gephart 1988).

However, the term now tends to be used very loosely. Instead of using 'paradigm' to refer to a topic or field of research (such as traditional physics) which might undergo a radical shift on the basis of evidence (e.g.

to quantum physics), some commentators now use it to refer to a whole approach to research including philosophy, values and method (Perlesz and Lindsay 2003). These commentators tend to use the term conservatively, to defend *themselves* against the need to change, or against contradictory evidence of a different nature to their own. The idea of normal science as a collection of individuals all working towards the solution of a closely defined problem has disappeared. The concept of paradigm has, thus, become a cultural cliché with many meanings (and some of this was inherent even in the original formulation). It is now almost meaningless.

The most unhelpful of the supposed paradigms in social science are the methodological ones of 'qualitative' and 'quantitative' approaches. Unfortunately, novice research students can quickly become imprisoned within one of these purported 'paradigms'. They learn, because they are taught, that if they use any numbers in their research then they must be positivist or realist in philosophy, and they must be hypothetico-deductive or traditional in style (see e.g. such claims by Clarke 1999). If, on the other hand, students disavow the use of numbers in research then they must be interpretivist, holistic and alternative, believing in multiple perspectives rather than truth, and so on. Sale *et al.* (2002: 44), for example, claim that 'The quantitative paradigm is based on positivism. Science is characterized by empirical research'. Whereas, 'In contrast, the qualitative paradigm is based on ... multiple realities. [There is] no external referent by which to compare claims of truth' (p. 45).

What is ironic about this use of the term 'paradigm' to refer to a methods- and value-based system in social research is that it has never been intended to be generally taken for granted, in the way that 'normal science' is. Rather, it was and is intended to split the field into two non-communicating parts. Therefore, a paradigm of this kind cannot be shifted by evidence, ideas or the fact that others reject it. It has become divisive and conservative in nature, leading to 'an exaggeration of the differences between the two traditions' (Gray and Densten 1998: 419) and an impoverishment of the range of methods deployed to try and solve important social problems.

When we act pragmatically in our non-research lives we do not usually invoke a paradigm as our starting point. In preparing a large formal party, for example, we would use documents, conversations and numeric accounts in an unproblematic way. We would not, presumably, reject the advice of the caterer simply because it was expressed verbally, nor would we refuse to calculate the amount of food or drink required simply because that would involve numbers. If we did, the organization of the party would suffer. 'We may consider ourselves utterly devoted to qualitative research methods. Yet when we think about investigations carried out in the normal course of our daily lives, how often do measuring and counting turn out to be essential to our purposes?' (Crotty 1998: 15). Why then do we behave any differently in our research, which is, presumably, just as important? According to Beyer (1992), quality research should inevitably lead us to *question* existing theory rather than set out to protect it. It will tend to develop new theory via an examination of relevant evidence, and will not restrict the nature of that evidence in order to protect the pre-existing theory. Methods will be used 'as a tool serving the questions pursued, rather than allowing them to constrict the range of inquiry' (p. 62).

Worldviews do not logically entail or privilege the use of specific methods (Guba 1990), but may only be thought to do so due to a common confusion between the logic of designing a study and the method of collecting data (according to de Vaus 2001; Geurts and Roosendaal 2001). 'The researcher's fidelity to principles of inquiry is more important than allegiance to procedural mechanics ... Research should be judged by the quality and soundness of its conception, implementation and description, not by the genre within which it is conducted' (Paul and Marfo 2001: 543–5). Nevertheless, some researchers 'evidently believe that the choice of a research method represents commitment to a certain kind of truth and the concomitant rejection of other kinds of truth' (Snow 2001: 3). Such researchers consider that the value of their methods can be judged apart from the questions they are used for. In real life, methods *can* be separated from the epistemology from which they emerge, so that qualitative work is not tied to a constructivist paradigm, and so on (Teddlie and Tashakkori 2003).

As we have shown in previous chapters, the distinction between 'quantitative' and 'qualitative' work, on which this notion of paradigms is based, is in any case exaggerated. Most methods of analysis use some form of number, such as 'tend', 'most', 'some', 'all', 'none', 'few' and so on. Whenever one talks of things being 'rare', 'typical', 'great' or 'related' this is a statistical claim, and can only be so substantiated, whether expressed verbally or in figures (Meehl 1998). The patterns in qualitative analysis are, by definition, numeric, and the things that are traditionally numbered are qualities. Quantification does not consist of simply assigning numbers to things, but of relating empirical relations to numeric relations (Nash 2002). The measurement of all useful quantities requires a prior consideration of theory leading to the identification of a quality to be measured. The numbers themselves are only valuable in so far as their behaviour is an isomorph of the qualities they are summarizing (see Chapters 1 and 2).

It is, therefore, somewhat impractical to sustain an argument that all parts of all methods, including data collection, carry epistemological or ontological commitments (Frazer 1995; Bryman 2001). Rather, researchers tend to confuse the issues, shuttling from technical to philosophical differences, and exaggerating them into a paradigm (Bryman 1988). No research design implies either qualitative or quantitative data even though reviewers commonly make the mistake of assuming that they do – that experiments can only collect numeric data, observation must be non-numeric, and so on. Qualitative and quantitative work are therefore *not* conducted in differing research paradigms in practice. The alleged differences between research paradigms (in this sense) prevail in spite of good evidence, not because of it (Quack Theories 2002).

As noted above, this schism of paradigms is sometimes supported by a philosophical 'argument' along the lines of 'but that is just positivist' (in Oakley 2001). Terms like 'positivist' referring to all numeric, or even all reasoned, approaches to research have become insults, used to dismiss opponents but never by those opponents themselves (in Fitz-Gibbon 2000 and Phillips 1992: 95). 'In the context of the critique of quantitative research that built up in the 1960s ... the attribution "positivist" was used glibly and indiscriminately by many writers and in fact became a term of abuse' (Bryman 1988: 13). Other than that, the word signifies very little (it is rare for a social scientist to declare themselves a 'positivist', whereas other terms that could be used of others in a similarly derogative way, such as 'relativist', are also commonly used as self-references). Perlesz and Lindsay (2003), who are not positivists, believe that positivists hold reality to be independent of and external to any observer. Constructivists, on the other hand, hold that there is no external reality, and that findings are 'created' solely through the research process (and triangulation between methods is therefore impossible since there cannot be different views of the same reality, because the reality *is* the different views). However, the key point about positivism, and the reason it is so seldom advocated today, is exactly the opposite. Positivism denotes a belief that entities do *not* exist independently of their measurement, and is therefore more similar to relativism than either logical empiricism or realism. This view has long been discredited (Cook and Payne 2002). Rather than worrying about rather petty distinctions between constructivism and social constructs, given that no one is suggesting that we have direct experience of an objective reality, we should be more concerned with finding better ways of describing what we *do* experience (Rorty 1999).

Theory and science

Objections to research as science are often based on a false ontological dualism. Science is not merely positivism with numbers (Swann 2003). Rather, research is science and vice versa, irrespective of the methods employed (Breault 2002). Research findings, and the models based on them, represent a simplified description of a system that assists us with calculations and predictions. They do not represent complete truth, and are good and useful only in so far as they enable us to make good decisions or improve performance (West and Harrison 1997). There are certain shared assumptions underlying all research, whatever methods are used, and there are no pure ontological or epistemological divisions in practice (Denscombe 2002). By analogy, a policy-maker who believes that human rights are an inalienable part of the soul and one who thinks that human rights are simply an admirable invention may both suggest the same policies. Similarly, in natural science the actual philosophy adopted by practitioners makes no difference to how they proceed (Rorty 1999). Scientists who support Kuhn's views are not going to do much different in their research to those who support Weinberg, for example.

Research requires rigorous reasoning supported by an appropriate mixture of methods, and findings leading to testable models or theories. A specific design or method does not make a study scientific, for 'the question drives the methods, not the other way around' (Feuer *et al.* 2002: 8). At its core, the nature of scientific inquiry is the same in all fields (National Research Council 2002). In fact, a consideration of how social science research is actually done, rather than how methodologists often claim it should be done, suggests that nearly all studies proceed in the same way – contextualized, value-attuned and 'post-positivist' (Eisenhart and Towne 2003).

Research has no universally agreed account of its nature or method, and offers no certainties (Chalmers 1999). Despite the fact that science is portrayed by outsiders and opponents as the mechanistic application of predetermined procedures, progress is actually achieved via the self-regulating norms of the scientific community (Collins and Pinch 1993). This is what we mean when we say that a knowledge claim is 'accepted as true'. In this way, natural science has been observed to behave very much like social science. The surface differences between the natural and social sciences are more to do with the phenomena being studied than the procedures observed as being employed (Cole 1994).

It would be a category mistake, therefore, to say that some social science research descriptions are not meant to be accepted as 'true', else why should we be concerned with them? Recognizing the existence of genuine multiple perspectives does not mean the end of truth as an ideal. We could, for example, view one research site in terms of its efficiency, economy, heating and lighting etc. Each account so generated may be true, but they are also, quite properly, orthogonal to all of the others. We cannot, because of this, seriously assert that anything must be true. But 'interpretivist methods and analyses are sometimes abused to *justify* a lack of rigour' (Denscombe 2002: 22). Such commentators are confusing the perfectly proper realization that one phenomenon can be viewed from many perspectives, with the idea that anything can be a perspective. They are confusing the widely accepted notion that knowledge is socially constructed with the invalid inference that any social construct can be deemed knowledge. Truth, according to Howe (1988), is a normative concept, like 'good'. It is what works in practice, for that is how we recognize its truth. Where research has been testable, and has practical consequences, a kind of evolutionary natural selection has led, over time, to the universality of logical empiricism. For, while there may be plausible arguments put forward to believe that pain is good, or that two plus two equals five, research based on such premises would be non-viable and actions based on that research could be dangerous (Tooley 1999). Researchers with such idiosyncratic views are, eventually, eliminated, just as someone who *genuinely* does not believe in an external reality might soon be knocked down by a bus. This slow evolutionary pressure means that we do not have to go as far as Kroto (2003) suggests by denying the benefits and results of the scientific approach (medicine, transport etc.) to those who decry scientific endeavours.

In fact, the researcher who claims not to be scientific may merely be insufficiently aware of the basis of their own approach – there are many examples of social scientists who claim to be relativists, for example, while behaving with respect to the ideas of others as nothing of the sort: 'So unconscious is the average social scientist ... of the gnoseological presuppositions of his study that he finds it only too easy to avow allegiance to doctrines wholly at variance with the philosophical prerequisites of his own researches ... intellectual fashions are made up of avowed philosophies and not assumed ones' (Postan 1971: ix; see also Bricmont and Sokal 2001). In the same way, many readers will have observed commentators decrying the ability of science to control or predict future events (with some justification), but then advocating astrology, for example.

The call for better and more responsible publicly-funded social science is largely a request for empirical evidence and reasoned argument, as opposed to prejudice and untestable opinion. It is in response to those people who seriously propose unscientific research that allows fictional drama, for example, to be treated as evidence rather than simply a way of disseminating evidence (in Mayer 2001): 'We have to put up with an appalling amount of bunk ... simply because we cannot draw a firm line between what is legitimate academic sociology and what is not' (Davis 1994: 188). However, mixing methods does not necessarily involve a commitment to social research as a natural or even a social science. Design science, for example, includes creativity, artisanship, craft principles, inspiration and fuzzy science. However, even in design science any artefact we create has to work for the design to be considered successful. There is little room for relativism here (Bailey 2001). Either the artefact works as the design intended, or it does not. The key point, again, is that a specific design or method does not make a study scientific (but only if it allows *direct* investigation of the question being asked). Dewey (1916: 200) summed up one advantage of science with a warning against 'our predilection for premature acceptance and assertion ... Even in the case of failure, we are inclined to put the blame not on the inadequacy and incorrectness of our data and thoughts ... Science represents the safeguard of the race against these natural propensities and the evils that flow from them'.

The role of theory in social science

Holmwood and Stewart (1983, 1991) have written about a distinction between 'productive' and 'non-productive' sociology. The former tradition of work uses theories that try to simplify and unify explanations of the social world, permitting any level of complexity only when those simpler attempts fail. It does not adhere to firm a priori categories or classifications, looking rather for straightforward and parsimonious explanations of social processes which are consistent with the evidence. This generally leads to new theories in the form of transferable and testable resources for researchers to help them both explain and predict empirical phenomena. The latter tradition of non-productive work, on the other hand, starts from a premise that social experience is confounding, contradictory and paradoxical, because that is how it often appears to new researchers. This tradition, therefore, preserves its prior theories for much longer because for its researchers a theory does not fail when it is contradicted by experience (that is merely further confirmation for their premise). Where such theory develops it tends to do so in an ad hoc fashion that is not clearly related to the findings of subsequent research.

Of course, the distinction between these traditions is not sharply delineated. Any theory can be affected by processes and phenomena unrelated to the empirical evidence, and the difference between the groups would therefore be one of degree. And any theory totally at odds with the evidence from the social phenomena it seeks to explain is likely to be overthrown eventually, even in the non-productive tradition. But this does not mean that the two extremes do not exist. To these two users of the term 'theory', we could also add a third group. This would consist of researchers within both traditions that deny any great value for theory at all.

For example, within education, despite the relative maturity of the field, there are so many important and basic practical questions to which we do not know the answer that our key starting point is often not much of a theory at all but genuine ignorance. These are often fairly straight-forward situations where we are ignorant of the consequences of important decisions we are forced to make in practice (Tymms and Fitz-Gibbon 2002). They include the cost/benefits of single-sex teaching, decreased class sizes, homework, group work, rote learning and many others. Now, of course, we *could* argue that class size is a social construct or that a sex dichotomy does not do justice to the continuous nature of gendered experience, but the people who fund public research in education – the taxpayers and charity-givers and their political repre-sentatives – know perfectly well what they mean by these concepts. If they want to know whether having more or fewer pupils in a class makes a difference to Key Stage 3 examination outcomes, for example, then the role of theory is severely limited in the ensuing research. As researchers we could simply vary class sizes in controlled ways over a large relevant sample, and monitor and measure the predefined outcome. If properly conducted, the research leads to an answer which is then advertised, and policy can be made on the basis of the answer (while it is not the fault of the researcher if this does not ensue). Public policy amelioration would then be more nearly based on proven models tested against their alter-natives in experimental comparisons (Slavin 2002). We *may* start the research with our own ideas and hunches about what will happen, but a fully-fledged prior theory, which may be no more than a belief or superstition, can actually be less than helpful. The need to make new explanations consistent with some already established body of theory tends to stifle progress (see also Feyerabend 1993). When setting out to test a practical question such as those above, imagining the eventual argument structure on which a knowledge claim will be based helps ascertain the form of data it would require, and so helps the planning of research. But theory, as it is usually envisaged, is largely irrelevant to such practical arguments (Toulmin 1958).

A similar point is made from a very different perspective by Thomas (2002: 419) who claims that 'educators' irrepressible interest in theory leads qualitative inquiry [in particular] into sterile terrain'. A lot of their writing is not about theory at all, but is simply 'theory talk', with the associated epistemological cachet and prestige that this creates for a certain type of peer reviewer. A theory can be a set of statements about the social world that can be tested empirically (clearly not its use in a lot of UK work), or a kind of tool for thinking often referred to as a 'lens'. Thomas claims that qualitative researchers presumably want the tool kind of theory, but that in practice they also want to use the knowledge-claiming properties of the first type of theory. They are trying to have their cake and eat it too, and their over-commitment to preordained theory is leading to mistakes of interpretation in what are otherwise relatively simple observation data. Theory use of this kind is, therefore, a hindrance to progress. It is too often confused with speculation or sub-jectivity (To 2000).

At the micro level it is easy to assent to the notion that all research data collection is theory-laden (Phillips 1999). Even such an apparently basic operation as the measurement of a length involves acceptance of a series of theories about the nature of length and the isomorphic behaviour of numbers (Berka 1983). It is important that we even revisit such theories on occasion (Prandy 2002), and their reconsideration could be part of a genuine paradigm shift (see above), but the ideas within them will have been tested, and found useful in making predictions about the future behaviour of the world. As with 'number' and 'length', so also with many of our basic concepts and classifications for use in social science – 'sex', 'time', 'place', 'family', 'class' or 'ethnicity'. Such ideas are tre-mendously powerful and useful, but they remain theories and so should be susceptible to change. Theory, in this sense, is part of our ordering of all experience (Dubin 1978).

On the other hand, at the meso level are those explanatory theories created by practising researchers, which generate hypotheses to be tested by subsequent research. A key identifying characteristic of these is that they are presented as one of a set of possible alternative explanations, and are argued only to be currently the best of those alternatives, usually due to making the fewest otherwise unnecessary assumptions. Over time they may become generally accepted and more like the taken-for-granted micro-level theories in nature, in that their alternatives become less explicitly acknowledged. At the macro level we have grand theories and the ideas of the big thinkers in the social sciences. What distinguishes these *big* theories from the others, apart from their scale, is that they are largely untested and generally untestable. They become, therefore, less like other forms of theory and more like articles of faith or even fashion. It is a critique of these, and the confusion they cause for other users of the term 'theory', that is the focus of the next section.

Problems in using big theories

By 'big theory' here we refer to second- and subsequent-generation grand theory, or subsequent-generation users of the ideas of purportedly great thinkers in social theory. The use of theory, in education research for example, often involves the 'adulation of great thinkers' such as Lyotard, Vygotsky or Foucault, according to Tooley and Darby (1998: 56). As they describe it, this is not a scientific approach to explanation through the use of theory, and does not involve testing or specifying criteria for failure of the theory. Rather, it appears to stem from a literary criticism background, which rewards ingenuity in applying literary ideas from one writer to the writing of another. It is common for 'researchers' in this tradition to try and explain some new phenomenon using the thinker's framework, but they do so by only arguing *for* it (using it as a 'lens', in their own terminology). Tooley and Darby (1998) give examples of journal articles where the theory palpably does not fit the data but remains apparently unhurt by the experience, at least in the eyes of each article's author. The use of vague definitions of unfamiliar terms, the easy creation of new terms and the perception of contradictions as attractive rather than anathema all mean that the theory cannot be easily tested by new evidence. There is also commonly a lack of consideration of any alternative explanations (Gorard 2002c).

Perhaps this is why the process of research does not seem either to alter these theories through a consideration of new data or help our under-standing of the data. The template for such work is rather: here is the evidence, here is the explanation, and here is its similarity to the writing of the great thinker. In the same way that evidence does not seem to affect theories, sociological theory has had little impact on any of the important findings of empirical study. 'This does not mean that general theorists are not cited by sociologists who do empirical research; but these citations usually appear at the beginning of the article as a cere-monial citation and have little influence on the actual conduct of the work' (Cole 1994: 140).

Referring to the theories of big thinkers like Freud or Marx, Hollis (1994: 72) comments that 'these theories were awash with confirming evidence but for the unsatisfactory reason that their adherents could square them with whatever happened'. Rather than specifying in advance the conditions under which a theory would be deemed to be false (however unlikely that might appear in prospect), adherents of big theories often defend their position in advance by arguing against logic itself. For example, MacLure (2003) treats poststructuralism as just such a big theory. She says, 'by "theory" I have in mind that loose collection of continentally influenced approaches with literary and/or psychoanalytic leanings that often go under the names of poststructuralism, post-modernism, deconstruction and discourse analysis' (p. 134). She defines poststructuralism as follows: 'Perhaps the nearest one could get to a common characteristic of poststructuralism would be a radical suspicion of reason, order and certainty' (p. 180). Therefore, this is a theory that can be defended against contrary evidence because it rejects the very notion of logic on which contradiction is based by conflating reasonable doubts about certainty in social science with doubts about reason itself.

'Reasoning is a way of testing and sifting ideas critically. It is concerned with how people share their ideas and thoughts in situations that raise the question of whether those ideas are worth sharing' (Toulmin *et al.* 1979: 10). The line of argument must be exposed, and stand up, to criticism. If theories make a difference compared to their alternatives (i.e. they lead to different, however subtly, accounts of the world) then the evidence for or against each theory can be presented, and all commentators can then argue from common ground (i.e. if theory T implies that event E will happen, then if E does not happen it affects the truth value of T). If theories lead to different accounts than their alternatives, then these differences can be sought in evidence and the persuasiveness of the theory can be reasoned. On the other hand, where they do not make a difference, then they are not testable. They become merely articles of faith (or 'religions'), a voice for their users' own 'rage against reason' (Hacking 1999: 67), and not part of the research process at all.

A similar approach to the rejection of reason and the celebration of contradiction is used by Usher and Edwards (1994) with the work of another big theorist: 'to make sense of Lyotard demands that we avoid totalisation and thus the argument that there are inconsistencies in his position' (p. 171). Whatever 'totalization' means, it is clear that Usher and Edwards will not treat logical contradiction within a theory as any kind of hindrance to its use. According to common definitions of the term – such as that of *The American Heritage Dictionary of the English Language* (2000) that theory is 'a set of statements or principles devised to explain a group of facts or phenomena, especially one that has been repeatedly tested or is widely accepted and can be used to make predictions about natural phenomena' – what MacLure and the others are talking about is not really a theory at all but a pre-existing stance for conducting their research.

Typical of the big theorists used frequently by subsequent researchers is Bourdieu (1990) who asserted that because the social world is complex (clearly plausible) then any theory about it must also be complex. The latter is not so plausible. It would appear that any theory will be a simplification of the social world it claims to help explain (otherwise it would simply repeat that world in its entirety). In fact, one of the main reasons that the physical world appears simpler than the social world to some observers is precisely because we currently have simpler theories to explain the physical world (Turner 2002). This is because the science of the physical world is more advanced than that of the social world, rather than because it is intrinsically simpler. If theories have to be simpler than the worlds they explain, then we have to decide how much simpler they can be. In scientific approaches the answer has tended to be that a theory should be as simple as possible while remaining faithful to the observed evidence (Morgan 1903). Bourdieu does not agree, but does not explain why. According to him, if critics do not agree with him it is because they do not understand. But, 'in my view, the real purpose served by the obscurity of Bourdieu's prose is to protect his own work from refutation' (Sullivan 2003: 26).

Leaving aside the actual value of Bourdieu's theories in explaining his *own* findings, it is harder to see the justification for using these ideas to help interpret work by others in different fields. Yet this happens frequently (Howe 1985). Such theory is used by (mainly) qualitative researchers to help their results and to try and influence practice or policy, but why it is necessary to do so is not usually explained. The problem, for qualitative work conducted in isolation, is that its findings are not usually generalizable – by its nature it is not used to make general claims, and in practice its conclusions are rarely presented in warranted fashion. So mono-methodic qualitative researchers tend to eschew generalization, but then they have to face the issue of why they are doing the work, and why anyone else should be interested in their results. There is a real danger then that the results from predominantly small-scale qualitative studies are largely and unfairly ignored (Swann and Pratt 1999). Howe (1985) believes that researchers use theory to suggest that their work provides them with something more epistemologically secure than mere ungeneralized observations.

Bourdieu's theory of habitus is ideal for such uses because it is vague. For example, 'Habitus can be viewed as a complex internalised core from which everyday experiences emanate' (Reay 1995: 357). What does that mean? Bourdieu gives habitus many meanings in his own work, and it is often used by others despite being very difficult to operationalize: 'It is unclear what the concept of habitus adds to such work' (Sullivan 2003: 16). Yet it may be this very slipperiness that is a key attraction: 'The conceptual *looseness* of habitus ... makes possible adaptation rather than the more constricting straightforward adoption of the concept within empirical work' (Reay 1995: 357, emphasis added). This is not theory as any scientist would understand it – it is, rather, an inkblot test used as a stimulus for the imagination.

Mills (1959) asks of this kind of theory use, 'after all the impediments to meaning are removed ... what then is being said?' (p. 27, although it should be recalled that Mills also warned of the dangers of empiricism abstracted entirely from theory). He translated examples of grand theory into simpler styles, and shows how anodyne their ideas often are. His purpose in doing so is to help theorists down from 'their useless heights' (p. 33). He claims that most commentators who appreciate grand theory do not, actually, understand it but find it fascinating precisely because of its unintelligibility. Users of grand theories have generally abdicated their responsibility to their audience for describing social processes plainly. Theory becomes, for them and us, an endless and pedantic elaboration of points and distractions. The advancement of any grand theory usually ceases with its founder in any case (To 2000). In future studies, 'rather than proceeding forward toward the testing and formulation of this theory, the data are made to fit it' (pp. 8–9). The theory has, therefore, become a system of belief. It may be easier to sustain such a belief in a social science rather than a natural science because the data are more fleeting. But while the general validity of social theory may therefore be limited by its specific geographic, social and temporal context, ironically the assumption of its extended applicability is 'usually held by followers and users who romanticise the function and power of the theory, [which] virtually forecloses the possibility for the advancement of the original inquiry' (p. 9).

Sceptical or clerical?

The standard approach to research is logical empiricism (see above, and Paul and Marfo 2001), which has gained its strength from its commitment to learning based on experience and experimentation. At heart it is sceptical rather than dogmatic. The results have been astounding in comparison to fields such as law or politics that did not adopt the same approach (Kroto 2003). In natural science, logical empiricism was the basis for the Enlightenment, and from the outset it appealed to the dispossessed and ordinary citizens. It was adopted in France by radicals as a means of reforming education and promoting social class harmony. Writing was couched in simple language wherever possible, to ensure that arguments were robust, to allow wider consideration and dissemination, and to keep things grounded and of practical use – thereby avoiding the chance of a Sokal hoax. Empiricism was deemed a radical approach offering resistance to authoritarian epistemologies, especially those of clericalism, which promoted the importance of doctrine (i.e. a big theory) over evidence. Empiricism also fitted well with a long-standing tradition in Britain of using the vernacular to make things clearer to everyone (Ackroyd 2002). As early as the thirteenth century this emancipatory approach meant that scholars and poets were deliberately writing in the middle-English of the common household, rather than the French of the aristocracy or the Latin of the Church. But one of the main reasons that practitioners and policy-makers do not use the findings of academic research today is that it tends to be written in a form of language that they cannot comprehend, for which the use of theory must take a substantial part of the blame (Hemsley-Brown *et al.* 2002). Those who might object to this analysis are probably confusing what Toulmin (1958) calls 'substantial' for 'analytic' arguments. In practical fields such as education, housing, health, crime and so on, we are primarily concerned with substantial arguments and should therefore, according to Toulmin, ground our claims in the practical context of each situation, rather than in the abstract principles that earlier philosophers and religious leaders wished to impose on us. It might be no exaggeration to say, in the twenty-first century, that the growth of research is still being retarded, as it was in previous centuries, by a kind of reactionary clericalism (Steele 2002).

Although postmodernism, for example, has been presented by some as the end of theory, for others it clearly *is* a theory (MacLure 2003). It casts doubt upon 'the self-evidence of the idea of knowledge as emancipatory' (Ramakers 2002: 636). As an intellectual approach to research (rather than in art and architecture whence it sprang) it is therefore the antithesis of the liberating anti-clerical tradition. Instead it resurrects the privileged position of clericalism, and emasculates people as activists (Gonzalez 2002). The idea that postmodernism (or poststructuralism) can be a force for social change or improving justice is probably an illusion, because 'those who describe themselves as postmodern ... are not as radical, original, or relevant to moral and political deliberation as they sometimes think' (Rorty 1999: 4). In this 'post' age, formal religion is faltering in developed countries, yet that same mindset of believing in grand accounts of the world in the absence of, or even despite, evidence is still powerful among an academic aristocracy.

It is not clear that the terms postmodern, or post-Fordist or post-industrial, describe the world in any meaningful or useful way. Their 'central ideas are that the world has fundamentally changed and that people are only interested in consumption and their individual lives. The evidence is overwhelmingly against them here' (Cole 2003: 31). However, these are not theories that exist to be tested, or subjected to evidence. Like solipsism, they cannot be tested in any practical way. Knowledge for them is only meaning: 'Realities are discursive; that is, there is no direct access to a reality "outside" "discourse"' (MacLure 2003: 180). Research is here merely the deconstruction of meaning rather than a search for the truth (or preference) or practicality (what works). And so, 'Post-modern theorizing alternates between banality and absurdity, between triviality posing as revelation and bizarre claims that conflict with common sense' (Bailey 1999: 162). As Gomm (2004) points out, by denying the possibility that there is any means of judging knowledge claims to be more or less true, postmodernism makes research a completely pointless activity. Theories such as these have become religions, contributing to a waste of research time and effort that could be devoted to useful reform and improving popular justice in the real world inhabited by the people who actually fund the research (Howe 1985).

'Being sceptical in some way or other can be considered to be the driving force behind human intellectual endeavour' (Ramakers 2002: 632). Scepticism can be converted from being simply a challenge to certainty, to being a component of good scientific research and theoretical development. It is something we need to foster (Shavelson *et al.* 2003), largely through the development of our ability to create and consider substantive (i.e. not solely methodological) alternatives to any of our research conclusions (Weiss 2002). However, the scepticism associated with postmodernism is very different to that traditional idea of *close* scrutiny. Rather, it is generally relativism 'of the worst kind' (Ramakers 2002: 631). The problem with this relativism is that it is inherently contradictory, being itself based upon a universal claim. It is standard practice for relativists to claim to know something which is not possible if their theory is correct (Winch and Gingell 1999). For example, if different social groups have different notions of truth that cannot be understood by outsiders then who is the observer who can see from outside? If middle-class teachers cannot understand working-class kids then how is it possible for middle-class education researchers to realize this? The observation that everyone has a different viewpoint is useful but commonplace, and it leads us to *relativity*, which is an injunction to researchers to express their findings in ways that would be true for all observers (Turner 2002). Relativism, however, is the precise opposite of this useful and simplifying relativity, even though commentators often seem to conflate the two.

There is a very real danger that big theory as a system of thought prescribes the conduct of the research by influencing the subject of which it is intended to be an investigation (To 2000). We need instead a healthy scepticism about all theory (Rossman and Wilson 1991). 'In many cases general theoretical/methodological stances are just stances: slogans, hopes, aspirations, not guidelines with clear implications that are followed in practice' (Platt 1996: 275), and the 'worship of theory [is] inhibiting cumulation' (Davis 1994: 196). By 1994, the National Opinion Research Center General Social Survey had received over 100 suggestions for extra questions to be added to the survey, but not one of these was based on the justification that they would test a social theory. Apparently the desire to test our cherished ideas is absent. One problem is that the widespread use of big theories in social research without recourse to testing leads to the adoption and rejection of alternative theories on an ad hoc basis. Theory becomes an intellectual fashion item which, through association with the research, creates a poor public image for all academic research.

Prejudged stances for research, such as feminism or anti-racism, may, like autobiography or even serendipity, help determine the nature of the research questions to be asked (Agozino 1999). They help us decide what is important to study, for while commitment to a cause is not the same as objectivity, neither is it, necessarily, in opposition. But such commitment or prior perspective/theory must *not* be allowed to predetermine the answer. An anti-racist researcher might be one who wished to uncover racism in a particular area, publicize it and ameliorate it. However, the logic and conduct of their research should be the same, as far as possible, as it would be for someone who felt sure that there was no racism in that area, or someone who simply wanted to find out if there was or was not. The kinds of evidence generated by the different starting points should be able to be set against each other – and in an ideal research world, the evidence uncovered by each researcher would be very similar whatever their starting point. *The first commitment of the researcher is to the quality of the research* – for poor research, with findings driven by the desires of the researcher, however worthy, is demonstrably unethical (Gorard 2002f). The chief criterion that identifies research as an enterprise *sui generis* has to be the capacity for surprise. If it is not possible for the research to bring us up against evidence that our preconceived ideas (our prior bets) are wrong, then we are not doing research (even if it is labelled as such).

Again, a comparison of progress in natural science can help us see how commitment to improve society or public life is totally compatible with genuine curiosity as a researcher. Of course, all scientists want good results, but if Watson and Crick had produced a different model of DNA that was just as useful then they would have had no reason to stick with a counter theory (Cole 1994). Compare this with someone who argues that social researchers should take sides before collecting data (Griffiths 1998), such as a feminist who may not propose a theory that sex discrimination is infrequent, for personal reasons, even when it fits the data better. Or a school effectiveness researcher who uses more and more complex statistical analysis to find the effect 'that must be there'. Their goal here is political rather than cognitive. This is one of the key barriers to progress in social science, and just about the only one that *can* be changed (e.g. we cannot change the complexity of our research sites or the mutability of our data). Progress could be seen as like a biological evolutionary process with no specific life-form destined to emerge from its pressures. Similarly, no specific theory has to be so, and we might have made equivalent or even better progress with other theories. So our ideas are not inevitable, even though they are based on 'reality'.

Discussion

Theory helps us to decide what and how we research. It helps us to measure and explain. It can be crucial in the transfer of research findings to new settings, and an important end-product of research. Above all, theories are cheap. They allow us to consider alternative positions simultaneously, to make progress in parallel and to accept failure without great cost. Theory and research are usually inseparable complements, since a piece of research tests ideas stemming from a theoretical model, leading to modification of the theory (Dubin 1978). Theories lead via logical deduction to hypotheses, via operationalization to observation, via scaling and measurement to empirical generalizations, and so to further theories.

But there must be a balance in our use of theory. A theory is a tentative explanation, used for as long as it usefully explains or predicts real-world events, not as an end in itself. As soon as theory itself becomes an obstacle to what or how research is conducted then it becomes worse than useless. Above all, theories must be subject to testing and then discarded whenever they consistently do not match up to empirical observation. Theories will always be under-determined by the evidence on which they rest, since any finite number of observations can be explained by a potentially infinite number of theories. By itself, theory rarely leads us to new inventions or the creation of useful artefacts.

All potential aviators in the 1900s followed the same Newtonian theories of physics, for example, but some of their ensuing planes flew and some did not – it was only the testing that sorted the one from the other. The theory alone is not *sufficient*. Nor is the theory *necessary*, for if, on the other hand, someone had managed to fly in some way that contradicted the prevailing theory then it would be the theory that would have to change. The act of flying would be far more powerful than the best theory could ever be. Science and technology, therefore, often advance through instrumentation rather than theory, with the theoreticians playing 'catch-up' (Davis 1994). But in social science, methods are often not as highly regarded (as opposed to being merely talked about). We have good methods for studying individuals in social settings, but many people study large groups and huge global or temporal trends using somewhat naive methods. Academic research funding tends to be given to big questions that we are likely to be unable to answer, and so on.

It is important for practical progress in our field that we begin to be more precise about the term 'theory' and its role, and cease criticizing a piece of work simply for not having a big theory framework. At one level, theory seems to be a framework, such as socioculturalism or constructivism, that is used as a tool to help generate ideas and questions for research. But these frameworks are protected by their advocates from any testing scrutiny or the consideration of counterfactuals. They are, in effect, articles of faith. This does not make them any worse, or indeed any better, for generating ideas than any other approach. What they must not be allowed to do is help determine the *results* of research. At its most abstract level, theory is about how and what we can know about the social world of our research. Theory at this level is often turned into paradigms. This is not a useful form of theory for most researchers, for two related reasons. First, while it is perfectly possible for a philosopher to have many views of the nature of knowledge that are logically consistent with our everyday observations – such as solipsism or a belief that everything is random – ethically, it is not possible to hold any such views while conducting applied and publicly-funded research. Second, if a 'paradigm' privileges particular forms of evidence then this leads to a kind of knowledge relativism in which the different parties cannot even argue coherently with each other, since each can legitimately reject the very nature of the argument used by the other party (note that this is a very different situation to querying the quality of the argument). If all research were to lead only to the finding that the results depend on the prior perspective of the researcher, then it would cease to be funded and cease to be listened to by outsiders with any respect at all.

Conclusion

As we have seen there are a number of constraints facing the combination of different methods in education and social science. Some of these limitations may reflect your own concerns. You may even be able to think of other factors. We hope that throughout this book, so far, we have addressed, either directly or indirectly, at least the most salient of these points. The preceding chapters have provided both practical examples of combining methods and the grammar or language of how to write about research that combines methods. In this chapter, we also discussed and attempted to rebut some of the philosophical arguments that have been attempted against combining methods in education and social science research. By now we hope you are beginning to develop your own understanding of what it means to do combined methods research, and whether it is feasible for your next project.

Prospects for the 'new' education and social science researcher

In the preceding chapters, we hope that we have demonstrated that research involving combined methods can be fairly unproblematic, that there is some overarching logic to all methods, and that methods can be classified in a variety of ways, such as direct or indirect and active or passive. The dichotomy between qualitative and quantitative is only one such classification, and it is not currently a very helpful one. It betrays a misunderstanding of the qualitative basis underlying all measurement, and of the importance of patterns in qualitative analysis, for example. To suggest that using a table of numbers in a piece of research makes you a 'positivist', with all that this entails, is absurd. To suggest that presenting the words of a research participant in your report means that you must be an 'interpretivist' is equally absurd. Yet this is what generations of novice researchers are being taught by their mentors in their confusing introductory courses on methods identities and epistemology. This wasteful, capacity-destroying strife between alleged 'paradigms' has to stop.

This chapter first considers one of the key components of the overarching logic for all research, the justification for any research claims. We continue with a brief discussion of the ethical responsibility we all have to conduct research of high quality, irrespective of method or ideology. We conclude the book with a summary of the prospects and pitfalls for the increased use of combined methods in education and social science.

What is a warrant?

We have written elsewhere about the importance of warranting research claims, and the fact that their logic is largely independent of the methods used in the research (e.g. Gorard 2002c). Warranting also has the advantage of fostering scepticism, when we define it in the following way. Consider, for any research claim (of ours or others), whether if that claim is not true, then how else could we explain the existence of the evidence leading to it? Only when all plausible alternative explanations, both methodological and substantive, have been shown to be inferior should the research claim be allowed to stand. As can be seen, this definition does not depend on how the evidence was generated, although, of course, the possibility that the evidence itself is wrong (either through error or deceit) is always a possible alternative explanation. Campbell *et al.* (2003: 5) argue, in their guide for novice researchers, that 'there are basics that relate to all [methods and approaches]' which lie at the heart of all good research. One of the most important of these is 'ensuring that what is reported is founded upon the evidence' (p. 5). In this, they are echoing the plea of Feuer *et al.* (2002) for more scientific research that involves posing significant questions, that are answerable empirically, linked to relevant testable theory, using appropriate methods, avoiding bias as far as possible, presenting a coherent chain of reasoning, reported logically and clearly, and disclosing to public scrutiny. Again, these are desirable characteristics for empirical research using all and any methods.

Research itself is quite easy. Everyone (even an infant) does it every day by gathering information to answer a question and so solve a problem (e.g. to plan a rail journey, Booth *et al.* 1995). In fact most of what we 'know' is research-based, but reliant on the research of others (such as the existence of Antarctica). Where we have no other choice we may rely on our judgement of the *source* of that information (an atlas may be more reliable than memory, the rail enquiries desk may be more reliable than last year's timetable). But where we have access to the research evidence on which any conclusions are based we can also examine their quality and the warrant that connects the two. Similarly, when we present our own research findings, we need to give some indication, via caveats, of the extent to which we would be prepared to bet on them being true, or the extent to which we would wish others to rely on them being true. This is part of our 'warrant'. Obviously, producing high-quality research is important in the first place, but even high-quality work can lead to inappropriate conclusions (Toulmin 1958).

Huck and Sandler (1979) remind readers of a humorous example in order to make an important point about warrants. An experimental psychologist trains a flea to jump in response to hearing a noise. Every time the noise is made the flea jumps. They then cut the legs off the flea, and discover that it no longer jumps when the noise is made. Conclusion: cutting off the legs has affected the flea's hearing. Of course, this is clearly nonsense but it is likely that we have all been persuaded by similar conclusions. If a physiologist cuts out a piece of someone's brain, and the person can no longer tell us about a memory (or perform a skilled action) that they were able to previously, then is this evidence that the specific memory or skill was 'stored' in that section of the brain? Many such claims have been made, and early maps of brain function were based on just this approach. However, the same effect of inability to report recall of memory (or skill) could have been achieved by cutting people's tongues out, or removing their hearts. All three operations may prevent memory recall for different reasons without showing that the part of the body removed in each case is the *site* of the memory. What is needed, in addition, is an argument leading from the evidence to the conclusion. This would be the warrant for those findings.

Brignell (2000) provides another example. The chemical industry routinely uses a chemical called 'dihydrogen monoxide'. While tremendously useful, this chemical often leads to spillages, and finds its way into our food supply. It is a major component of acid rain, and a cause of soil erosion. As a vapour it is a major greenhouse gas. It is often fatal when inhaled, and is a primary cause of death in several UK accidents per year. It has been found in the tumours of terminally ill patients. What should we do about it? In a survey the clear majority of respondents believed that *water*, for that is what it is, should be either banned or severely regulated. All of those statements about water are basically 'true', yet clearly none of them mean that water should be banned. Replace water with another, less abundant, chemical. How do we feel about banning it now? We have no obvious reason to change our mind. Yet we will all probably have accepted just such evidence as we have about water in order to accept the banning of other chemicals. This shows how difficult, but also how important, the warrants for research conclusions are. In both the flea and the water example the problem was not principally the research quality (or put another way, the problem was separate from any reservations we may have about the quality of the evidence). The problem was that the conclusions drawn were not logically entailed by the research evidence itself.

'Reasoning ... is a way of testing and sifting ideas critically. It is concerned with how people share their ideas and thoughts in situations that raise the question of whether those ideas are worth sharing' (Toulmin *et al.* 1979: 10). On a weak interpretation, a warrant is the form in which 'people furnish rationales as to why a certain voice ... is to be granted superiority ... on the grounds of specified criteria' (Gergen 1989: 74). Perhaps, for present purposes, a warrant is more simply summarized as that 'which makes the difference between knowledge and mere true belief' (Plantinga 1993a: 3). The warrant of an argument can be considered to be its general principle – an assumption that links the evidence to the claim made from it (Booth *et al.* 1995). The claim itself must be substantive, specific and contestable. The evidence on which the claim is based ought to be precise, sufficient, representative, authoritative and clear to the reader (as far as possible). In logical terms, if we imagine that our simplified research evidence is that a specific phenomenon (A) has a certain characteristic (B), then our evidence is that A entails B. If we want to conclude from this that phenomenon A therefore also has the characteristic C, then the third component of our syllogism (the classic form of our argument) is missing or implicit. This third component is that: everything with characteristic B also has characteristic C. Thus, our complete syllogism is:

This A is B
All B are C
Therefore, this A is also C

If the first part (A is B) may be likened to the evidence in a research study (e.g. water can be fatal), and the third (A is C) is the conclusion (e.g. water should be banned), then the second (B is C) is like the warrant (e.g. everything that can be fatal should be banned). In research reporting this step is often missed, as it is tacitly assumed by both the author and the reader. However, where the research is intended to change the views of others it is necessary to make the warrant explicit. This warrant can then be challenged, but unlike a challenge to the evidence it is not about quality but rather about the *relevance* of the evidence to the conclusion. In the water example the warrant is clearly nonsense. Water can be fatal, but we cannot ban everything that *could* be fatal. But accepting that this warrant is nonsense also means that no evidence, however good, can be used with this precise format of argument to justify banning anything at all simply because it is fatal.

For Toulmin *et al.* (1979) a warrant is an argument that stands up to criticism, and that moves from a valid dataset to a claim. They present a similar example to the one above. The empirically based claim that Harry is a British citizen can be warranted from the evidence that Harry was born in Bermuda, and the warrant that anyone born in Bermuda at that time will be a British citizen. The chief difference between this chain of reasoning and the classic syllogism is that it may also contain qualifying phrases (such as 'probably'), backing (in the form of other evidence or statutes), and any known conditions for rebuttal (e.g. 'unless both of his parents were aliens'). There is often considerable confusion, even in textbooks on methods, between this issue of warrant (are the conclusions justified?) and considerations of the quality of the evidence. It is important to realize that, in an extreme case, the evidence from a study may be ideal but the inferences drawn from that evidence totally erroneous. Instead of emphasizing this, many standard texts overemphasize notions of validity and reliability, giving the erroneous impressions that these are attributes of a whole study (which either has, or has not, validity). Rather, Tashakkori and Teddlie (2003) remind us that the issue of validity and of warrant is not a characteristic of a study (such as that the dataset generated is of high quality), but needs to be established via the kind of argument that Toulmin describes for each and every conclusion within a study.

Consider next an example of a warrant involving a causal model. Death rates due to cancer (of all types) increased over the course of the twentieth century in the UK, and they look set to continue to rise. One possible conclusion is that 'modern' lifestyle is to blame, including perhaps the food we eat and damage to our environment. The warrant here would be largely based on causation as correlation. Two sets of events, growth of cancer and lifestyle changes, are contemporaneous. Therefore, we assume that they are causally related and, of course, they may be. But we should also automatically start seeking alternative explanations, and see how these shape up. Another very plausible alternative is based on the fact of mortality. We all die. Therefore, a change in the probability of death by any one cause affects the probability of death by all other causes (put in statistical terms – the degrees of freedom of our model are fixed). As death rates due to typhoid, smallpox and war have declined so the death rates due to heart disease or cancer must be expected to rise (this is progress). If we add some more evidence, that people in the UK now live longer, on average, than at the start of the twentieth century, then the lifestyle theory becomes a much poorer explanation for the rise in cancer than the simple reduction of other avoidable causes of death. The latter explanation makes fewer assumptions for which we do not have direct evidence, and is therefore currently more 'scientific'. This example highlights another characteristic of a desirable warrant: it should be simple as well as transparent.

The history of epistemology has seen clashes between realists and relativists, and empiricists and rationalists. It is not the purpose of this chapter to revisit these debates (but see Musgrave 1993; Bonjour 1998; and Chapter 9). The purpose, rather, is to argue that when drawing conclusions from evidence, researchers should draw attention to those parts of their chain of reasoning that *could* be disputed. It should not matter, for example, whether a researcher believes in the existence of an external reality or not as long as they are clear about this when drawing conclusions. Our guess would be that once ideas such as extreme relativism are made explicit in research claims, then 'financial evolution' will play a large part in deciding whether the taxpayer or charity-giver wishes to continue funding research by researchers who do not believe in the reality of the world they are researching. Similarly, policy-makers, once genuinely aware of the epistemological positions of researchers with opposing conclusions, will use that knowledge in making a judgement about them one way or the other. Also, despite these earlier debates, most researchers appear to end up working with a mixture of pragmatic rationalism and fallible empirical realism (Platinga 1993b).

Only a clear and robust warrant, along with high-quality and relevant research, provides the necessary foundation for changes in evidence-informed policy (or practice), and then ensuring that the proclaimed benefits of change actually arise. At heart a warrant for change contains a causal claim (Gorard 2002b), which states that if the practitioner (policy-maker) does one thing then another will ensue. The warrant may be part of the research design, as it is with a closely controlled experiment, but it is generally independent of any particular method of data collection (de Vaus 2001). The National Research Council (2002) suggest principles for scientific research in education, of which the fourth is: 'Provide a coherent and explicit chain of reasoning' (p. 4). An important part of this involves 'systematically ruling out plausible counterexplanations in a rational, compelling way' (p. 4). The results should be disclosed to critique, and the warrant is intended to be persuasive to a sceptical reader (rather than playing to a gallery of existing 'converts'). Gorard *et al.* (2001b), for example, present a set of findings about changes over time in the social composition of UK secondary schools. They follow this with eight separate competing explanations for these findings, and spend the rest of the paper considering the relative merits of each. This is conducive to the scepticism felt necessary for research to prosper according to Shavelson *et al.* (2003), whose guiding principles for warrants are:

> To what extent can rival narrative accounts of the same action be ruled out? To what extent would another narrator replicate the account? To what extent does the narrative generalize to other times and places? There is nothing in the use of narrative form, by itself, that guarantees the veracity of the content of the account or which vitiates the need for the usual epistemic warrants used in science. How can it be determined that the narrative being used is complete, or does not misrepresent events?
>
> (p. 27)

This boxing off of plausible rival explanations is generally at the heart of effective warrants (Weiss 2002). For any real system of variables there are nearly infinite models that could explain them (Glymour *et al.* 1987), in the same way that an infinite number of equations can join any two points on a graph. This is also referred to as the underdetermination of theory by data, which perhaps expresses better the need to add something to the data in order to draw conclusions. This is the 'warrant'. The purpose of the warrant is to show readers that the proposed explanation is the best we have at this point in time. A useful short cut is to employ parsimony to eliminate many of the potential alternatives. Parsimony is the canon attributed to Morgan (1903: 53), 'In no case may we interpret an action as the outcome of the exercise of a higher psychical faculty, if it can be interpreted as the outcome of one which stands lower in the psychological scale'. It is, for example, simpler, and usually safer, for a doctor to diagnose a complaint of headache, neck stiffness, fever and confusion as meningitis, rather than as a combination of brain tumour, whiplash, tuberculosis and acute porphyria. Of course, the latter could be correct, but parsimony encourages us to eliminate the more mundane and simplest explanations first. We therefore limit our potential explanations to those that employ in their chain of reasoning the fewest (ideally none) assumptions for which we have no direct evidence. This claim is common to *all* methods of research, and forms the basis for their overarching logic.

Ethical considerations

Another important part of the overarching logic for all research methods, that we have not discussed so far in this book, is an ethical responsibility. This can be summed up in the phrase 'quality is paramount'. There is a wide literature on the role of ethics in social science research, yet most of the discussion focuses on the actions of the researcher with respect to the participants. Any ethical considerations from the point of view of non-participants in the research are, therefore, largely ignored. This is inequitable. Where research is publicly funded or has practical implications (i.e. nearly all education research, and much of the rest of social science), a more equitable perspective means that major issues of quality become more important than minor issues of ethics. Of course, the welfare of research participants must be protected, but there is a lot more to research ethics than this.

For any research using any method, the one outcome that would be of no use to anyone is where the research is of insufficient quality to reach a safe and believable conclusion about the question being asked. In this case, all of the risk to participants has been run for no reason and no gain. From this it would not be too much of a stretch to say that, in general, poor research leading to indefinite answers tends to be unethical in nature, while good trustworthy research tends to be more ethical. Poor research wastes the time, at the least, of the participants, but is perhaps particularly unethical from the point of view of those outside the research situation.

In many of the fields in which we wish to research, our influence over ethical situations is marginal. One may have to 'befriend' convicted serial killers, however repugnant the task, in order to find out about their motivations (if this is felt to be important to know), for example. But one can still conduct both good and bad research involving these killers. Our control over the quality of our work is, therefore, generally greater than our control over ethical factors. Thus, ethically, the first responsibility of all research should be to quality and rigour. If it is decided that the best answer to a specific research question is likely to be obtained via a combined methods approach, then this is at least part of the justification in ethical terms for its use. In this case, a combined methods approach may be the *most* ethical approach, even where it runs a slightly greater risk of 'endangering' participants than another less appropriate design. Pointless research, on the other hand, remains pointless however 'ethically' it appears to be conducted. Good intentions do not guarantee good outcomes. Such a conclusion may be unpalatable to some readers, but where the research is potentially worthwhile, and the 'danger' (such as the danger of wasting people's time) is small relative to the worth, this conclusion is logically entailed in the considerations above.

Thus, there should be considerable ethical pressure on the researcher to use the best mix of methods. To stick to a mono-methods identity in all circumstances would be wrong, both in practical research terms and for ethical reasons. For further discussion of the points in this section, and examples from research, see Gorard (2002f).

Problems facing increased combination of methods

We have argued in this book that combined methods research can be done, and that in many cases it *should* be done. There is sufficient skill among the UK education research community, and sufficient encouragement from research funders, for more combined methods work. It faces no real philosophical or technical barriers. In this final section we mention two further possible problem areas – research training and peer recognition for combined work.

Research training

Pellegrino and Goldman (2002) argue that we need a thorough reconsideration of the training provided for new researchers, and perhaps even for the professional development of existing researchers. Trainers have a responsibility to start preparing their students for the real world better, and that real world, according to Tashakkori and Teddlie (2003), is one where there is considerable practical pressure for more experts able to combine methods approaches easily. But at present 'an examination of research method books in education, psychology and sociology would result in much verbiage regarding the separateness, or even incompatibility, of quantitative and qualitative methods' (p. 62). Current approaches to methods teaching generally consider qualitative and quantitative methods separately (Bernard 2000; Gomm 2004), and make very little effort to link them. Texts, for example, discuss them in two unlinked sections or in books in isolation. So we continue to prepare students for a dichotomous world that no longer exists. Our own personal experience of trying to overcome this illustrates the pressures brought to bear to keep the status quo.

The publishers of one of our books insisted that its title should be *Quantitative Methods in Educational Research* (see Gorard 2001b) even though the author disliked the term quantitative, and felt that the title 'The simple use of numbers in everyday research' was a better description of the content and intent of the book. The publisher's argument was that without the term 'quantitative' people would not know what the book was about (and it would not appear so easily in internet searches). Similarly, when we have attempted to redesign methods courses in our own institution without reference to, or division by, qualitative and quantitative methods other members of our department have objected. Their objections include the concern that students will not know, when the course is over, which methods are qualitative and which quantitative (precisely!). People, apparently, do not want to teach *general* research methods, and do not want anyone else teaching them either. It is, therefore, not enough merely to abolish modules with qualitative or quantitative in the title. The models of lectures within modules need to be changed also, so that the distinction appears only at a very late stage, as one consideration among many of the ways in which research might be classified for ease of description in academic writing. Our experience of teaching, assessing and external examining of methods courses suggests that the training of novice researchers should start with substantive but generic issues of research – sampling, warranting, clarity, referencing, sources of secondary data and so on. This is proposed instead of modules and lectures on identity and epistemology which, however well-intentioned, merely act to reinforce the supposed schism between qualitative and quantitative paradigms.

The peer review process

Another practical problem, at least in the short term, will be to gain appropriate recognition for combined approaches when trying to get work published. Journals tend to display considerable cronyism, which distorts the review process (Travis and Collins 1991). Although the two are not wholly distinct, this cronyism is more dangerous when it is cognitive (based on intellectual similarity) rather than institutional (which tends to be more visible). Papers are routinely rejected by their expert referees, perhaps for ideological reasons, or because they dispute the views of current 'experts' in the field (i.e. the referees). In this case, peer review actually becomes *competitor review*. Papers and proposals are generally rejected where the reviewers disagree with each other, since this is seen as the protection of quality. Therefore, new work, radical approaches, divergent thinking and even new techniques are likely to lead to rejection. The mechanisms of review provide short-term inequity and a longer-term encouragement of orthodoxy. The worst acceptance rates are for interdisciplinary work, and the same fate could befall combined methods work. Capacity-building in this area risks hostility from established groups with vested interests in maintaining the status quo. Journals tend to send papers to reviewers who are methodologically in sympathy with them. Ethnographies are more likely to be reviewed by ethnographers, and complex statistical models by experienced statisticians, for example. Who, therefore, gets the combined approach papers, and if they are the traditional mono-methodic researchers will they be happy to comment on all of the paper? If not then, rather than being seen as combining approaches, the paper may be judged as falling between two stools. Editors, generally, need to be more sensitive to these issues.

The 'new' education and social science researcher

According to Teddlie and Tashakkori (2003: 45), social science research has passed through its quantitative and qualitative phases and is entering the 'third methodological movement', where it is increasingly OK for us to act in a way that Rossman and Wilson (1991) approve of as 'shamelessly eclectic' in our use of methods. As with any change, this third phase will take time to mature and will face hurdles such as those above. Perhaps research capacity in this area will only truly advance 'funeral' by 'funeral', as the referees, funders and research mentors of today begin to give way to newer people with new ideas. Perhaps though, through their control today of grant-funding allocation, peer-review publication and research training for tomorrow, the establishment can preserve their precious methodological schism by creating another generation just like themselves. Perhaps we need a revolution in thinking. One fairly radical change would be acceptance of the fact that it is not up to pragmatists to explain why all methods *are* compatible, it is up to opponents to convince us where they are not.

Conclusion

The research process can be viewed as a series of interwoven concerns. These concerns present themselves as a set of choices which require the researcher to maximize conflicting desirables. These desirables include:

- generalizability over populations;
- precision in the control and measurement of variables related to the behaviours of interest;
- contextual realism for the participants.

All things being equal, the goal of the researcher is to maximize the capacity for the findings of a specific study (through the choice of design) to simultaneously generalize across all three of these desirables. However, each of these separate generalizations is associated with very different research strategies. They cannot all be simultaneously *maximized* in a single activity. Surveys, for example, emphasize generality over populations. Laboratory experiments emphasize precision in the measurement of behaviour. And field studies emphasize the role of context. The implications of choosing any one research strategy severely limits the type of generalizations we may make. Maximizing a single type of generality negatively affects the researcher's capacity to generate general knowledge and make general statements regarding either of the other two desirables. Moreover, designing a study that forms a compromise between any two types of generality will also automatically minimize the researcher's capacity to make appropriate statements about the third type of generality – a cross between a survey and an experiment would tend to neglect context, for example. This is part of the reason why we argue that no one method is intrinsically superior to any other, and why mixing the approaches traditionally seen as 'qualitative' and 'quantitative' is so powerful in practice.

References

Ackroyd, P. (2002) *Albion: The Origins of the English Imagination*. London: Chatto & Windus.

Adair, J. (1973) *The Human Subject*. Boston, MA: Little, Brown & Co.

Adonis, A. and Pollard, S. (1998) *A Class Act*. Harmondsworth: Penguin.

Agozino, B. (1999) Committed objectivity in race-class-gender research, *Quality and Quantity*, 33: 395–410.

Altman, D., Machin, D., Bryant, T. and Gardiner, M. (2000) *Statistics with Confidence*. London: BMJ Books.

Anfara, V., Brown, K. and Mangione, T. (2002) Qualitative analysis on stage: making the research process more public, *Educational Researcher*, 31(7): 28–38.

Association of Teachers and Lecturers (2000) Social selection, *Report*, 22(5).

Badger, D., Nursten, J., Williams, P. and Woodward, M. (2000) Should all literature reviews be systematic? *Evaluation and Research in Education*, 14(3&4): 220–30.

Bailey, R. (1999) The abdication of reason: postmodern attacks upon science and reason, in J. Swann and J. Pratt (eds) (1999) *Improving Education: Realist Approaches to Method and Research*. London: Cassell.

Bailey, R. (2001) Overcoming veriphobia – learning to love truth again, *British Journal of Educational Studies*, 49(2): 159–72.

Bannan-Ritland, B., Gorard, S., Middleton, J. and Taylor, C. (2004) The 'compleat' design experiment: from soup to nuts, in E. Kelly, and R. Lesh, (eds) *Design Research: Investigating and Assessing Complex Systems in Mathematics, Science and Technology Education*. Mahwah, NJ: Lawrence Erlbaum.

Barbour, R.S. (1998) Mixing qualitative methods: quality assurance or quality quagmire? *Qualitative Health Research*, 8: 352–61.

Bartholomew, D., Steele, F., Moustaki, I. and Galbraith, J. (2002) *The Analysis and Interpretation of Multivariate Data for Social Scientists*. Florida: Chapman & Hall.

Beinart, S. and Smith, P. (1998) *National Adult Learning Survey 1997*. London: DfEE.

Benn, C. and Chitty, C. (1996) *Thiry Years On: Is Comprehensive Education Alive and Well or Struggling to Survive?* London: David Fulton Publishers.

Berka, K. (1983) *Measurement: Its Concepts, Theories and Problems*. London: Reidel.

Bernado, J. and Smith, A. (1994) *Bayesian Theory*. Chichester: John Wiley.

Bernard, R. (2000) *Social Research Methods: Qualitative and Quantitative Approaches*. London: Sage.

Beyer, J. (1992) Researchers are not cats, in P. Frost and R. Stablein (eds) *Doing Exemplary Research*. London: Sage.

Blau, P. and Duncan, O. (1967) *The American Occupational Structure*. New York: Wiley.

Bonjour, L. (1998) *In Defense of Pure Reason*. Cambridge: Cambridge University Press.

Booth, W., Colomb, G. and Williams, J. (1995) *The Craft of Research*. Chicago: University of Chicago Press.

Boruch, R. and Mosteller, F. (2002) Overview and new directions, in F. Mosteller and R. Boruch (eds) *Evidence Matters: Randomized Trials in Education Research*. Washington: Brookings Institution Press.

Bourdieu, P. (1990) *In Other Words*. Cambridge: Polity Press.

Breault, D. (2002) The sources of a science of educational research: a response to Eisner, presentation at AERA, New Orleans, April.

Bricmont, J. and Sokal, A. (2001) Science and sociology of science: beyond war and peace, in J. Labinger and H. Collins (eds) *The One Culture?* Chicago: University of Chicago Press.

Brignell, J. (2000) *Sorry, Wrong Number! The Abuse of Measurement*. Brussels: European Science and Environment Forum.

Brown, A. (1992) Design experiments: theoretical and methodological challenges in creating complex interventions in classroom settings, *Journal of the Learning Sciences*, 2(2): 141–78.

Brown, A. and Dowling, P. (1998) *Doing Research/Reading Research: A Mode of Interrogation for Education*. London: Falmer.

Brown, S. (2003) *The History and Principles of Q Methodology in Psychology and the Social Sciences*, //facstaff.uww.edu/cottlec/Qarchive/Bps.htm (accessed 2 October 2003).

Bryman, A. (1988) *Quantity and Quality in Social Research*. London: Unwin Hyman.

Bryman, A. (2001) *Social Research Methods*. Oxford: Oxford University Press.

Butler, R. (1988) Enhancing and undermining intrinsic motivation: the effects of task-involving evaluation on interest and performance, *British Journal of Educational Psychology*, 58: 1–14.

Campanario, J. (1996) Using citation classics to study the incidence of serendipity in scientific discovery, *Scientometrics*, 37(1): 3–24.

Campbell, A., Freedman, E., Boulter, C. and Kirkwood, M. (2003) *Issues and Principles in Educational Research for Teachers*. Southwell: British Educational Research Association.

Campbell, D. and Fiske, D. (1959) Convergent and discriminant validation by the multitrait-multimethod matrix, *Psychological Bulletin*, 56: 81–105.

Campbell, M., Fitzpatrick, R., Haines, A., Kinmouth, A., Sandercock, P., Spiegelhalter, D. and Tyrer, P. (2000) Framework for design and evaluation of complex interventions to improve health, *British Medical Journal*, 321: 694–6.

Carlin, J., Taylor, P. and Nolan, T. (1998) School based bicycle safety education and bicycle injuries in children: a case control study, *Injury Prevention*, 4: 22–7.

Chalmers, A. (1999) *What is This Thing Called Science?* Buckingham: Open University Press.

Chioncel, N., van de Veen, R., Wildemeersch, D. and Jarvis, P. (2003) The validity and reliability of focus groups as a research method in adult education, *International Journal of Lifelong Education*, 22(5): 495–517.

Clarke, A. (1999) *Evaluation Research*. London: Sage.

Cobb, P., Confrey, J., diSessa, A., Lehrer, R. and Schauble, L. (2003) Design experiments in educational research, *Educational Researcher*, 32(1): 9–13.

Cole, M. (2003) Might it be in the practice that it fails to succeed? A Marxist critique of claims for postmodernism and poststructuralism as forces for social chance and social justice, *British Journal of Sociology of Education*, 24(4): 487–500.

Cole, S. (1994) Why doesn't sociology make progress like the natural sciences? *Sociological Forum*, 9(2): 133–54.

Coleman, J., Campbell, E., Hobson, C., McPartland, J., Mood, A., Weinfield, F. and York, R. (1966) *Equality of Educational Opportunity*. Washington: US Government Printing Office.

Collins, A. (1992) Toward a design science of education, in E. Scanlon and T. O'Shea (eds) *New Directions in Educational Technology*. New York: Springer-Verlag.

Collins, A., Bielaczyc, K. and Joseph, D. (2001) *Design Experiments: Theoretical and Methodological Issues*, mimeo.

Collins, H. and Pinch, T. (1993) *The Golem: What You Should Know About Science*. Cambridge: Cambridge University Press.

Commission on the Social Sciences (2003) *Great Expectations: The Social Sciences in Britain*. London: Academy of Learned Societies for the Social Sciences.

Cook, T. and Campbell, D. (1979) *Quasi-experimentation: Design and Analysis Issues for Field Settings*. Chicago: Rand McNally.

Cook, T. and Payne, M. (2002) Objecting to the objections to using random assignment in educational research, in F. Mosteller and R. Boruch (eds) *Evidence Matters: Randomized Trials in Education Research*. Washington: Brookings Institution.

Cooper, H. (1998) *Synthesizing Research: A Guide for Literature Reviews*. London: Sage.

Cox, D. and Snell, E. (1981) *Applied Statistics*. London: Chapman & Hall.

Creswell, J. (2003) *Research Design: Qualitative, Quantitative and Mixed Methods Approaches*. Thousand Oaks, CA: Sage.

Crotty, M. (1998) *The Foundations of Social Research*. Thousand Oaks, CA: Sage.

Curtis, D. and Araki, C. (2002) Effect size statistics: an analysis of statistics textbooks, presentation at AERA, New Orleans, April.

Davis, J. (1994) What's wrong with sociology? *Sociological Forum*, 9(2): 179–97.

Dawes, R. (2001) *Everyday Irrationality*. Oxford: Westview Press.

de Corte, E., Verschaffel, L. and van De Ven, A. (2001) Improving text comprehension strategies in upper primary school children: a design experiment, *British Journal of Educational Psychology*, 71: 531–59.

de Vaus, D. (2001) *Research Design in Social Science*. London: Sage.

de Vaus, D. (2002) *Analyzing Social Science Data: 50 Key Problems in Data Analysis*. London: Sage.

Debats, D., Drost, J. and Hansen, P. (1995) Experiences of meaning in life: a combined qualitative and quantitative approach, *British Journal of Psychology*, 86(3): 359–75.

Denscombe, M. (2002) *Ground Rules for Good Research*. Buckingham: Open University Press.

Department of Health (1997) *Research and Development: Towards an Evidence-based Health Service*. London: Department of Health.

Dewey, J. (1916) *Democracy and Education*. New York: Macmillan.

Diamond, I. (2002) Towards a quantitative Europe, *Social Sciences*, 51: 3.

Dixon-Woods, M., Fitzpatrick, R. and Roberts, K. (1999) Including qualitative research in systematic reviews, *Journal of Evaluation in Clinical Practice*, 7: 125–33.

Dubin, R. (1978) *Theory Building*. New York: Macmillan.

Dyson, A. and Desforges, C. (2002) *Building Research Capacity: Some Possible Lines of Action*, report to National Educational Research Forum.

Eisenhart, M. and Towne. L. (2003) Contestation and change in national policy on 'scientifically based' education research, *Educational Researcher*, 32(7): 31–8.

Eiser, J. and van der Plight, J. (1988) *Attitudes and Decisions*. London: Routledge.

Eisner, E. (1981) On the differences between scientific and artistic approaches to qualitative research, *Educational Researcher*, 10(4): 5–9.

Eisner, E. (1998) A vision for educational research and AERA in the twenty-first century, *Educational Researcher*, 7(9): 34.

Ellmore, P. and Woehilke, P. (1998) *Twenty Years of Research Methods Employed in American Educational Research Journal, Education Researcher and Review of Educational Research from 1978 to 1997* (mimeo), ERIC ED 420701.

Erzberger, C. and Prein, G. (1997) Triangulation: validity and empirically-based hypothesis construction, *Quality and Quantity*, 31: 141–54.

Evans, J. and Benefield, P. (2001) Systematic reviews of educational research: does the medical model fit? *British Educational Research Journal*, 27(5): 527–42.

Faber, J. and Scheper, W. (2003) Social scientific explanations? *Quality and Quantity*, 37: 135–50.

Feldman, A. (2003) Validity and quality in self-study, *Educational Researcher*, 32(3): 26–8.

Feuer, M., Towne, L. and Shavelson, R. (2002) Scientific culture and educational research, *Educational Researcher*, 31(8): 4–14.

Feyerabend, P. (1993) *Against Method*. London: Verso.

Fitz, J., Gorard, S. and Taylor, C. (2002) School admissions after the School Standards and Framework Act: bringing the LEAs back in? *Oxford Review of Education*, 28(2): 373–93.

Fitz-Gibbon, C. (1985) The implications of meta-analysis for educational research, *British Educational Research Journal*, 11(1): 45–9.

Fitz-Gibbon, C. (2000) Education: realising the potential, in H. Davies, S. Nutley and P. Smith (eds) *What works? Evidence-based policy and practice in public services*. Bristol: Policy Press.

Flay, B. (1986) Efficacy and effectiveness trials (and other phases of research) in the development of health promotion programs, *Preventive Medicine*, 15: 451–74.

Frazer, E. (1995) What's new in the philosophy of science? *Oxford Review of Education*, 21(3): 267.

French, S. and Smith, J. (1997) Bayesian analysis, in S. French and J. Smith (eds) *The Practice of Bayesian Analysis*. London: Arnold.

Gallie, D. (1994) Methodological appendix: the social change and economic life initiative, in D. Gallie, C. Marsh and C. Vogler (eds) *Social Change and the Experience of Unemployment*. Oxford: Oxford University Press.

Gephart, R. (1988) *Ethnostatistics: Qualitative Foundations for Quantitative Research*. London: Sage.

Gergen, K. (1989) Warranting voice and the elaboration of self, in J. Shotter and K. Gergen (eds) *Texts of Identity*. London: Sage.

Geurts, P. and Roosendaal, H. (2001) Estimating the direction of innovative change based on theory and mixed methods, *Quality and Quantity*, 35: 407–27.

Gewirtz, S., Ball, S. and Bowe, R. (1995) *Markets, Choice and Equity in Education*. Buckingham: Open University Press.

Gigerenzer, G. (2002) *Reckoning with risk*. London: Penguin.

Gilchrist, W. (1984) *Statistical Modelling*. New York: Wiley.

Glass, G., McGaw, B. and Smith, M. (1981) *Meta-analysis in Social Research*. Beverley Hills, CA: Sage.

Glymour, C., Scheines, R., Spirtes, P. and Kelly, K. (1987) *Discovering Causal Structure*. Orlando, FL: Academic Press.

Godfrey, R. (2004) Meta-analysis and qualitative data: insights from the history of probability, *Building Research Capacity*, 7: 9–11.

Goldhaber, D. (2000) School choice: do we know enough? *Educational Researcher*, 29(8): 21–2.

Goldthorpe, J. with Llwellyn and Payne, C. (1987) *Social Mobility and Class Structure in Modern Britain*. Oxford: Clarendon Press.

Gomm, R. (2004) *Social Research Methodology: A Critical Introduction*. Basingstoke: Palgrave Macmillan.

Gonzalez, M. (2002) Against post-modernism, *Concept*, 12(2): 27–31.

Goodson, V. (1999) *Does the Method of Assessing Affect Performance?* TERSE report, http://ceem.dur.ac.uk/ebeuk/research/terse/Goodson.htm (accessed 15 December 2002).

Gorard, S. (1997) *School Choice in an Established Market*. Aldershot: Ashgate.

Gorard, S. (1999) 'Well. That about wraps it up for school choice research': a state of the art review, *School Leadership and Management*, 19(18): 25–47.

Gorard, S. (2000a) *Education and Social Justice*. Cardiff: University of Wales Press.

Gorard, S. (2000b) 'Underachievement' is still an ugly word: reconsidering the relative effectiveness of schools in England and Wales, *Journal of Education Policy*, 15(5): 559–73.

Gorard, S. (2001a) International comparisons of school effectiveness: a second component of the 'crisis account'? *Comparative Education*, 37(3): 279–96.

Gorard, S. (2001b) *Quantitative Methods in Educational Research: The Role of Numbers Made Easy*. London: Continuum.

Gorard, S. (2002a) Can we overcome the methodological schism? Four models for combining qualitative and quantitative evidence, *Research Papers in Education*, 17(4): 345–61.

Gorard, S. (2002b) The role of causal models in education as a social science, *Evaluation and Research in Education*, 16(1): 51–65.

Gorard, S. (2002c) Fostering scepticism: the importance of warranting claims, *Evaluation and Research in Education*, 16(3): 135–149.

Gorard, S. (2002d) Political control: a way forward for educational research? *British Journal of Educational Studies*, 50(3): 378–89.

Gorard, S. (2002e) The role of secondary data in combining methodological approaches, *Educational Review*, 54(3): 231–7.

Gorard, S. (2002f) Ethics and equity: pursuing the perspective of non-participants, *Social Research Update*, 39: 1–4.

Gorard, S. (2003a) *Quantitative Methods in Social Science: The Role of Numbers Made Easy*. London: Continuum.

Gorard, S. (2003b) Understanding probabilities and re-considering traditional research methods training, *Sociological Research Online*, 8(1): 12 pages.

Gorard, S. (2003c) What is multi-level modelling for? *British Journal of Educational Studies*, 51(1): 46–63.

Gorard, S. (2003d) In defence of a middle way: a reply to Plewis and Fielding, *British Journal of Educational Studies*, 51(4): 420–6.

Gorard, S. (2003e) Lifelong learning trajectories in Wales: results of the NIACE Adults Learners Survey, in F. Aldridge and N. Sargant (eds) *Adult Learning and Social Division*, vol. 2. Leicester: National Institute of Adult Continuing Education.

Gorard, S. (2004a) Comments on modelling segregation, *Oxford Review of Education*, 30(3).

Gorard, S. (2004b) *Judgement-based Statistical Analysis*, occasional paper 60, Cardiff School of Social Sciences.

Gorard, S. and Fitz, J. (1998) The more things change ... the missing impact of marketisation, *British Journal of Sociology of Education*, 19(3): 365–76.

Gorard, S. and Rees, G. (2002) *Creating a Learning Society?* Bristol: Policy Press.

Gorard, S. and Roberts, K. (2004) What kind of creature is a design experiment? *British Educational Research Journal*, 30: 3.

Gorard, S. and Smith, E. (2004) What is 'underachievement'? *School Leadership and Management*, 24: 2.

Gorard, S. and Taylor, C. (2001) Specialist schools in England: track record and future prospect, *School Leadership and Management*, 21(4): 365–81.

Gorard, S. and Taylor, C. (2002) What is segregation? A comparison of measures in terms of strong and weak compositional invariance, *Sociology*, 36(4): 875–95.

Gorard, S., Rees, G. and Fevre, R. (1999a) Two dimensions of time: the changing social context of lifelong learning, *Studies in the Education of Adults*, 31(1): 35–48.

Gorard, S., Rees, G. and Fevre, R. (1999b) Patterns of participation in lifelong learning: do families make a difference? *British Educational Research Journal*, 25(4): 517–32.

Gorard, S., Fevre, R. and Rees, G. (1999c) The apparent decline of informal learning, *Oxford Review of Education*, 25(4): 437–54.

Gorard, S., Rees, G., Fevre, R. and Welland, T. (2001a) Lifelong learning trajectories: some voices of those in transit, *International Journal of Lifelong Education*, 20(3): 169–87.

Gorard, S., Fitz, J. and Taylor, C. (2001b) School choice impacts: what do we know? *Educational Researcher*, 30(7): 18–23.

Gorard, S., Taylor, C. and Fitz, J. (2003a) *Schools, Markets and Choice Policies*. London: RoutledgeFalmer.

Gorard, S., Selwyn, N. and Madden, L. (2003b) Logging on to learning? Assessing the impact of technology on participation in lifelong learning, *International Journal of Lifelong Education*, 22(3): 281–96.

Gorard, S., Rushforth, K. and Taylor, C. (2004) Is there a shortage of quantitative work in education research? *Oxford Review of Education*, 30(3).

Graham, A., Dawson, N. and Moore, L. (2000) Emergency contraception: a survey of knowledge and attitudes among PSHE co-ordinators in Avon secondary schools, *Health Education Journal*, 59: 329–39.

Gray, J. and Densten, I. (1998) Integrating quantitative and qualitative analysis using latent and manifest variables, *Quality and Quantity*, 32: 419–31.

Gray, J. and Wilcox, B. (1995) *'Good school, bad school': evaluating performance and encouraging improvement*. Buckingham: Open University Press.

Griffiths, M. (1998) *Educational Research and Social Justice*. Buckingham: Open University Press.

Guba, E. (1990) The alternative paradigm dialog, in E. Guba (ed.) *The Paradigm Dialog*. London: Sage.

Hacking, I. (1999) *The Social Construction of What?* London: Harvard University Press.

Hakuta, K. (2000) *Perspectives on the state of education research in the US*, presentation at AERA, New Orleans, April.

Hammersley, M. (1996) The relationship between qualitative and quantitative research: paradigm loyalty versus methodological eclecticism, in J. Richardson (ed.) *Handbook of Research Methods for Psychology and the Social Sciences*. Leicester: BPS.

Hammersley, M. (2001) *Some questions about evidence-based practice in education*, presentation to BERA, Leeds, 13–15 September.

Hargreaves, D. (1999) Revitalising educational research: lessons from the past and proposals for the future, *Cambridge Journal of Education*, 29(2): 239–49.

Harker, R. (2004) *Compositional effects in school effectiveness studies: a New Zealand case study*, presentation at AERA Annual Conference, San Diego, April.

Harlow, L., Mulaik, S. and Steiger, J. (1997) *What if there were no Significance Tests?*. Marwah, NJ: Lawrence Erlbaum.

Harris, D. and Corcoran, T. (2002) *Impact and quasi-experimentation: the challenge of researching whole school reform*, presentation at AERA Annual Conference, New Orleans, April.

Hartigan, J. (1983) *Bayes Theory*. New York: Springer-Verlag.

Hausman, C. (2000) *Reviewing the review process: what can we learn?* Presentation at AERA, New Orleans, April.

Hayes, E. (1992) The impact of feminism on adult education publications: an analysis of British and American Journals, *International Journal of Lifelong Education*, 11(2): 125–38.

HEFCE (1992) *Research Assessment Exercise 1992: The Outcome*, http://www.niss. ac.uk/education/hefc/rae92/c26_92.html (accessed 4 March 2003).

HEFCE (1996) *Research Assessment Exercise 1996: The Outcome.* Bristol: Higher Education Funding Council.

HEFCE (1999) *Research Assessment Exercise 2001: Assessment Panels' Criteria and Working Methods,* www.rae.ac.uk.

HEFCE (2001) *2001 Research Assessment Exercise: The Outcome.* Bristol: Higher Education Funding Council.

Hemsley-Brown, J., Wilson, R. and Easton, C. (2002) How are LEAs helping schools to use research and what are the benefits? Presentation to NFER/LGA conference on Using Research for School Improvement, London, 5 December.

Hillage, J., Pearson, R., Anderson, A. and Tamkin, P. (1998) *Excellence on Research in Schools.* Sudbury: DfEE.

Hodkinson, P. (1998) Naivete and bias in educational research: the Tooley Report, *BERA Research Intelligence,* http://www.bera.ac.uk/ri/no65hodkinson.html (accessed 6 March).

Hollis, M. (1994) *The Philosophy of Social Science.* Cambridge: Cambridge University Press.

Holmwood, J. and Stewart, A. (1983) The role of contradictions in modern theories of social stratification, *Sociology,* 17(2): 234–54.

Holmwood, J. and Stewart, A. (1991) *Explanation and Social Theory.* London: Macmillan.

Horowitz, R. and Maimon, O. (1997) Creative design methodology and the SIT method, *Proceedings of the ASME International Design Engineering Technical Conferences,* September, Sacramento, CA.

Howard, G., Maxwell, S. and Fleming, K. (2000) The proof of the pudding: an illustration of the relative strengths of null hypothesis, meta-analysis, and Bayesian analysis, *Psychological Methods,* 5(3): 315–32.

Howe, K. (1985) Two dogmas of educational research, *Educational Researcher,* 14: 10–18.

Howe, K. (1988) Against the quantitative-qualitative incompatibility thesis, *Educational Researcher,* 17: 10–16.

Huck, S. and Sandler, H. (1979) *Rival Hypotheses: Alternative Interpretations of Data-based Conclusions.* New York: Harper & Row.

Kacapyr, E. (1996) Are you middle-class? *American Demographics,* www.demographics.com.

Kelle, U. (2001) Sociological explanations between micro and macro and the integration of qualitative and quantitative methods, *Qualitative Research,* http://qualitative-research.net/fqs.

Kelly, A. (2003) Research as design, *Educational Researcher,* 31(1): 3–4.

Kelly, A. and Lesh, R. (2000) *Handbook of Research Design in Mathematics and Science Teaching.* Mahwah, NJ: Lawrence Erlbaum.

Kroto, H. (2003) Chemists should remove scientific inventions, *Times Higher Educational Supplement,* 18 April: 13.

Kuhn, T. (1970) *The Structure of Scientific Revolutions.* Chicago: University of Chicago Press.

Lakatos, I. (1978) *The Methodology of Scientific Research Programmes.* Cambridge: Cambridge University Press.

Lambert, P. (2002) Handling occupational information, *Building Research Capacity,* 4: 9–12.

Lauder, H., Hughes, D., Watson, S., Waslander, S., Thrupp, M., Strathdee, R., Dupuis, A., McGlinn, J. and Hamlin, J. (1999) *Trading Places: Why Markets in Education Don't Work*. Buckingham: Open University Press.

Lawson, T. (2003) *Reorienting Economics*. London: Routledge.

Lee, C. (2003) Why we need to re-think race and ethnicity in educational research, *Educational Researcher*, 32(5): 3–5.

Leech, D. and Campos, E. (2000) *Is comprehensive education really free? A study of the effects of secondary school admissions policies on house prices*, University of Warwick Economic Research Paper 581.

MacKenzie, D. (1999) The zero-sum assumption, *Social Studies of Science*, 29(2): 223–34.

MacLure, M. (2003) *Discourse in Educational and Social Research*. Buckingham: Open University Press.

Marshall, G., Swift, A. and Roberts, S. (1997) *Against the Odds? Social Class and Social Justice in Industrial Societies*. Oxford: Oxford University Press.

Matthews, R. (1998a) *Statistical Snake-oil: The Use and Abuse of Significance Tests in Science*. Cambridge: European Science and Environment Forum, Working Paper 2/98.

Matthews, R. (1998b) *Facts Versus Factions: The Use and Abuse of Subjectivity in Scientific Research*, ourworld.compuserve.com/homepages/rajm/twooesef.htm (accessed 29 July 2003).

Matthews, R. (2002) The cold reality of probability theory, *Sunday Telegraph*, 5 May: 31.

Mayer, R. (2001) Resisting the assault on science: the case for evidence-based reasoning in educational research, *Educational Researcher*, 30(7): 29–30.

McGee, S., Dimitrov, D., Kirby, J. and Croft, S. (2002) *Using design experiments to investigate long-term program success*, presentation at AERA Annual Conference, New Orleans, April.

McIntyre, D. and McIntyre, A. (2000) *Capacity for Research into Teaching and Learning*. Swindon: Report to the ESRC Teaching and Learning Research Programme.

McNay, I (2003) Assessing the assessment: an analysis of the UK Research Assessment Exercise, 2001, and its outcomes, with special reference to research in education, *Science and Public Policy*, 30(1): 47–54.

McNiff, J. and Whitehead, J. (2002) *Action Research: Principles and Practice*. London: RoutledgeFalmer.

Meehl, P. (1998) *The power of quantitative thinking*, speech delivered upon receipt of the James McKeen Cattell Fellow award at the American Psychological Society, Washington, 23 May.

Meijer, P., Verloop, N. and Beijaard, D. (2002) Multi-method triangulation in a qualitative study on teacher's practical knowledge, *Quality and Quantity*, 31: 145–67.

Mills, C. (1959) *The Sociological Imagination*. London: Oxford University Press.

Moore, L. (2002) Lessons from using randomised trials in health promotion, *Building Research Capacity*, 1: 4–5.

Moore, L., Campbell, R., Whelan, A., Mills, N., Lupton, P., Misslebrook, E. and Frohlich, J. (2002) Self-help smoking cessation in pregnancy: a cluster randomised controlled trial, *British Medical Journal*, 325: 1383–6.

Morgan, C. (1903) *Introduction to Comparative Psychology*. London: Walter Scott.

Morrison, K. (2001) Randomised controlled trials for evidence-based education: some problems in judging 'what works', *Evaluation and Research in Education*, 15(2): 69–83.

Mortimore, P. (2000) Does educational research matter? *British Educational Research Journal*, 26(1): 5–24.

Mortimore, P. and Sammons, P. (1997) Endpiece: a welcome and a riposte to the critics, in J. White and M. Barber (eds) *Perspectives on School Effectiveness and School Improvement*. London: Institute of Education.

MRC (Medical Research Council) (2000) *A Framework for Development and Evaluation of RCTs for Complex Interventions to Improve Health*. London: MRC.

Murtonen, M. and Lehtinen, E. (2003) Difficulties experienced by education and sociology students in quantitative methods courses, *Studies in Higher Education*, 28(2): 171–85.

Musgrave, A. (1993) *Common Sense, Science and Scepticism*. Cambridge: Cambridge University Press.

Narodowski, M. and Nores, M. (2002) Socio-economic segregation with (without) competitive education policies, *Comparative Education*, 38(4): 429–51.

Nash, R. (2002) Numbers and narratives: further reflections in the sociology of education, *British Journal of Sociology of Education*, 23(3): 397–412.

Nash, R. (2003) Is the school composition effect real? A discussion with evidence from the UK PISA data, *School Effectiveness and School Improvement*, 14(4): 441–57.

National Institute of Health (1999) *Qualitative Methods in Health Research: Opportunities and Considerations in Application and Review*, www.nih.gov/icd (accessed 12 February 2002).

National Research Council (2002) *Scientific Research in Education*. Washington: National Academy Press.

NERF (2001) *A Research and Development Strategy for Education: Developing Quality and Diversity*. Nottingham: National Educational Research Forum.

Newton, P. (1997a) Measuring comparability of standards across subjects: why our statistical techniques do not make the grade, *British Educational Research Journal*, 23(4): 433–9.

Newton, P. (1997b) Examining standards over time, *Research in Education*, 12(3): 227–48.

Nuttall, D. (1979) The myth of comparability, *Journal of the National Association of Inspectors and Advisers*, 11: 16–18.

Nuttall, D. (1987) The validity of assessments, *European Journal of the Psychology of Education*, II(2): 109–18.

Oakley, A. (2001) Making evidence-based practice educational: a rejoinder to John Elliott, *British Educational Research Journal*, 27(5): 575–6.

Onwuegbuzie, A. and Wilson, V. (2003) Statistics anxiety: nature, etiology, antecedents, effects and treatments – a comprehensive review of the literature, *Teaching in Higher Education*, 8(2): 195–209.

Oppenheim, A. (1992) *Questionnaire Design, Interviewing and Attitude Measurement*. London: Continuum.

Park, R. (2000) *Voodoo Science: The Road from Foolishness to Fraud*. Oxford: Oxford University Press.

Parsons, E., Chalkley, B. and Jones, A. (2000) School catchments and student movements: a case study in parental choice, *Educational Studies*, 26(1): 33–48.

Paterson, L. (2001) *Education and inequality in Britain*, presentation to British Association for the Advancement of Science, Glasgow, 4 September.

Paul, J. and Marfo, K. (2001) Preparation of educational researchers in philosophical foundations of inquiry, *Review of Educational Research*, 71(4): 525–47.

Paulos, J. (2000) *Once Upon a Number: The Hidden Mathematical Logic of Stories*. London: Penguin.

Pawson, R. (2003) *Assessing the Quality of Evidence in Evidence-based Policy*. Manchester: ESRC Research Methods Programme, Working Paper 1.

Pedhazur, E. (1982) *Multiple Regression in Behavioural Research*. London: Holt, Rhinehart & Winston.

Pellegrino, J. and Goldman, S. (2002) Be careful what you wish for – you may get it, *Educational Researcher*, 31(8): 15–17.

Perlesz, A. and Lindsay, J. (2003) Methodological triangulation in researching families: making sense of dissonant data, *International Journal of Social Research Methodology*, 6(1): 25–40.

Petrosino, A., Turpin-Petrosino, C. and Finckenauer, J. (2000) Programs can have harmful effects! Lessons from experiments of programs such as Scared Straight, *Crime and Delinquency*, 46(1): 354–79.

Petroski, H. (1996) *Invention By Design*. Boston, MA: Harvard University Press.

Phillips, D. (1992) *The Social Scientist's Bestiary*. Oxford: Pergamon Press.

Phillips, D. (1999) How to play the game: a Popperian approach to the conduct of research, in G. Zecha (ed) *Critical Rationalism and Educational Discourse*. Amsterdam: Rodopi.

Plantinga, A. (1993a) *Warrant and Proper Function*. Oxford: Oxford University Press.

Plantinga, A. (1993b) *Warrant: The Current Debate*. Oxford: Oxford University Press.

Platt, J. (1996) *A History of US Sociological Research Methods 1920–1960*. Cambridge: Cambridge University Press.

Plewis, I. and Fielding, A. (2003) What is multi-level modelling for? A critical response to Gorard (2003), *British Journal of Educational Studies*, 51(4): 420–6.

Popkewitz, T. (1984) *Paradigm and Ideology in Educational Research*. Lewes: Falmer Press.

Porter, T. (1986) *The Rise of Statistical Thinking*. Princeton, NJ: Princeton University Press.

Postan, M. (1971) *Fact and Relevance: Essays on Historical Method*. Cambridge: Cambridge University Press.

Prandy, K. (2002) Measuring quantities: the qualitative foundation of quantity, *Building Research Capacity*, 2: 3–4.

Quack Theories (2002) *Russell Turpin's 'Characterization of Quack Theories'*, htttp://quasar.as.utexas.edu/billinfo/quack.html (accessed 9 May 2002).

Ramakers, S. (2002) Postmodernism: a 'sceptical' challenge in educational theory, *Journal of Philosophy of Education*, 36(4): 629–51.

Reay, D. (1995) 'They employ cleaners to do that': habitus in the primary classroom, *British Journal of Sociology of Education*, 22(3): 331–46.

Rendall, M. (2003) *Quantitative Research: A Scoping Study*. London: Learning and Skills Research Centre.

Richardson, W. (2002) Educational studies in the United Kingdom, *British Journal of Educational Studies*, 50(1): 3–56.

Roberts, I. (2000) Randomised trials or the test of time? The story of human albumin administration, *Evaluation and Research in Education*, 14 (3&4): 231–6.

Roberts, K. (2002) Belief and subjectivity in research: an introduction to Bayesian theory, *Building Research Capacity*, 3: 5–6.

Roberts, K., Dixon-Woods, M., Fitzpatrick, R., Abrams, K. and Jones, D. (2002) Factors affecting uptake of childhood immunisation: an example of Bayesian synthesis of qualitative and quantitative evidence, *The Lancet*, 360: 1596–9.

Robertson, D. and Symons, J. (2004) Self-selection in the state school system, *Education Economics*, 11(3): 259–72.

Rogers, A. and Nicolaas, G (1998) Understanding the patterns and processes of primary care use: a combined quantitative and qualitative approach, *Sociological Research Online*, 3: 4.

Rorty, R. (1999) Phony science wars, review of Hacking, I. (1999) The social construction of what? London: Harvard University Press, *The Atlantic Monthly online*, November.

Rossman, G. and Wilson, B. (1991) *Numbers and Words Revisited: Being 'Shamelessly Eclectic'*, ERIC Document Reproduction Service No. 337235, Washington DC: Office of Educational Research and Improvement.

Sale, J., Lohfeld, L. and Brazil, K. (2002) Revisiting the quantitative-qualitative debate: implications for mixed-methods research, *Quality and Quantity*, 36: 43–53.

Schmidt, C. (1999) *Knowing What Works: The Case for Rigorous Program Evaluation*, IZA DP 77. Bonn: Institute for the Study of Labor.

Scholz, R. and Tietje, O. (2002) *Embedded Case Study Methods: Integrating Quantitative and Qualitative Knowledge*. London: Sage.

Schorr, R. and Firestone, W. (2001) Changing mathematics teaching in response to a state testing program, presentation at AERA Annual Conference, Seattle WA, April.

Shavelson, R., Phillips, D., Towne, L. and Feuer, M. (2003) On the science of education design studies, *Educational Researcher*, 32(1): 25–8.

Sheffield, P. and Saunders, S. (2002) Using the British Education Index to survey the field of educational studies, *British Journal of Educational Studies*, 50(1): 165–83.

Shipman, M. (1997) *The Limitations of Social Research*. Harlow: Longman.

Shvyrkov, V. (1997) The new statistical thinking, *Quality and Quantity*, 31: 155–71.

Silverman, D. (1985) *Qualitative Methodology and Sociology*. Aldershot: Gower.

Skinner, C., Holt, D. and Smith, T. (1989) *Analysis of Complex Surveys*. Chichester: Wiley.

Slavin, R. (1986) Best evidence synthesis: an alternative to meta-analytic and traditional reviews, *Educational Researcher*, 15(9): 5–11.

Slavin, R. (2002) Evidence-based education policies: transforming educational practice and research, *Educational Researcher*, 31(7): 15–21.

Sloane, F. and Gorard, S. (2003) Exploring modeling aspects of design experiments, *Educational Researcher*, 31(1): 29–31.

Snow, C. (2001) Knowing what we know: children, teachers, researchers, *Educational Researcher*, 30(7): 3–9.

Sooben, P. (2002) Developing quantitative capacity in UK social science, *Social Sciences*, 50: 8.

Speller, V., Learmonth, A. and Harrison, D. (1997) The search for evidence of effective health promotion, *British Medical Journal*, 315: 361–3.

Spencer, L., Ritchie, J., Lewis, J. and Dillon, L. (2003) *Quality in Qualitative Evaluation: A Framework for Assessing Research Evidence*. London: Cabinet Office Strategy Unit.

Spillane, J. and Zeuli, J. (1999) Reform and teaching: exploring patterns of practice in the context of national and state mathematics reforms, *Educational Evaluation and Policy Analysis*, 21(1): 1–28.

Statistics Canada (2003) *Non-probability Sampling*, www.statcan.ca/english/power/ch13/ (accessed 5 January 2004).

Steele, T. (2002) The role of scientific positivism in European popular educational movements: the case of France, *International Journal of Lifelong Education*, 21(5): 399–413.

Stillman, A. (1990) Legislating for choice, in M. Flude and M. Hammer (eds) *The Education Reform Act 1988: Its Origins and Implications*. Lewes: Falmer.

Sullivan, A. (2003) Bourdieu and education: how useful is Bourdieu's theory for researchers? *Netherlands Journal of Social Sciences* (forthcoming).

Sutcliffe, J. (2000) Home front in war on poverty, *Times Educational Supplement*, 10 March: 24.

Suter, L. and Frechtling, J. (2000) *Guiding Principles for Mathematics and Science Education Research Methods*. Arlington, VA: National Science Foundation.

Swann, J. (2003) How science can contribute to the improvement of educational practice, *Oxford Review of Education*, 29(2): 253–68.

Swann, J. and Pratt, J. (1999) *Improving Education: Realist Approaches to Method and Research*. London: Cassell.

Taeuber, K. and James, D. (1982) Racial segregation among public and private schools, *Sociology of Education*, 55(2/3): 133–43.

Taeuber, K., Wilson, F., James, D. and Taeuber, A. (1981) A demographic perspective in school desegregation in the USA, in C. Peach, V. Robinson and S. Smith (eds) *Ethnic Segregation In Cities*. London: Croom Helm.

Tashakkori, A. and Teddlie, C. (2003) Issues and dilemmas in teaching research methods courses in social and behavioural sciences, *International Journal of Social Research Methodology*, 6(1): 61–77.

Taylor, C. (2002) *The RCBN Consultation Exercise: Stakeholder Report*, Occasional Paper 50. Cardiff: Cardiff University School of Social Sciences.

Taylor, C. and Gorard, S. (2001) The role of residence in school segregation: placing the impact of parental choice in perspective, *Environment and Planning A*, 30(10): 1829–52.

Taylor, E. (2001) From 1989 to 1999: a content analysis of all submissions, *Adult Education Quarterly*, 51(4): 322–40.

Teddlie, C. and Tashakkori, A. (2003) Major issues and controversies in the use of mixed methods, in A. Tashakkori and C. Teddlie (eds) (2003) *Handbook of Mixed Methods in Social and Behavioural Research*. London: Sage.

The American Heritage Dictionary of the English Language (2000) 4th edn. Boston, MA: Houghton Mifflin.

The United Kingdom Parliament (2002) Select Committee on Science and Technology, http://www.parliament.the-stationery-office.co.uk/pa/cm200102/cmselect/cmsctech/507 (accessed 31 October 2002).

Thomas, G. (2002) Theory's spell – on qualitative inquiry and educational research, *British Educational Research Journal*, 28(3): 419–34.

Thompson, B. (2002) What future quantitative social science could look like: confidence intervals for effect sizes, *Educational Researcher*, 31(3): 25–32.

To, C. (2000) *The Scientific Merit of the Social Sciences*. Stoke-on-Trent: Trentham.

Tooley, J. (1999) The Popperian approach to raising standards in educational research, in J. Swann and J. Pratt (eds) (1999) *Improving Education: Realist Approaches to Method and Research*. London: Cassell.

Tooley, J. and Darby, D. (1998) *Educational Research: A Critique*. London: Ofsted.

Torgerson, C. and Torgerson, D. (2001) The need for randomised controlled trials in educational research, *British Journal of Educational Studies*, 49(3): 316–28.

Toulmin, S. (1958) *The Uses of Argument*. Cambridge: Cambridge University Press.

Toulmin, S., Rieke, R. and Janik, A. (1979) *An Introduction to Reasoning*. New York: Macmillan.

Travis, G. and Collins, H. (1991) New light on old boys: cognitive and institutional particularism in the peer-review system, *Science, Technology and Human Values*, 16(3): 322–41.

Turner, D. (2002) *The class struggle: the place of theory in education?* Inaugural lecture, School of Humanities and Social Sciences, Glamorgan University.

Tymms, P. (2003a) *Standards over time*, presentation at BERA annual conference, Edinburgh, September.

Tymms, P. (2003b) *School Composition Effects*. Durham: School of Education, Durham University.

Tymms, P. and Fitz-Gibbon, C. (2002) Theories, hypotheses, hunches and ignorance, *Building Research Capacity*, 2: 10–11.

Usher, R. and Edwards, R. (1994) *Postmodernism and Education*. London: Routledge.

Verschuren, P. (2001) Holism versus reductionism in modern social science research, *Quality and Quantity*, 35: 389–405.

Wainer, H. and Robinson, D. (2003) Shaping up the practice of null hypothesis significance testing, *Educational Researcher*, 32(7): 22–30.

Weiss, C. (2002) What to do until the random assigner comes, in F. Mosteller and R. Boruch (eds) *Evidence Matters: Randomized Trials in Education Research*. Washington: Brookings Institution.

West, M. and Harrison, J. (1997) *Bayesian Forecasting and Dynamic Models*. New York: Springer.

White, P., Gorard, S., Fitz, J. and Taylor, C. (2001) Regional and local differences in admission arrangements for schools, *Oxford Review of Education*, 27(3): 317–37.

Winch, C. and Gingell, J. (1999) *Key Concepts in the Philosophy of Education*. London: Routledge.

Woodhead, C. (1998) Academia gone to seed, *New Statesman*, 26 March: 51–2.

Wright, D. (1999) Science, statistics and the three 'psychologies', in D. Dorling and L. Simpson (eds) *Statistics in Society*. London: Arnold.

Wright, D. (2003) Making friends with your data: improving how statistics are conducted and reported, *British Journal of Educational Psychology*, 73: 123–36.

Wright, D. and Williams, S. (2003) How to produce a bad results section, *The Psychologist*, 16(12): 646–8.

Zaritsky, R., Kelly, A., Flowers, W., Rogers, E. and O'Neill, P. (2003) Clinical design sciences: a view from sister design efforts, *Educational Researcher*, 31(1): 32–4.

Index